Dewey or Don't We? Librarians Cook

edited by

Susan Henricks

[signature]

D1253665

"Cookbooks have always intrigued and seduced me. When I was still a dilettante in the kitchen they held my attention, even the dull ones, from cover to cover, the way crime and murder stories did."

Gertrude Stein (1874-1946) American author

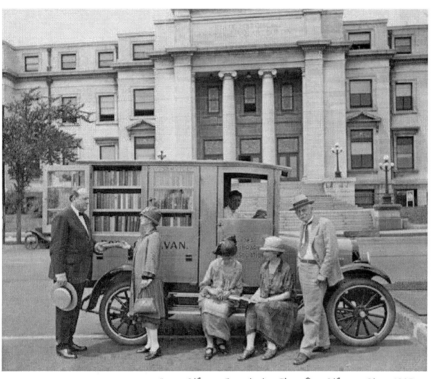

Iowa Library Association Traveling Library, Circa 1927
From the archives of the State Library of Iowa

Introduction

The Iowa Library Association (ILA) was established in 1890. It is the second oldest state library association in the country with a current membership of 1,400.

Organized in 1983, the Iowa Library Association Foundation (ILAF) awarded its first continuing education grant of $250 just three years later. Since 1986 the dollars awarded by ILAF have grown to more than $60,000. The more than 60 awards made by ILAF since 1986 have funded scholarships, continuing education workshops, and the Endowed Speaker at the ILA annual conferences.

ILA has long been a positive influence in my career beginning with when I was a library school student. I was fortunate to be awarded a scholarship by the ILAF and the Iowa Library Trustees division of ILA. The cookbook is my way to give back to the Association.

Thank you for purchasing this cookbook. Profits from this book will be donated to the ILAF Endowed Speakers Fund. This fund is used to underwrite keynote speaker fees at the annual conference ensuring that librarians will continue to be inspired by motivating speakers for years to come.

Table of Contents

598.07234 Birds-Food.

Bluebird Banquet

1 cup peanut butter
4 cups yellow cornmeal
1 cup rendered suet, melted
1 cup flour
1 cup currants
1 cup small sunflower chips
1 cup peanut hearts

Mix all ingredients together well. The mixture should be granular but stick together. If too sticky, add a little more cornmeal. Offer to Bluebirds in an open tray, platform, or Bluebird feeder.

Denise S. Crawford, Glenwood Public Library, Glenwood, IA

599.67 Elephants.

Elephant Stew

1 elephant
Salt and Pepper (to taste)
Brown Gravy (lots)
2 rabbits*

Cut elephant into small bite size pieces. (This will take about two months.)
Add enough gravy to cover.
Cook over kerosene fire for about four weeks.
This will serve about 3,800 people. If more guests are expected add the two rabbits, but do this only if necessary, as most people do not like to find "Hare" in their stew!

*Rabbits can be found on any country road in Iowa after dark.

Maybeth Gilliam, retired, Blairstown Public Library, Blairstown, IA

636.084 Horse-Feeding.

Special Cookies for Horses

1 cup uncooked oatmeal
1 cup flour
1 cup shredded carrots
1 teaspoon salt
1 tablespoon granulated sugar
2 tablespoons corn oil
¼ cup water
¼ cup molasses

Mix ingredients in a bowl in the order listed. Make small balls and place on cookie sheet sprayed with vegetable cooking spray such as Pam. Bake at 350 degrees for 15 minutes or until golden brown. Horses love these.

From recipegoldmine.com/pets

Winter Salad for Horses

6 apples, quartered
8 carrots, cut in three inch pieces
2 cups oatmeal, such as Quaker oats
1 cup sweet feed
Molasses

Combine all ingredients and fold in enough molasses to make the oatmeal and grain stick to the fruit. Chill overnight and serve.

From recipegoldmine.com/pets

636.70855 Dogs-Food.

Canine Carrot Cookies

2 cups carrots, boiled and pureed
2 eggs
2 tablespoons garlic, minced
2 cups unbleached all purpose flour, rice, or rye flour
1 cup rolled oats
¼ cup wheat germ

Combine carrots, eggs and garlic. Mix until smooth. Add dry ingredients. Roll out on heavily floured surface and cut into bars or desired shapes. Bake at 300 degrees for 45 minutes or to desired crunchiness. The centers will continue to harden as they cool. Brush with egg white before baking for a glossy finish.

From Dog Fancy Magazine, February 1999

Milk Bone-Style Dog Biscuits

¾ cup hot water
1/3 cup margarine
½ cup powdered milk
Pinch salt
1 egg, beaten
3 cups whole wheat flour

In large bowl pour hot water over the margarine. Stir in powdered milk, salt, and egg. Add flour, ½ cup at a time. Knead for a few minutes to form stiff dough. Pat or roll to ½ inch thickness. Cut into bone shapes. Bake at 325 degrees for 50 minutes. Cool. They will dry out quite hard. Makes about 1¼ pounds of biscuits.

Susan Henricks, Carnegie-Stout Public Library, Dubuque, IA

Catnip Cookies

1 cup whole-wheat flour
2 tablespoons wheat germ
¼ cup soy flour
1/3 cup confectioners' milk
1 tablespoon kelp
½ teaspoon bonemeal
1 teaspoon crushed dried catnip leaves
1 tablespoon unsulfured molasses
1 egg
2 tablespoons oil, butter or fat
1/3 cup milk or water

Mix the dry ingredients together. Add the molasses, egg, oil, butter or fat and milk or water. Roll out flat on an oiled cookie sheet and cut into narrow strips or ribbons. Bake at 350 degrees for 20 minutes or until lightly toasted. Break into pea-size pieces, suitable for cats. Good for treats, exercising gums and cleaning teeth, but too low in protein to use for regular fare.

From Dr. Pitcairn's Complete Guide to Natural Health for Dogs and Cats

Crunchies for Kitties

1½ cups whole-wheat flour
1½ cups rye flour
1½ cups brown rice flour
1 cup wheat germ
1 teaspoon dried kelp or alfalfa
1 teaspoon garlic powder
4 tablespoons vegetable oil
1½ cups chicken broth or beef broth
1 pound ground chicken
1 to 2 tablespoons brewer's yeast

Preheat the oven to 350 degrees. In a large bowl, combine the first six dry ingredients. Slowly add oil, broth and chicken, and mix well. On a lightly floured surface, roll the dough to a thickness of 1/8 inch, then place it on a greased cookie sheet. Bake until golden brown. Cool, then break into bite-size pieces. Place pieces in a bag with the brewer's yeast and shake to coat them. Store leftovers in an airtight container in the refrigerator. Makes 2-3 dozen pieces.

Susan Henricks, Carnegie-Stout Public Library, Dubuque, IA

641.255 Liqueurs.

Di's Homemade "Baileys"

2 eggs
1 can sweetened condensed milk
1 tablespoon chocolate ice-cream topping
1 300 milileters carton thickened cream
1 cup Scotch whiskey bottle

Beat the eggs. Slowly add sweetened condensed milk, chocolate syrup, cream, and whiskey. Blend until smooth; pour into a bottle; cap and refrigerate. This is best kept for about a week before consumption... if you can wait that long!

Di Cranwell, Mount Barker Community Library, Mount Barke, South Australia

"Alcohol is a misunderstood vitamin."
P.G. Wodehouse (1881-1975) English novelist

5

641.52 Breakfasts.

Banana-stuffed French Toast with Streusel Topping

2 tablespoons plus ¼ cup unsalted butter
2 tablespoons plus ½ cup sugar
2 tablespoons water
2 large ripe bananas, peeled, cut into ½-inch-thick rounds
1 pound unsliced loaf of egg bread, ends trimmed, and cut into 6 slices about 1 ½"
2 cups milk
6 large eggs
2½ teaspoons ground cinnamon
¼ teaspoon vanilla extract
1½ cups thinly sliced almonds, toasted
¼ cup light brown sugar, packed
¼ cup quick-cooking oats
2 tablespoons flour
Maple syrup

Melt 2 tablespoons butter in heavy large skillet over medium heat. Add 2 tablespoons sugar and 2 tablespoons water and stir until sugar dissolves. Continue stirring until mixture is foamy, about 2 minutes. Add bananas; cook until tender stirring occasionally, about 5 minutes. Transfer to small bowl; cool. (Can be prepared 4 hours ahead. Cover and chill.)
Preheat oven to 350 degrees. Using small sharp knife, cut a 2" long slit in 1 side of each bread slice, cutting ¾ of way through bread and creating pocket that leaves 3 sides of bread intact. Divide banana mixture equally among pockets in bread. Whisk milk, eggs, ½ teaspoon cinnamon, vanilla and ½ cup sugar in large bowl to blend. Pour into large glass baking dish. Place bread in egg mixture; let soak 10 minutes, turning occasionally.
Place almonds in shallow bowl. Carefully remove bread from egg mixture and coat both sides with almonds. Place bread on heavy large baking sheet. Mix brown sugar, oats, flour and remaining 2 teaspoons cinnamon in medium bowl. Add ¼ remaining butter and rub in using fingertips, until moist clumps form. Sprinkle topping over bread.
Bake French toast until topping golden brown and filling is hot, about 25 minutes. Transfer toast to plates and serve with maple syrup. 6 Servings

Christine Lind Hage, Clinton-Macomb Public Library, Clinton Township, MI

"Only dull people are brilliant at breakfast."
Oscar Wilde (1854-1900) Irish novelist and dramatist

6

Christmas Brunch French Toast

French bread, enough to fill 3 loaf pans
6 ounces cream cheese
1 cup nuts, chopped
1¼ cup brown sugar
¼ cup margarine
2 tablespoons light corn syrup
1 cup raspberry pie filling
1 cup whole cranberry sauce
2 cups whole milk
6 eggs
1 teaspoon vanilla
¼ teaspoon salt

Cut bread into 1" slices. Mix the cream cheese and nuts and spread on each slice of bread. Put the loaf back together. Combine the sugar, margarine, and syrup and bring to a boil. Reduce heat and simmer 2 minutes. Stir in pie filling and cranberry sauce. Pour sauce evenly into bottoms of the bread pans. Place bread in the pans, upside down. Beat the milk, eggs, vanilla and salt well. Pour the egg mix evenly over the bread in each pan. Cover and refrigerate 8-10 hours or overnight. Bake, covered, at 350 degrees for 55 minutes. Let stand 5 minutes before inverting pan and removing. Makes 3 loaf pans

Mary Frisbie, Kinney Memorial Library, Hanlontown, IA

"'When you wake up in the morning, Pooh,' said Piglet at last, 'what's the first thing you say to yourself?' 'What's for breakfast?' said Pooh. 'What do you say, Piglet?' 'I say, I wonder what's going to happen exciting today?' said Piglet. Pooh nodded thoughtfully. 'It's the same thing,' he said."
A. A. Milne (1882-1956) *The House at Pooh Corner*, 1928

Easy Egg Casserole

8 slices bread
8 eggs
3 cups milk
3 cups cheese, shredded
3 cups ham, bacon, or sausage

Mix eggs and milk. Cut bread into bite size pieces. Place bread in a greased 13" x 9" baking dish. Pour egg mixture over top. Sprinkle meat and cheese on top. Refrigerate overnight. Bake at 350 degrees for 1 hour.

Michelle Minerd, Kent District Library, East Grand Rapids Branch, East Grand Rapids, MI

"I think breakfast so pleasant because no one is conceited before one o'clock."
Sydney Smith (1771-1845) English writer

641.53 Snack foods.

Lazy Librarian's Choco-Peanut Butter Blast

1 jar creamy peanut butter (chunky NOT allowed)
1 bag semi-sweet chocolate morsels, such as Nestles
The biggest spoon you can find

Open peanut butter jar. Carefully rip open the bag of semi-sweet morsels, making sure you do not rip the sides of the bag. Pick up spoon, stick it into the peanut butter jar and swirl it around. Make sure as much peanut butter sticks to the spoon as humanly possible. Remove spoon from jar and stick it into the semi-sweet morsels. Make sure as many morsels are imbedded into the peanut butter as humanly possible. Lick and/or nibble at the spoon while watching your favorite reality television show. When finished, drink at least a six-pack of Diet Pepsi Twists to wash away the calories you've just ingested.

Linda Absher, The Lipstick Librarian http://www.lipsticklibrarian.com

"A man accustomed to American food and American domestic cookery would not starve to death suddenly in Europe, but I think he would gradually waste away, and eventually die." Mark Twain (Samuel Langhorne Clemens) American novelist, (1825-1910) *A Tramp Abroad,* 1879

Oven Baked Carmel Corn

7½ quarts popped popcorn.
2 cups brown sugar
1 cup margarine
½ cup white corn syrup
1 teaspoon salt
1 teaspoon baking soda

Put popcorn in a large roaster pan. Boil together brown sugar, margarine, corn syrup and salt for 5 minutes at 245 degrees. Use a candy thermometer. Remove syrup from heat and add baking soda. Pour over popped popcorn and mix. Bake 1 hour at 200 degrees, stirring every 15 minutes.

Lisa Torgerson, Waukee Public Library, Waukee, IA

Popcorn Cake

1 cup sugar
½ cup light Karo syrup
1 tablespoon vinegar
1 teaspoon vanilla
1 cup unpopped popcorn, popped

Cook the sugar, syrup, vinegar and vanilla until the mixture reaches 260 degrees. Pour this mixture over the popcorn. Pack into a well-buttered Bundt pan.

Christine Lind Hage, Clinton-Macomb Public Library, Clinton Township, MI

Seasoned Pretzels

2 bags pretzel sticks
1 cup of popcorn oil, such as Orville Redenbacher
1 teaspoon lemon pepper seasoning
1 package dry ranch dressing, such as Hidden Valley

Mix the popcorn oil, lemon pepper seasoning, and dry ranch dressing very well. Place pretzels in two 13" x 9" pans. Pour mixture over pretzels. Turn over every 20 minutes until they dry.

Ann Garas, patron, Rockford Public Library patron, Rockford, IL

"Eat first, morals after."
Bertolt Brecht (1898-1956) *The Threepenny Opera*, 1928

641.57 Quantity cookery.

Sloppy Joes

12 pounds ground beef
1 cup sugar
6-8 small onions, chopped
1 cup regular mustard
2 teaspoons salt
1 cup vinegar
6 cups catsup
1 cup Worcestershire sauce

Brown meat slowly in skillet with onion and salt. Meanwhile, make sauce by mixing together the other ingredients and cooking slowly over low heat for 15 minutes. Add meat to sauce and stir. Let simmer 30 minutes or longer before serving so that the meat absorbs the sauce. Serves 50

Susan Sterling, Dimmick Memorial Library, Jim Thorpe, PA

641.5884 Electric cookery, Slow.

Barbecued Ribs

3 pounds ribs (pork or beef)
2 tablespoons margarine
2 tablespoons onion, chopped
1 tablespoon green pepper, chopped
1 teaspoon celery seed
2 tablespoons brown sugar
2 tablespoons lemon juice
1 teaspoon mustard
1 cup water

Brown ribs on both sides. After browning, transfer to a slow cooker. Mix other ingredients and pour over ribs. Cook on low for 8 hours until tender.

Joan Schultz, Upham Memorial Library, Fredericksburg, IA

Best Ever Slow Cooker Stew

2 pounds beef chuck, cut into 1" cubes, or stew meat
¼ cup flour
1½ teaspoon salt
½ teaspoon pepper
1½ cups beef broth
1 teaspoon Worcestershire sauce
1 clove garlic, minced
1 bay leaf
1 teaspoon paprika
4 carrots, sliced
3 potatoes, diced
1 onion, chopped
1 stalk celery, sliced

Place meat in slow cooker. Mix flour, salt and pepper and pour over meat stirring to coat. Add remaining ingredients and stir to mix well. Cover and cook on low about 10-12 hours or high for 4-6 hours. Stir stew thoroughly before serving.

Denise S. Crawford, Glenwood Public Library, Glenwood, IA

"It is, of course, entirely possible to cook without using wine. It is also possible to wear suits and dresses made of gunny sacks, but who wants to?" Morrison Wood (1893- ?) newspaper columnist, *With a Jug of Wine* 1949

Crockpot Beef Burgundy

1-1 ½ pounds round steak, cut in 1" pieces
1 can cream of chicken soup
1 small can of mushrooms, drained
1 envelope dry onion soup mix, such as Lipton's
½ cup dry red wine

Mix all ingredients and pour into greased crockpot. Cook on low for 6 hours. Serve over rice that has been tossed with parsley flakes. Add a tossed salad and a crusty French bread for an easy meal.

Judy Havlik, Algona Community Schools, Algona, IA

Crockpot Corn

2 cans cream-style corn
2 cans whole-kernel corn, drained
1 cup uncooked elbow macaroni
1 cup American cheese, cubed
1 stick butter or margarine
Salt and pepper to taste

Mix all ingredients and place in a slow cooker. Cook on high for 1½ hours.

Teresa Buckingham, Glenwood Public Library, Glenwood, IA

Crockpot Roast Beef

1 beef roast
1 can cream of mushroom soup
2 tablespoon Worcestershire sauce
1 package dry onion soup mix

Place roast in slow cooker. Mix other ingredients together and pour over roast. Cover and cook on low for 10 hours.

Joan Schultz, Upham Memorial Library, Fredericksburg, IA

"All cooking is a matter of time. In general, the more time the better."
John Erskine (1879-1951) American novelist, *The Complete Life*, 1943

"There is no love sincerer than the love of food."
George Bernard Shaw (1856-1950) Irish playwright and critic

Crockpot Vegetarian Bean Soup

2 tablespoons olive oil
1 onion, chopped
1 bell pepper, chopped
2 stalks celery, chopped or sliced
3 cloves garlic, minced
2 carrots, chopped or sliced
4 15-ounce cans pinto beans
4 cubes vegetable bouillon
1 15-ounce can tomato sauce, or diced tomatoes
1 6-ounce package sliced mushrooms
1 can water or beer or broth

In medium saucepan, sauté onions, celery, bell pepper and garlic in olive oil until vegetables are tender. Place in crockpot with rest of ingredients. Cook on low for 6 - 8 hours. *Enjoy!*

Lisa Colcord, Glendale Public Library, Glendale, AZ

Delicious Pot Roast

1 arm roast (roast beef of any size)
1/3 cup cooking sherry
1/3 cup water
¼ cup soy sauce
1 cube beef bouillon
2 cinnamon sticks
Potatoes, optional
Vegetables, optional

Place all ingredients in a slow cooker. Add roast. Cook on low for 8 hours.

Mary Cameron, State Library of Iowa, Des Moines, IA

"Give them great meals of beef and iron and steel, they will eat like wolves and fight like devils."
William Shakespeare (1564-1616) *King Henry V*

Potluck Beans

1 16-ounce can kidney beans
1 16-ounce can small white beans
1 16-ounce can butter beans
1 16-ounce can black beans or small red beans
1 cup onion, chopped
2 teaspoons dry mustard
½ teaspoon hickory smoke flavoring
½ cup dark brown sugar
½ cup honey
1 cup barbecue sauce
2 tablespoons apple cider vinegar

Drain and rinse beans. Combine all ingredients in a slow cooker. Cover and cook on low 3-4 hours.

Margaret McCoy, Cordova District Library, Cordova, IL

Ratatouille

1 large eggplant, peeling and cut into 1" chunks
Salt
2 medium onions, chopped
2 cups fresh tomatoes, chopped (about 3 medium)
1 large green pepper, cut into ½" squares
1 large red or yellow bell pepper, cut into ½" squares
3 medium zucchini, sliced
3 tablespoons olive oil
3 tablespoons dried basil
2 garlic cloves, crushed
½ teaspoon freshly ground pepper
1 6-ounce can tomato paste
1 5 ¾-ounce can pitted ripe olives, drained and coarsely chopped
3 tablespoons fresh basil, chopped

Sprinkle eggplant with salt; let stand in a colander ½-1 hour to drain. Press out excess moisture. Rinse the eggplant with water and pat dry with paper towels. Place the eggplant in a 5 or 6 quart electric slow cooker. Add the onions, tomatoes, bell peppers, zucchini, olive oil, basil, garlic, pepper, and ½ teaspoon salt. Mix well. Cover and cook on high heat setting about 3 hours, until the vegetables are tender but still hold their shape. Stir in the tomato paste, olives, and fresh basil. Serve hot, at room temperature, or chilled.

Susan Henricks, Carnegie-Stout Public Library, Dubuque, IA

Slow-Cooker Roasted Chicken

1 4-pound chicken
1 teaspoon paprika
½ teaspoon dried thyme leaves
½ teaspoon dried basil
½ teaspoon Beau Monde seasoning
½ teaspoon seasoned salt
½ teaspoon garlic powder
½ teaspoon freshly ground pepper
1 tablespoon olive oil

Remove the giblets from the chicken. Remove as much fat and skin from the chicken as possible. Rinse and drain the chicken; pat dry inside and out with paper towels. Mix all the seasonings with the olive oil to make a paste. Spread a little of the seasoning paste inside the cavity. Place the chicken, breast side up, in a 3 ½ quart or 4-quart electric slow cooker. Spread the remaining seasoning over the top of the chicken. Cover and cook on high heat setting 3-3 ½ hours, or on low heat setting for 6 ½-7 ½ hours, or until the chicken is cooked through and the juices run clear.

Susan Henricks, Carnegie-Stout Public Library, Dubuque, IA

"I rose at 5 o'clock in the morning and read a chapter in Hebrew and 200 verses in Homer's Odyssey. I ate milk for breakfast, I said my prayers . . . I danced my dance. I read law in the morning and Italian in the afternoon. I ate tough chicken for dinner."
Diary of William Byrd (1709)

Tortellini and Vegetable Soup

2 14 ½ -ounce cans vegetable broth
1 15 ¼-ounce can whole kernel corn, drained
1 medium leek (white and tender green part), rinsed well and chopped
2 garlic cloves, crushed through a press
¼ cup fresh basil, chopped
1 28-ounce can diced, peeled tomatoes
1 red pepper, chopped
2 cups zucchini, chopped (about 1 medium)
1 9-ounce package fresh cheese tortellini
½ teaspoon garlic pepper
Parmesan cheese, grated

In a 4-quart electric slow cooker, mix together all the ingredients except the grated cheese. Cover and cook on the high heat setting for 3½-4 hours, or until the tortellini are tender. Do not overcook or the tortellini will become mushy. Serve immediately, topped with a sprinkling of Parmesan cheese.

Susan Henricks, Carnegie-Stout Public Library, Dubuque, IA

"There are two types of onions, the big white Spanish and the little red Italian. The Spanish has more food value and is therefore chosen to make soup for huntsman and drunkards, two classes of people who require fast recuperation."
Alexander Dumas (1802-1870) French author

Corn Fritters

1½ cups flour
¾ teaspoon salt
2/3 cups milk
1½ teaspoon baking powder
¼ cup sugar
1 egg, well beaten
1½ cups whole kernel corn, well drained

Sift together flour, baking powder, salt, and sugar. In an electric mixer, blend the egg and milk. Add gradually to dry ingredients. Stir in corn. Drop by tablespoons in hot deep fat fryer (365-375 degrees). Fry 2-5 minutes. Drain on paper towels.

Kim Robinson, Waukee Public Library, Waukee, IA

Corn with Jalapeños and Cream

4 cups corn (fresh or frozen)
¼ cup butter
1 small onion, finely chopped
2/3 cup pickled jalapeño chile slices, drained
2/3 cup cream cheese
1/3 cup Parmesan cheese, plus extra for garnish, freshly grated
Salt and pepper

Melt the butter in a saucepan. Add the chopped onion and sauté for 4-5 minutes, stirring occasionally, until the onion has softened and is translucent.
Add the corn kernels and cook for 4-5 minutes, until they are just tender. Chop the jalapeños finely and stir them into the corn mixture. Stir in the cream cheese and the Parmesan cheese. Cook over low heat until both cheeses have melted and the corn kernels are coated in the mixture. Season to taste, transfer into a heated dish and serve, topped with shredded Parmesan cheese. Good as a side dish or with tortilla chips.

Megan VanderHart, Rock Island Public Library, Rock Island, IL

"Sex is good, but not as good as fresh sweet corn."
Garrison Keillor (1942 -) American author and host of *A Prairie Home Companion*

Scalloped Corn and Oysters

1 8-ounce package of cream cheese
1 can creamed corn
1 stick margarine
1 can kernel corn
1 package corn muffin mix such as Jiffy
1 small can of oysters

Drain only the oysters; chop and then mix with all other ingredients together. Bake at 350 degrees for 30-35 minutes or until set.

Linda Mack, Waukee Public Library, Waukee, IA

"He was a very valiant man who first adventured on eating of oysters."
James I (1608-1661) Quoted in Thomas Fuller's *The History of the Worthies of England*

641.641 Cookery (Apples)

Healthy Baked Apples

4 apples, cored and sliced
2/3 cup brown sugar
¾ cup quick cooking oatmeal
1 teaspoon cinnamon
½ cup sifted flour
1/3 cup pecans, chopped
½ cup melted butter

Layer the apples in a 9" square pan. Mix together the brown sugar, oatmeal, cinnamon, flour, pecans, and butter; cover the apples. Bake 45 minutes at 350 degrees.

Jim Lander, Pfohl Health Science Library, Mercy Hospital, Dubuque, IA

641.42 Canning and preserving.

Spaghetti Sauce to Can

5 pounds fresh tomatoes, stemmed and peeled weight
1 pound onion, finely chopped (may substitute dried minced onion)
4-5 large cloves garlic, chopped fine
4 tablespoons canning salt
1 tablespoon chili powder
¼ heaping teaspoon black pepper
3 heaping tablespoons Italian seasoning
2 rounded teaspoons oregano
¾ cup sugar
1 rounded teaspoon basil
2 12-ounce cans tomato paste

Cook peeled fresh tomatoes in at least an 8-quart heavy saucepan. Boil until tomatoes are cooked through. Grind cooked tomatoes in a blender, food processor, or run through a sieve. Pour tomato puree back into saucepan. Grind fresh onions and garlic in blender or food processor and add to tomato puree with salt, chili powder, pepper, Italian seasoning, oregano, sugar and basil. Bring to a boil and then simmer until slightly thickened. Return to a boil. Lower heat and stir in tomato paste until all lumps of paste are incorporated. Keep this mixture at a low simmer. Secure prepared lids to clean rims. Either water bath method for 10 minutes or use a pressure cooker for recommended pressure or time.

Sue Padilla, Newton Public Library, Newton, IA

"Be it known that I, John L. Mason .. have invented new and useful Improvements in the Necks and Bottles, Jars & c., Especially intended to be air and water tight, such as are used for sweetmeats.
John L. Mason's (1832-1902) patent file, 1858

Sweet Pickle Relish

4 cups cucumbers, chopped
2 cups onion, chopped
1 cup green pepper, chopped
1 cup red pepper, chopped
¼ cup salt
3 ½ cups sugar
2 cups cider vinegar
1 tablespoon celery seed
1 tablespoon mustard seed

Combine cucumbers, onions, and green and red peppers in a bowl. Sprinkle with salt and cover with cold water. Let stand for two hours. Drain thoroughly. Press out excess liquid. Combine sugar, vinegar, and spices in a large saucepan and heat till boiling. Add drained vegetables and simmer for 10 minutes. Pack into hot pint jars, leaving ¼" headspace. Adjust caps. Process jars for 10 minutes in a boiling water bath. Yields 4 pints

Denise S. Crawford, Glenwood Public Library, Glenwood, IA

"On a hot day in Virginia, I know nothing more comforting than a fine spiced pickle, brought up trout-like from the sparkling depths of the aromatic jar below the stairs of Aunt Sally's cellar."
Thomas Jefferson (1743-1826) third President of the United States

641.5636 Vegetarian cookery.

Hearty Lentil Stew

1 head garlic, finely chopped
2 medium onions, finely chopped
1½ tablespoons olive oil
2 cups green lentils (but any kind will do)
½ bunch celery, chopped
1-2 medium zucchini, sliced
6-8 whole sliced carrots
2 15-ounce cans of green beans
2 medium potatoes
8-10 cups water or stock (you can use chicken or vegetable stock)
2 28-ounce cans "Italian Style" tomatoes with juice
2 bay leaves
1 tablespoon fresh parsley, finely chopped
1 teaspoon dried thyme
1 teaspoon oregano
Salt and pepper to your taste

Sauté onions and garlic in olive oil over medium heat in a stock pot for about 5 minutes or until soft. Add onions and garlic and all the remaining ingredients. Simmer, stirring occasionally for at least 1 hour. Remove bay leaves.

You can make this recipe vegan or add some lean stew beef for those that prefer meat in your meals. You can use a variety of vegetables in this stew (please see variations below). This recipe is very versatile, flexible, has flavors that improve in the refrigerator, and it freezes wonderfully!

Variations and Suggestions:
- Other vegetables to include: corn, peas, mushrooms, asparagus, bell peppers, etc.
- You can use frozen vegetables if you would like to cut down on preparation time
- Add lean stew beef to the stock pot, no pre-cooking necessary, if you do not have any vegetarians in your house
- Try fresh herbs
- If you want it more "soup like" you can add more tomatoes or stock
- Serve with a hearty wheat bread and a salad for a satisfying and filling meal
- This stew freezes wonderfully, and it tastes even better after it has been in the refrigerator for a few days

Angela Palmer, MSIS candidate, School of Information, University of Texas at Austin

Portobello Burgers

¼ cup vegetable broth
2 tablespoons olive oil
2 teaspoons balsamic vinegar
1 teaspoon fresh thyme leaves
1/8 teaspoon salt
1/8 teaspoon coarsely ground black pepper
4 medium (about 4" diameter) portobello mushrooms, stems discarded
4 large buns

In a glass baking dish, just large enough to hold mushrooms in a single layer, mix broth, olive oil, vinegar, thyme, salt and pepper. Add mushrooms, turning to coat. Let stand 30 minutes, stirring occasionally. Prepare outdoor grill, or heat a 10" grill pan over medium heat until hot. Add mushrooms and cook about 8-10 minutes per side, turning occasionally and brushing with remaining marinade, until mushrooms are browned and cooked through. Place warm mushrooms on buns to serve.

Susan Henricks, Carnegie-Stout Public Library, Dubuque, IA

"Animals are my friends . . . and I don't eat my friends."
George Bernard Shaw (1856-1950) Irish playwright and critic

State Library Gumbo Open Records Recipe

1 cup onions, chopped
3 cups water
2 tablespoons vegetable oil
3 cups vegetable stock
2 bay leaves
1 16-ounce can chopped tomatoes
½ teaspoon dried oregano
1 cup corn
½ teaspoon dried basil
1 cup uncooked rice
2 celery stalks, finely chopped
1 tablespoon cider vinegar
1 medium potato, diced
¼ teaspoon file gumbo
1 red bell pepper, diced
2 carrots, diced
Salt and pepper to taste
Tabasco to taste

Sauté the onions in the vegetable oil until just translucent. Add the herbs (except for the file gumbo), celery, bell pepper, carrots, and potatoes. Cook for about 10 minutes, stirring continuously to prevent sticking. When tender, add the tomatoes, vegetable stock, and water. Simmer for 10-15 minutes. Add the corn, rice, and the vinegar. Add the file gumbo. Simmer until the rice is cooked. Remove the bay leaves. Add the Tabasco and salt and pepper. Best when left to season over night. If the gumbo becomes too thick (or if more people than expected need to be served), add additional stock to thin. If using non-government funds, meat, shrimp, or other additional ingredients may be added. Serves 4-6 Texans (or 8-12 non-Texans) *Enjoy!*

Jeanette Larson, Austin Public Library, Austin, TX

"I seem to you cruel and too much addicted to gluttony, when I beat my cook for sending up a bad dinner. If that seems too trifling a cause, pray tell for what cause would you have a cook flogged?"
Martial (1st century B.C.E.) Roman poet

Vegetarian Gravy

2 tablespoons of flour
2 tablespoons of olive oil
2 teaspoons of soy sauce (or tamari)
1 cup of vegetable broth (or water, if it's all you have)
A wire whisk (believe me)
One capful of "Kitchen Bouquet Gravy Enhancer," optional

Mix the first three ingredients in a saucepan over low flame till smooth. Wisk in the cup of veggie broth, raise the flame to low/medium and continue stirring constantly until it thickens (10-15 minutes or so, I always try to have a book on tape going at the same time).
Serves two or three people. This recipe can be doubled or tripled at will. One may also add hot sautéed mushrooms when thick, if that's to your taste. Very good over mashed potatoes. Serve hot.

Stella Herzig, O'Keefe Library St. Ambrose University, Davenport, IA

"I like a cook who smiles out loud when he tastes his own work. Let God worry about your modesty; I want to see your enthusiasm." Robert Farrar Capon (1925-) author, teacher of cooking, and Episcopal parish priest

641.5941 Cookery, English.

Aunt Aggie's Parkin

1 pound cake flour
Pinch salt
2 teaspoons ground ginger
8 ounces sugar
2 ounces butter
8 ounces treacle
One egg beaten with 5 ounces of milk

Mix flour, salt, ginger, and sugar thoroughly. Warm the butter and treacle; beat together. Gradually add dry ingredients alternately with the egg and milk mixture until well blended. Pour into a greased 8" x 8" baking pan and bake at 325 degrees for 60-90 minutes.

Susan Henricks, Carnegie-Stout Public Library, Dubuque, IA

"Seeing is deceiving. It's eating that's believing."
James Thurber (1894-1961) American writer and cartoonist

Eclairs

5 ounces water
2 ounces butter or margarine
3 ounces flour
3 medium eggs
1 teaspoon vanilla

Melt margarine in a saucepan over low heat. Add water and bring to a quick boil. Remove from heat right away and add flour. Beat well. Return to a low heat and beat continually until the mixture becomes slightly glossy and leaves the sides of the pan. Remove from heat. Gradually beat in the eggs and vanilla until mixture is very glossy and drops easily from a spoon. Drop onto a cookie sheet using a knife which has been dipped in cold water. Bake at 475 degrees on the second shelf to the top of the oven for 15 minutes, then 20-25 minutes at 375 degrees. Cool. Fill with cream or filling of choice and frost with chocolate icing.

Ann Drought, patron, St. Helens Central Library, St. Helens, Merseyside, England

English Apple Cake

8 ounces plain flour
½ teaspoon mixed spice (apple pie spice)
½ teaspoon baking soda
4 ounces margarine
6 ounces caster sugar
2 eggs, beaten
8 ounces sultanas
2 ounces currants
8 ounces apples, peeled, cored, and grated roughly
Crushed sugar lumps

Grease and line an 8" round cake pan. Sift flour, spice and baking soda. Beat the margarine and sugar till light and creamy. Beat in the eggs and gradually fold in the flour. Stir in the dried fruit and apple. Turn into the pan, scatter crushed sugar over the cake mixture. Bake at 350 degrees for 1¼ -1½ hours. Leave in the pan for 10 minutes before turning onto a wire rack to cool.

Linda Magley, patron, Mesa Family History Center Library, Mesa, AZ

Meringue Cream with Raspberries

6 egg whites
12 ounces granulated sugar
1½ pints double cream
2 8-10-ounce packets quick frozen raspberries, thawed
1 ½ ounces pistachio nuts, blanched and chopped

Cover several baking sheets with parchment paper. Whisk the egg whites until stiff. Lightly whisk in half the granulated sugar, then fold in the rest of the sugar. With two small teaspoons, heap the meringue mixture in very small peaks on to the baking sheets. Sprinkle with sugar and bake at 240 degrees for about 1¼ hours. Cool. Whip the cream. Fold in half of the small meringues and the pistachio nuts. Pile the mixture high on a serving dish. Chill. Just before serving, put the raspberries around the edge of the serving dish.

Zoe Lodge, patron, Guildford Library, Surrey, England

Savory Crusted Lamb

1 small leg English lamb
2 crushed cloves garlic
3 tablespoons dry English mustard
1 teaspoon powdered rosemary
1 teaspoon powdered thyme
1 tablespoon mint, freshly chopped
1 teaspoon salt
½ teaspoon pepper
1 small onion finely grated
Small glass white wine
3 ounces butter, melted
2 cups fine white bread crumbs

Place the leg in a roasting tin and cook in a pre-heated oven at 450 degrees for 10 minutes. Do not butter or lard the joint. Set oven to 350 degrees and continue cooking for one hour. Meanwhile mix the crushed garlic, dry mustard, herbs, seasoning and grated onion well. Mix to a smooth paste with the wine. Make sure the mixture is free from lumps. Drip melted butter in gradually, beating well at the same time. Remove the lamb from the oven and allow to cool a little. The mixture should now look like a thick, quite light cream. Spread this thickly all over the joint. Pat the bread crumbs on firmly to make a coating to cover the joint almost completely. Dribble a little of the roasting fat over the crust and put the joint back into the oven for another 20-30 minutes until the coating is crisp and good color. Serve on a heated platter. Serves 4-6

Zoe Lodge, patron, Guildford Library, Surrey, England

From the archives of the Carnegie-Stout Public Library,
Dubuque, Iowa

641.5945 Cookery, Italian.

Grandma Columbo's Ravioli

¾ pound ground pork
¾ pound ground veal
¾ pound ground beef
1 egg
Onion to taste, chopped
1 hand full Parmesan cheese, freshly grated
1 package frozen spinach, thawed, drained, and squeezed dry
Salt, pepper and your choice of seasonings to taste
Bread crumbs

Mix ground meats, egg, onion, cheese, spinach, and seasonings together with hands. Add enough bread crumbs until the mixture comes together and holds a shape, but not too dry or firm.

Pasta

3 cups flour
4 eggs, beaten
2 half egg shells of water
1 tablespoon olive oil

Measure flour into a mixing bowl. Make a well and add the eggs, water, and olive oil. Mix by hand. Dough should be soft and tender, only slightly sticky. Roll out sheets of dough (easiest to do using a pasta machine) and place a sheet of dough on a ravioli tray. Fill each with meat mixture. Brush dough with an egg white and water mixture before placing the second sheet of dough on top and pressing to cut out individual ravioli. Can be frozen. Cook in gently boiling water. Length of cooking time will depend upon the thickness of the pasta. Yields about 33 dozen

Susan Henricks, Carnegie-Stout Public Library, Dubuque, IA

"The trouble with eating Italian food is that 5 or 6 days later you're hungry again."
George Miller, British writer

Italian Cheese and Ham Pie

1 16-ounce container cottage cheese
1 15-16-ounce container ricotta cheese
2 cups cooked ham (3/4 pound), diced
2/3 cup Parmesan cheese, freshly grated
3 eggs
2 teaspoons Italian seasoning
½ teaspoon salt
¼ teaspoon pepper
Pie crust, enough for a 9" crust
1 egg yolk, slightly beaten

In a medium bowl, mix the cottage cheese, ricotta cheese, ham, 3 eggs, and all seasonings until well blended. Prepare pie crust. Shape 2/3 of the pie crust into a ball, and the same with the remaining 1/3. Roll the large ball into a 16" circle, about 1/8" thick. Fold circle into fourths and lift into a 10" springform pan; unfold and press into bottom and sides to make crust even with the rim of the pan. Brush with some beaten egg yolk. Spoon the cheese and ham mixture into the pan. Fold edges of pastry crust over filling and brush with some beaten egg yolk. Roll remaining pastry into a 10" circle. Place the pastry circle over the filling in the pan pressing lightly to seal; top with remaining egg yolk. Bake the pie for 1 hour at 350 degrees of until a knife inserted in the center of the pie comes out clean. Cool in the refrigerator. To serve, carefully remove the sides of the springform pan. Cut into wedges.

Susan Henricks, Carnegie-Stout Public Library, Dubuque, IA

"There are two Italies. . . The one is the most sublime and lovely contemplation that can be conceived by the imagination of man; the other is the most degraded, disgusting, and odious. What do you think? Young women of rank actually eat - - you will never guess what - - garlick! Our poor friend, Lord Byron is quite corrupted by living among these people, and in fact, is going on in a way not worthy of him."
Percy Bysshe Shelleyin a letter from Naples, 22 December 1918

The etymology of the word lasagna is amusing. It starts with the Greek lasanon which means 'chamber pot!' The Romans borrow it as lasanum to humorously refer to a 'cooking pot.' Later, the Italian word lasagne (plural of lasagna) came to refer to a dish cooked in such a pot – flat sheets of pasta layered with minced meat and tomatoes topped with grated cheese. Soon the word lasagna was applied to the pasta itself. foodreference.com

Literary Lasagna

1½ pounds lean ground beef
1 medium onion, finely chopped
1 medium bell pepper, finely chopped
2 cloves garlic, minced
2 teaspoons basil (fresh preferred), chopped
1 teaspoon dried oregano
3 tablespoons brown sugar
1½ teaspoons salt
1 29-ounce can diced tomatoes
2 6-ounce cans tomato paste
12 dry lasagna noodles
2 eggs, beaten (may use egg substitute such as Egg Beaters)
1 pint part-skim ricotta cheese
3/4 cup Parmesan cheese, grated
2 tablespoons dried parsley
1 teaspoon salt
1 pound mozzarella cheese, shredded

In a skillet over medium heat, brown ground beef, onion, bell pepper, and garlic; drain fat. Mix in basil, oregano, brown sugar, 1½ teaspoons salt, diced tomatoes and tomato paste. Simmer for 30-45 minutes, stirring occasionally.
Preheat oven to 375 degrees. Fill a large pot ¾ full of water and add a pinch of salt. Bring pot to boil. Add lasagna noodles, and cook for 5- 8 minutes stirring occasionally; drain. Lay noodles flat on towels to dry. In a medium bowl, mix together eggs, ricotta, ½ cup Parmesan cheese, parsley and 1 teaspoon salt.
Layer 1/3 of the lasagna noodles in the bottom of a 13" x 9" inch-baking dish (spray with non-stick vegetable oil if desired). Cover noodles with ½ ricotta mixture, ½ of the mozzarella cheese and 1/3 of the sauce. Repeat. Top with remaining noodles and sauce. Sprinkle additional (up to ¼ cup) Parmesan cheese over the top. Bake in the preheated oven 30 minutes. Let stand 10 minutes before serving. Serves 8

Denette Kellogg, Carnegie-Stout Public Library, Dubuque, IA

30

Manicotti

1 pound sweet Italian sausage links
1 pound ground beef
1 8-ounce package of manicotti shells (16 shells)
1 medium onion, chopped
1 15-ounce can tomatoes
1 29-ounce can tomato puree
1 6-ounce can tomato paste
1 teaspoon sugar
½ teaspoon pepper
2 teaspoons oregano
1 ¾ teaspoon basil
2 cloves garlic, minced
4 cups ricotta cheese
1 8-ounce package shredded mozzarella cheese
2 tablespoons parsley, chopped
Parmesan cheese, freshly grated

In a covered 5-quart Dutch oven, over medium heat and in ¼ cup of water, cook sausage links for five minutes. Uncover, brown well and drain on paper towels. Spoon off any fat from the Dutch oven. Over a medium heat, brown ground beef and onion. Stir in tomato products, sugar, pepper, 1 teaspoon basil, 1 ½ teaspoons salt, and 1 cup of water. Simmer, covered for 45 minutes. Cut sausage into bite-sized pieces. Add to tomato mixture and cook for 15 more minutes stirring occasionally. Meanwhile, cook manicotti as label directs. Drain. Preheat oven to 375 degrees. In a large bowl combine ricotta and mozzarella cheeses, parsley, ¾ teaspoon basil and ½ teaspoon salt. Mix well. Stuff into the cooked manicotti shells. Spoon ½ of the meat sauce into a 13" x 9" baking pan. Place half of the stuffed manicotti shells over the sauce in one layer. Cover with all but ¾ cup of the remaining sauce. Top with remaining shells in one layer. Spoon reserved sauce over the top. Sprinkle with Parmesan cheese. Bake for 30 minutes

Susan Henricks, Carnegie-Stout Public Library, Dubuque, IA

"Tomatoes and oregano make it Italian; wine and tarragon make it French. Sour cream makes it Russian; lemon and cinnamon make it Greek. Soy sauce makes it Chinese; garlic makes it good."
Alice May Brock (of Alice's Restaurant fame)

Mushroom Risotto Cakes

3 tablespoons olive oil
1 large onion, diced
4 whole garlic cloves
2 bay leaves
10 sprigs fresh thyme
½ pound Arborio rice
1 cup dry white wine
4 cups vegetable stock
Salt & pepper to taste
1 bunch basil, julienned
1 bunch parsley, chopped
¼ bunch thyme, chopped
3 cups mushrooms (crimini, white, portabella, etc.), roasted
¼ pound Parmesan cheese, grated

Heat 1 tablespoon of oil in a large skillet over medium heat. Add onion, garlic, bay leaves, and thyme. Cook until onions are translucent. Add rice and cook until grains separate. Add wine and cook until it evaporates. Add stock slowly, 1 cup at a time, stirring constantly. Take out the bay leaves, garlic cloves, and thyme sprigs. Add salt and pepper to taste. Stir in chopped herbs, roasted mushrooms, and cheese. Spoon risotto onto a sheet pan and cool.

Shape risotto into 8 equal cakes. Heat 2 tablespoons oil in a large skillet over medium-high heat. Cook rice cakes until browned on each side (approximately 5 minutes). Serve on a bed of lettuce with a light salad, stir-fried mixed vegetables, or fresh olives and sweet pickles.

Sarah Houghton, Marin County Free Library, San Rafael, CA

"Leave the gun. Take the cannolis." Clemenza in *The Godfather*

641.59485 Cookery, Swedish.

Fingerklatchens

1 1/3 cups soft butter
1 cup sugar
4 egg yolks
1 teaspoon almond extract
1 teaspoon salt
3 ½ cups flour, sifted

Mix ingredients in order. Roll into small balls in palm of hand (approximately 1 tablespoon of dough per ball.) Place on ungreased cookie sheet and indent with finger to make a well in the center of the cookie. Bake at 325 degrees for 25-30 minutes or until cookies look *very light* brown. When cool, fill the center with favorite preserves. Sprinkle with confectioner's sugar just before serving.

Katherine Mazzella, Tappan Library, Tappan, NY

"Cooking is like love, it should be entered into with abandon or not at all."
Harriet van Horne (1920 -) American columnist

Jansson's Frestelse (Temptation)

6 potatoes
2 yellow onions
1 can anchovy fillets
2½ to 3 diliter (1¼-1½ cups) light cream
2 tablespoon margarine or butter

Peel the potatoes, cut into thin slices or grate. Slice the onions. Drain the anchovies (reserve liquid) and cut into pieces. Put potatoes, onions and anchovies in layers in buttered baking dish, making the first and last layers potatoes. Dot with butter. Pour in a little of the liquid from the anchovies and half of the cream. Bake in a 200 degree oven for about 20 minutes. Pour in the remaining cream and bake for another 30 minutes or until the potatoes are tender.

Linda Magley, patron, Mesa Family History Center Library, Mesa, AZ

Pepparkakor (Swedish Gingerbread Cookies)

½ pound butter
1 tablespoon each: cloves, cinnamon, ginger, cardamom
Grated rind of 1 orange
1½ cups sugar
1 beaten egg
2 tablespoons Karo syrup (dark or light)
2 teaspoon baking soda - with just enough warm water to wet the soda
3 cups flour

In a small saucepan, melt the butter with the spices being careful not to burn the mixture; cool. Mix sugar, egg, and Karo syrup and baking soda. Add the butter mixture and the flour mixture alternating dry/wet. Form a dough; place in a bowl, let stand in refrigerator overnight. Roll and cutout with your favorite cookie cutters. Bake 350 degrees for 8-10 minutes.

Linda Magley, patron, Mesa Family History Center Library, Mesa, AZ

Sill Salad

1 salt herring/sill (or ½ small jar of pickled herring sliced)
1½ cups boiled potatoes
1½ cups pickled beets, diced
1/3 cup gherkin diced
½ cup apples diced
¼ onion chopped
4 tablespoons vinegar
2 tablespoons water
2 tablespoons sugar
White pepper to taste
½ cup whipped cream
1-2 hard-boiled eggs and parsley for garnish

Clean fish removing head, and soak overnight in cold water; drain skin and fillet. Dice fillets, add potatoes, beets, apples, onion and gherkin; mix carefully. Blend vinegar, sugar and pepper. Add to mixture. Add whipped cream before serving.

Linda Magley, patron, Mesa Family History Center Library, Mesa, AZ

Swedish Soft Gingerbread (Mjuk Pepparkaka)

1½ cups sugar
1 cup plain yogurt or sour cream
3 eggs slightly beaten
1 cup margarine, melted
2 cups flour
1 teaspoon each: ginger, cloves, cinnamon, nutmeg
1 teaspoon baking soda with a tablespoon warm water
Grated orange and lemon peel (I use about 1 tablespoon orange marmalade if fresh peel isn't available.)

Mix in order given; bake at 350 degrees for 50 minutes. Enough for 3 loaf pans or one Bundt pan

Linda Magley, patron, Mesa Family History Center Library, Mesa, AZ

"Had I but a penny in the world, thou shouldst have it for gingerbread."
William Shakespeare (1564-1616) English poet and playwright

Swedish Pancakes

1/3 cup sugar
1½ cups all-purpose flour
½ teaspoon salt
8 eggs
3 cups milk
3 tablespoons butter, melted

In a bowl combine flour, salt and sugar. Beat eggs, milk, and butter. Stir into dry ingredients and mix well. Pour batter by ½ cupfuls onto a lightly greased hot griddle; cook until set and lightly browned. Turn; cook 1 minute longer. Keep warm while preparing the rest of the pancakes. Yields 1 dozen

Susan Henricks, Carnegie-Stout Public Library, Dubuque, IA

641.59495 Cookery, Greek.

Baklava is the ancestor of strudel. It was brought to Hungary by Turkish invaders in the 16th century. foodreference.com

Baklava

3 cups shelled walnuts (about ¾ pound)
½ cup sugar
1 ½ teaspoon cinnamon
2 8-ounce packages of phyllo dough
½ cup unsalted butter, melted
1 tablespoon water
Honey syrup (recipe follows)

Place walnuts on a 15" x 10" x 1" jellyroll pan and toast in a 350 degree oven for 10 minutes. Grind walnuts ½ cup at a time in a blender while still warm. Mix in sugar and cinnamon. Brush the bottom of a 13" x 9" pan with melted butter. Fold two leaves of phyllo in half, place on the bottom of the pan; brush with butter. (Note: You would fold two leaves of phyllo in half if your package of phyllo contains one roll of dough. Phyllo dough is also sold in two smaller rolls per box. If you get two rolls per box, you would take four leaves of phyllo which will just fit the pan, and do not fold them in half.) Remember to keep the rest of the phyllo pastry covered with a damp cloth to prevent drying while you work with it. Phyllo dries out very quickly. Next, sprinkle the layer of phyllo with ½ cup of the nut mixture. Add two more sheets of phyllo, fold over and brush with butter (or four smaller sheets, not folded) and sprinkle ½ cup of nut mixture. Repeat four more times. End with a layer of phyllo and brush with butter. Sprinkle with 1 tablespoon of water. With a knife mark the baklava squares, cutting only through the top layer. Begin with 5 lengthwise x 1 ½" apart strips, then mark diagonally 1 ½" apart forming 9 strips. Bake at 325 degrees for 50 minutes or until the top is golden. Remove. Cut all the way through the diamonds, separating slightly. Pour cooled honey syrup over the baklava and cool thoroughly. Cover and let stand overnight for the syrup to be absorbed. No refrigeration is necessary.

Honey Syrup

1 small lemon
1 cup sugar
1 cup water
1 2" piece stick cinnamon
2 whole cloves
1 cup honey
1 tablespoon brandy

36

Pare the rind of the lemon; just the thin yellow part; no white. Squeeze out 1 ½ teaspoons lemon juice and set aside. Place lemon rind, sugar, water, cinnamon stick, and cloves in a heavy medium-sized saucepan. Bring to a boil. Lower the heat and continue to cook without stirring for 25 minutes or until the mixture is syrupy; 230 degrees on a candy thermometer. Stir in honey. Pour the mixture through a strainer, or cheesecloth, into a 2 cup measure. Stir in the reserved lemon juice and the brandy. Cool to room temperature.

Susan Henricks, Carnegie-Stout Public Library, Dubuque, IA

Greek Cookies

1 ½ pounds of unsalted butter
2 egg yolks
1 egg, whole
¼ cup powdered sugar
1 ounce cognac
¼ teaspoon almond extract
2 pounds cake flour, such as Swan's Down
2 teaspoons baking soda mixed with the juice from ½ lemon

Beat butter until light and fluffy. Beat in everything but the flour. Mix the flour in by hand, then knead. The dough will be quite stiff. Form into small balls. Bake at 350 degrees until very lightly browned. Roll in powdered sugar while warm.

Ann Garas, patron, Rockford Public Library, Rockford, IL

"If more of us valued food and cheer and song above hoarded gold, it would be a merrier world."
J.R.R. Tolkein (1892-1972) English author

641.5952 Cookery, Japanese.

"Laver, purple laver, redware, or sea tangle is one of the most commonly eaten seaweeds. Sheets of dried laver look somewhat like purple cellophane. It is called nori by the Japanese." foodreference.com

Salad Roll Recipe (Sushi)

Sushi is the marriage of vinegar rice to other ingredients. There are four basic categories of sushi: nigiri sushi (finger or oval shaped sushi rice), maki sushi (rolled sushi rice), oshi sushi (pressed sushi rice) and chirashi sushi (scattered sushi rice). This recipe is for maki sushi (rolled sushi rice), salad roll.

Ingredients for rice:

1½ cups of uncooked rice, use only short grain white rice
2 cups of water
1 package of sushi nori (toasted seaweed) - in this recipe, you need approximately 5 sheets of them
2/3 cup of seasoned rice vinegar

Ingredients for sushi roll filling:

Lettuce, shredded
Tuna fish mixed with a little mayonnaise
2 eggs cooked to omelet style and sliced into strips
1 cucumber, peeled, seeded and sliced into strips
Imitation crab or boiled shrimp, diced

Sushi supplies:

Bamboo mat (maki-su or sushi mat) to make the sushi rolls
Rice paddle, or large flat plastic spoon, or wooden spoon
Shallow wooden bowl , large flat plastic container or glass container

Cook rice. Try this or follow directions on your rice bag. Use a heavy bottom medium size pot, add rice and water. Cover and cook over medium-high heat, bringing to a boil for 2 minutes. Turn down the heat to medium and boil for 5 minutes. Reduce heat to very low and cook for 15 minutes or till water is absorbed. Turn off the heat and let stand on burner with lid still on for 10-15 minutes.

Transfer the rice to large shallow mixing bowl. (Do not use any metal because the vinegar reacts with it causing an unpleasant taste.) Using horizontal, cutting strokes, gently cut into the rice with a watery wooden paddle. Pour a small amount of vinegar on the top of the rice. Cut through the rice several times to evenly distribute

38

vinegar. Taste test. Add more vinegar as necessary and repeat. You may not have to use all the vinegar dressing. Do not add too much or it will become mushy. When rice has cooled, it is ready to use for sushi rolls. Watch out to keep the rice from drying out. (You may want to place it in a container and cover it with a damp cloth or paper towel.). Meanwhile, prepare filling ingredients by mixing the lettuce, tuna, cucumbers, eggs and crab or shrimp in a bowl.

Roll sushi: Lay your bamboo mat on a cutting board with bamboo strips going horizontally from you. Place one sheet of nori on it leaving 1-2" border around the outside of the nori. In the center of the nori spread rice. Place the remaining nori sheets on the filling ingredients. Lift the bamboo mat and roll once to make a long sushi log - slightly squeeze along entire roll. Slightly lift the bamboo mat and roll again till you get to the end of the nori sheet. The roll should be nice and tight with ingredients directly in the center. Using a sharp knife slice the sushi log into 1/2" rolls. I recommend you wipe the knife with a damp cloth or paper towel after cutting each one. Place flat on a plate. If you like, serve with dipping sauce - soy sauce and wasabi.

Nanako Hashini, patron Meitokukai Library, Tadotsu, Kagawa, Japan

"If white wine goes with fish, do white grapes go with sushi?"

"Cuisine is when things taste like themselves."
Curnosky (Maurice Edmond Sailland) (1872-1956) French writer

Pansit Canton

A popular dish from the Philippines; essential for any celebration.

1-2 pounds of pork, cubed
4 garlic cloves, diced or crushed
1 medium onion, chopped
1 teaspoon salt
½ teaspoon pepper
2 cups water
4 tablespoons soy sauce
4 tablespoons vinegar
1 pound green beans, cut in long strips
1 carrot, cut in long thin strips
3 leaves of cabbage, cut in long strips
1 medium package of canton (or kanton) noodles. *(These are available in the oriental aisle of stores. If you cannot find these use 2-3 packages of Ramon noodles.)*
Key limes

In a wok or large pan, brown the pork, garlic, and onions. Add salt, pepper, and water. Cook until meat is tender Add soy sauce, vinegar, green beans, carrot, and cabbage. Cook 5 minutes adding more water if needed. Add canton noodles. The noodles should soak up virtually all of the water. Stir constantly until heated through. Serve garnished with lemon or lime slices, to be squeezed on top as desired. Key limes cut in half are the most authentic. Variations: Use chicken instead of pork, or use a mixture of chicken and pork. Add small shrimp when adding the canton noodles. Serves 4-6

Mary Mastraccio, MARCIVE, Inc. San Antonio, TX

"Next to eating good dinners, a healthy man with a benevolent turn of mind, must like, I think, to read about them."
William Makepeace Thackeray (1811-1863) English author

Pork Adobo

2 pounds pork, cubed (or mixture of pork and chicken; with or without bone)
2 large cloves garlic, cut in fourths
¼ cup vinegar
1 large bay leaf
¼ teaspoon pepper
½ teaspoon salt
1 tablespoon soy sauce
1 teaspoon brown sugar
1½ cups water

Sauté the pork cubes and garlic in hot fat until browned. Add vinegar, bay leaf, pepper, salt, soy sauce, brown sugar and water. Simmer until meat is tender. Serve with rice. Serves 6-8

Mary Mastraccio, MARCIVE, Inc. San Antonio, TX

Sweet Potato Vine Salad

This is a popular salad in the Philippines.

Remove leaves from sweet potato vine* and wash thoroughly. You will want at least one packed colander-full of leaves. Pour boiling water over washed leaves. Cover and let steam about 5 minutes. Drain well. Add:

½ small onion, chopped onion
1 small tomato, diced
2 teaspoons (or to taste) fresh ginger, minced
1 tablespoon lemon juice
1 teaspoon soy sauce

Serves 2-4
*Substitute fresh spinach if you don't have sweet potato vines.

Mary Mastraccio, MARCIVE, Inc. San Antonio, TX

"The true essentials of a feast are only fun and feed."
Oliver Wendell Holmes, Sr. (1809-1894) American author and physician

641.5962 Cookery, Egyptian.

Bamia Masloukah(Egyptian-Style Boiled Okra)

1½ pounds fresh okra pods
1 tablespoon vegetable oil
1 medium onion, minced
2½ cups beef stock
1 teaspoon lemon juice, freshly squeezed

Wash and top and tail okra, discarding hard pods or any blemishes. Heat the oil in a saucepan and sauté the onion until it is translucent. Add okra, cook for 3 minutes, constantly stirring. Add stock, cover, and cook for 10 additional minutes, until okra is tender. Add lemon juice and serve hot. Serves 5-6

Barbara Feist Stienstra, Middletown Thrall Library, Middletown, NY

Bamia (Sweet and Sour Okra)

1 pound small okra pods
2 tablespoons olive oil
1 tablespoon honey
Salt
Black pepper, freshly ground to taste
1 tablespoon lemon juice, freshly squeezed
½ cup water

Wash the okra and pat dry with paper towels. Top and tail it, discarding any hard pods or blemishes. Heat the olive oil in a saucepan and sauté the okra in the oil for 3-5 minutes, turning each pod once. Add honey, salt, pepper, lemon juice, and water. Cover, lower heat, and simmer for 15 minutes, adding water, when necessary. Serve hot. Serves 4-6

Barbara Feist Stienstra, Middletown Thrall Library, Middletown, NY

Dukkah (spice mixture)

This spice mixture is an Egyptian household staple. It can be made in large quantities and stored in jars; this recipe yields 1½ cups.

¼ cup coriander seeds
¼ cup unsalted peanuts
1 tablespoon cumin seeds
2 tablespoons sesame seeds
2 tablespoons dried chickpeas
½ cup salt
2 tablespoons dried mint leaves
1 teaspoon black peppercorns

Roast the coriander seeds, peanuts, cumin, sesame seeds separately by placing them in a heavy skillet over medium heat and stirring them with a wooden spoon until they release a full aroma. (Times vary per spice, let your nose be your guide!) When all seeds are roasted, place the ingredients in a mortar and pound until seeds are finely crushed. (If using a food processor, do not allow mixture to become paste!) Pour mixture into a jar and seal tightly. The spice mixture will keep for several weeks at room temperature.

Barbara Feist Stienstra, Middletown Thrall Library, Middletown, NY

Ful Medames (Beans)

2 cups dried Egyptian broad beans or dried Italian fava beans
4 cups water
6 cloves garlic
1 teaspoon sea salt
1 tablespoon lemon juice, freshly squeezed
¼ cup olive oil
1½ tablespoons parsley, minced
Radishes, scallions, and hard-boiled eggs to use as garnishes.

Wash the beans and remove blemished ones and "stones." Place beans in heavy large pot with water, for them to soak overnight. Next morning, add more water to cover the beans, and over medium heat, bring beans to a boil. Lower the heat, cover, and simmer the beans for two hours, or until tender, adding more *boiling* water when needed. (Otherwise at tap temperature, the beans will become tough.) As the beans cook, mash garlic, sea salt in a bowl. Mix in lemon juice, olive oil, and parsley to garlic mixture. After the beans have been cooked, drain and reserve two teaspoons of cooking liquid. Add garlic mixture and the reserved cooking liquid to beans and combine. Serve warm, with toasted pita bread. Serves 4-6

Barbara Feist Stienstra, Middletown Thrall Library, Middletown, NY

Gebna Makleyah (Fried Cheese)

1 cup firm feta cheese, or other mild cheese, finely crumbled
1 tablespoon flour
1 egg
Salt to taste
Pepper to taste, freshly ground
Olive oil for deep frying
Lemon wedges for serving
Pita triangles for serving

Place the cheese, flour, egg and pepper in a bowl and mix well with your hands. Roll the mixture into 1-inch balls. If it is too loose, add a touch more flour. If it is too dry, add some liquid from the feta cheese. Heat oil (375 degrees) for deep frying in a deep fryer, Dutch oven, or heavy pot. When the oil is hot, add the cheese balls one at a time. Fry until they are golden brown. Remove with a slotted spoon and drain on paper towel. Serve warm with lemon wedges and pita bread. Serves 6

Barbara Feist Stienstra, Middletown Thrall Library, Middletown, NY

641.6318 Rice.

Gourmet Rice

1 box seasoned long grain and wild rice, such as Uncle Ben's
1 can onion soup
1 can beef consommé
2/3 stick margarine
2 cans mushrooms with liquid
1 tablespoon brandy or sherry

Combine all ingredients. Bake uncovered at 350 degrees for 1½ hours. Since it is very rich it is best served with plain meat such as roast.

Susan Radosti, South O'Brien High School Library, Paullina, IA

"Rice is the best, most nutritive and unquestionably the most widespread staple in the world."
Esoffier (1846-1935) Chef and cookbook writer was called the "emperor of chefs and "emperor of the world's kitchens by Emperor William II of Germany

Rice Delight

1 cup raw rice
1 small can mushrooms (stems and pieces) undrained
1 stick margarine, cut up
1 can dried onion soup mix
1 can beef broth
¼ cup sliced almonds

Combine all ingredients in a two-quart casserole dish. Bake, covered, at 350 degrees for 1 hour.

Jan Buenning, Waverly Public Library, Waverly, IA

Variations on Low Calorie Rice Recipes

Sesame Rice -- Toast sesame seeds in oven or in a hot ungreased skillet. Stir into rice that has been cooked in beef broth. Add a dash of Worcestershire sauce, if desired.

Seafood Rice -- Cook rice in clam juice and toss with sautéed sliced green onions before serving.

Fruited Rice -- Lightly sauté in a little margarine some shredded carrot, chopped onion, and diced apples. Stir into hot cooked rice. If desired, garnish with a sprinkling of toasted sesame seeds.

Green Rice -- Finely chop green pepper, parsley, green onions, and celery (lightly sauté if desired). Add to hot cooked rice and steam for a minute or two to heat thoroughly.

Susan Radosti, South O'Brien High School Library, Paullina, IA

641.638 Cookery (Salad dressing)

Aunt Helen's French Dressing

This was the house dressing at my Aunt's (Helen Reed Johnson) restaurant in Oregon, IL in the 1930's.

¾ cup oil
¾ cup white vinegar
1 teaspoon prepared mustard
½ cup ketchup
¼ cup Roquefort cheese
1 small onion, chopped

Put all the ingredients in a fruit jar and shake well.

Jim Lander, Pfohl Health Science Library, Mercy Hospital, Dubuque, IA

"... the seede of Mustard pounded with vinegar is an excellent sauce, good to be eaten with any grosse meates, either fish or flesh, because it doth help digestion, warmeth the stomache and provoketh appetite."
John Gerard (1564-1637) A Jesuit, well known for his autobiography

Thousand Island Dressing

2¾ cups mayonnaise
1 cup chili sauce
4 tablespoon parsley, chopped
2 tablespoon ground onion
¼ green pepper, chopped
2 teaspoons pimento, chopped
2 hard-boiled eggs, chopped, optional

Combine all ingredients, mixing well. Keep refrigerated.

Christine A. Cowles, Fort Madison Public Libraries, Fort Madison, IA

📖📖📖📖📖

641.65 Cookery (Vegetables)

Artichokes

Artichokes
Butter
Salt and pepper to taste

Take the most beautiful artichoke you can find. Trim the stem and the top so the artichokes will sit in a saucepan with a lid on. Place in boiling water for 20 minutes or more. Let drain. Melt butter and serve in a small dish next to the artichoke. Peel the leaves one by one dipping them into the butter eating the tender portion which grows in proportion to your nearness to the heart. When you get to the choke, cut it out with a small paring knife. Cut up the heart in the butter dish and eat it. Salt or pepper are welcome. I have also prepared this dish with olive oil.

Kelly Prewett, Greensboro Public Library, Greensboro, NC

Question: What did the carrot say to the wheat?
Answer: Lettuce rest, I'm feeling beet.
Shel Silverstein (1932-1999) American poet, author, and illustrator

Broccoli and Rice Casserole

1 package frozen broccoli, chopped
1 can cream of mushroom soup
1 cup milk
3 teaspoons butter
1 cup rice, uncooked
1 cup Velveeta cheese diced, or the shredded type

Mix all ingredients together and place in 350 degree oven for 50 minutes. This is a really easy and fast dish to make. It is great for taking to parties or church.

Bonnie Webster, Taylor County Public Library Campbellsville, KY and
Sarah Kennedy, Waukee Public Library, Waukee, IA

"I do not like broccoli. And I haven't liked it since I was a little kid and my mother made me eat it. And I'm president of the United States and I'm not going to eat any more broccoli."
George H.W. Bush, (1924 -) 41st President of the United States

47

Broccoli Holiday Casserole

2 packages frozen broccoli, chopped
1 can cream of mushroom soup
½ cup mayonnaise
1 tablespoon lemon juice
½ cup sharp cheese, grated
1 2-ounce jar pimento
1 cup Ritz crackers, crushed
¼ cup almonds, slivered

Cook broccoli as directed. Arrange in buttered casserole. Mix soup, mayonnaise, lemon juice and cheese; spoon over broccoli. Top with pimento, nuts and crackers. Bake at 350 degrees for 20 minutes.

Susan Elgin, Waukee Public Library, Waukee, IA

Broccoli with Black Olives

1 bunch (1½ pounds) fresh broccoli, trimmed
3 tablespoons olive oil
1 clove garlic, finely chopped
3 tablespoon Parmesan cheese, grated
Salt and pepper to taste
¼ cup small black olives, pitted and diced

Parboil the broccoli about 10 minutes in small amount of salted water. Drain. Heat the oil, add the garlic and sauté until lightly browned. Add the broccoli and season with salt and pepper. Cook slowly over low heat 10 minutes, adding a little of the water in which the broccoli was cooked if the pan goes too dry. Add the olives and heat 2 minutes longer. Serve immediately, sprinkled with the grated cheese.

Susan Radosti, South O'Brien High School Library, Paullina, IA

"Vegetables are a must on a diet. I suggest carrot cake, zucchini bread, and pumpkin pie."
Jim Davis (1945-) cartoonist, *Garfield*

Cauliflower and Broccoli Casserole

1 package California blend vegetables, frozen, or 1 package frozen broccoli, plus package frozen cauliflower
1 cup instant rice, such as Minute Rice
1 can cream of chicken soup
3/4 cup milk

Prepare vegetables as label directs; drain. Add the rice, soup and milk to the vegetables. Place in a two-quart baking dish and bake at 350 degrees for about 30 minutes.

Pat Boe, Dike Public Library, Dike, IA

Quick and Easy Hawaiian Vegetables

Fresh vegetables - your preference
Mrs. Dash Seasoning
Lawry's Hawaiian Marinade Sauce

Boil the vegetables until tender crisp. Drain; return vegetables to pan and add Mrs. Dash seasoning to taste. Add the Hawaiian marinade sauce to taste and simmer gently for 5 minutes.

Hope Smith, Louisville Free Public Library, Louisville, KY

"Cauliflower is nothing but a cabbage with a college education."
Mark Twain (Samuel Langhorne Clemens) (1835-1910) American author

Simple Way to Serve Avocados

Avocado(s) - 1 or 2 servings
Extra virgin olive oil
Lemon
Salt
Pepper

Avocado should be slightly soft when squeezed. Slice each avocado in half the long way. Scoop the pit out, leaving a well in each half. Fill each well about three fourths full with olive oil. Squeeze lemon juice into the olive oil. Salt and pepper each half. Use spoon to scoop out part of the avocado nearest the well and to get some of the olive oil/lemon on it.

Susan Radosti, South O'Brien High School Library, Paullina, IA

Spinach Casserole

6 eggs, beaten
1 quart cottage cheese
½ pound American cheese, cubed
1 box frozen spinach, chopped
6 tablespoons flour
½ cup butter, melted

In a large bowl mix the eggs, cottage cheese, and American cheese together. Break frozen spinach into small pieces and add to the egg/cheese mixture. Add flour and stir until blended. Pour into a 13" x 9" baking pan. Pour melted butter over the top. Bake at 300 degrees for 1 hour.

Kay K. Runge, Des Moines Public Library, Des Moines, IA

"Happy is said to be the family which can eat onions together. They are, for the time being, separate from the world and have a harmony of aspiration."
Charles Dudley Warner (1829-1900) *My Summer in a Garden*, 1871

Vegetable Oven Baked Egg Dish

2 tablespoons butter
6 eggs
2-3 tablespoons milk
¼ teaspoon salt
Pinch of pepper
8 ounces cauliflower, broccoli, carrot mixture, frozen and partially cooked
1/3 cup green onion, chopped
2 cups cheddar cheese, shredded

Heat oven to 350 degrees. Melt butter in a glass pie plate. Combine eggs, milk, salt and pepper; beat well. Put vegetables and onion in pie pan with butter. Pour egg mixture over all. Put cheese evenly over the top. Bake 25-30 minutes or until eggs are set in the center. Serve with salsa.

Bette Jollifee, Marathon Public Library, Marathon, IA

Mother: "It's broccoli, dear."
Child: "I say it's spinach, and I say the hell with it."
E.B. White (1899-1985) From a cartoon in the *New Yorker*

Zucchini Provençale

1 medium onion, sliced
1 clove garlic, minced
¼ cup salad oil
2 pounds zucchini, sliced
4 tomatoes, sliced
1 green pepper, chopped
Parsley, minced
Parmesan cheese
Mozzarella cheese, sliced

In a skillet sauté onion and garlic, in salad oil. Add zucchini, tomatoes, green pepper, salt and pepper to taste. Cook until tender. Sprinkle with minced parsley and Parmesan cheese before serving. Add slices of mozzarella cheese. Serves 8

Nancy Voltmer, Hiatt Middle School Library, Des Moines, IA

"The first zucchini I ever saw I killed it with a hoe."
John Gould (1908-2003) American author, *Monstrous Depravity*, 1963

641.6521 Potatoes.

German Potato Salad

6 medium potatoes
6 slices bacon, cooked crisp
1/3 cup bacon grease
¾ cup onion, chopped
2 tablespoons flour
2 tablespoons sugar
1½ teaspoons salt
Dash pepper
½ teaspoon celery seed
¾ cup water
1/3 cup vinegar

Cook potatoes until tender. Slice and place in a 2 quart casserole dish.
Fry onion slowly in the bacon grease. Add flour, sugar, salt, and celery seed. Stir in water and vinegar. Boil one minute until thick. Pour over potatoes. Top with bacon; serve warm.

Susan Henricks, Carnegie-Stout Public Library, Dubuque, IA

Hashed Brown Potato Casserole

½ cup melted margarine
2 pounds frozen hash browns, thawed
1 10 ¾ ounce can creamy chicken mushroom soup
½ cup green onion, chopped
1 pint sour cream
2 cups cheddar cheese, shredded
1 cup cracker crumbs, crushed, such as Ritz or Club crackers
2 tablespoons margarine, melted

Pour melted margarine into a 13" x 9" baking dish. Add ½ of the frozen hashed brown potatoes. Mix soup, milk, sour cream and onions in a bowl. Pour half of this mixture over the potatoes. Sprinkle 1 cup shredded cheddar cheese over top. Add remaining hashed browns, sauce, and cheese. Sprinkle top with crushed cracker crumbs. Drizzle two tablespoons melted margarine over top. Bake at 350 degrees for 45 minutes to 1 hour.

Cheryl Boothe, Newton Public Library, Newton, IA and
Denise Crawford, Glenwood Public Library, Glenwood, IA

Holiday Refrigerator Mashed Potatoes

5 pounds red potatoes, peeled
2 3-ounce packages of cream cheese
1 cup sour cream
2 tablespoons butter or margarine
1 teaspoon salt
¼ teaspoon pepper
2 teaspoons dill weed

Boil the peeled potatoes in salted water until tender. Drain. Mash until smooth and then add remaining ingredients. Beat until light and fluffy. Cool and cover then place in refrigerator for up to 2 weeks. To heat, place desired amount in greased casserole. Dot with butter and bake at 350 degrees for about 30 minutes. Makes 8 cups or 12 servings

Linda Mack, Waukee Public Library, Waukee, IA

Potato Scramble

2 russet potatoes, cubed
1 can of corn, drained
1 yellow onion, chopped
1 red or green pepper, diced
Handful of mushrooms, sliced
Handful of spinach, chopped
2 cloves garlic, minced or crushed
1 tablespoon olive oil
1 cup cheese, of your choice (more or less to taste), grated

Heat oil in skillet, add potatoes and onions. Stir till soft, then add other vegetables. Continue stirring until all veggies are cooked through, adding a bit more oil or a bit of water to prevent sticking. Once the vegetables are cooked, sprinkle grated cheese over all and mix thoroughly. Serve plain, with sour cream, or salsa. Note: The quantities are to serve 4 as a side dish, or two to three as a main dish; change amounts to your taste and number of people. Also feel free to substitute any vegetables you; like this recipe is very flexible.

Penny Scott, Gleeson Library/Geschke Center, University of San Francisco
San Francisco, CA

"Peace of mind and a comfortable income are predicted by a dream of eating potatoes in any form."
Ned Ballantyne and Stella Coeli, *Your Horoscope and Your Dreams*, 1940

Sliced Oven Potatoes

6 potatoes, unpeeled
1 or 2 onions
¼ teaspoon celery seed
1 clove garlic, crushed
¼ teaspoon paprika
¾ teaspoon salt
¼ teaspoon pepper
¾ cup butter, melted

Scrub potatoes. Slice potatoes (with skins on) into ¼" slices. Slice onions into ¼" slices. Alternate potato and onion slices in 13"x 9" baking pan. Blend celery seed, garlic, paprika, salt and pepper. Add seasonings to melted butter; pour over the potatoes and onions. Bake at 400 degrees for 40 minutes.

Karen Keller, Johnston Middle School Library, Johnston, IA

641.6522 Cookery (Sweet potatoes)

Mama Graziana's Sweet Potato and Apple Casserole

8 large sweet potatoes
6 large Granny Smith apples
3 tablespoons butter
¼ cup Jack Daniels, dark rum, or apple cider
¼ cup dark brown sugar

Peel the potatoes and cut them in half. Put in cold water, bring to a full boil, covered, and boil for about 20 minutes. Drain, cool, and slice into rounds. Peel, core, and slice the apples so that you have apple circles. Place in a pot with the brown sugar, 2 tablespoons of the butter, and the Jack Daniels or cider and cook over medium high heat, stirring, until the apples begin to soften (about ten minutes). Remove from heat. Butter a baking pan (I use a lasagna pan) and put in a layer of sweet potato, a layer of apple, etc. until you have used all you have. End with a layer of apple. Pour the liquid the apples were cooked in into the pan. Dot the top with a bit more butter and brown sugar and cover loosely with aluminum foil. Bake in a preheated 350-degree oven for about 1 hour; take the aluminum foil cover off for the last 15 minutes. This reheats beautifully both in the oven and in the microwave.

GraceAnne Andreassi DeCandido, Blue Roses Consulting, New York City, NY

"Zen . . . does not confuse spirituality with thinking about God while one is peeling potatoes. Zen spirituality is just to peel the potatoes."
Alan W. Watts (1915-1973) *The Way of Zen*, 1957

Special Sweet Potato Casserole

2 cups cooked sweet potatoes, mashed
2/3 cup evaporated milk
½ cup pecans or walnuts, chopped
½ cups flaked coconut
1½ cups miniature marshmallows
1½ cups sugar
½ cup margarine, melted
3 eggs

Combine sweet potatoes with remaining ingredients in a bowl in order listed, mixing well after each addition. Spoon into 3 quart baking dish. Bake at 350 degrees for 45 minutes. Serves 12

Sarah Kennedy, Waukee Public Library, Waukee, IA

"Let the sky rain potatoes."
William Shakespeare (1564-1616) English poet and playwright, *The Merry Wives of Windsor*

641.6565   Cookery (Lentils)

Baked Lentils and Rice

2 2/3 cups chicken or vegetable broth
¾ cup dry lentils
¾ cup onion, chopped
½ cup brown rice
¼ cup dry white wine
½ teaspoon dried basil
¼ teaspoon salt
¼ teaspoon oregano
¼ teaspoon thyme
1/8 teaspoon garlic powder
1/8 teaspoon pepper
½ cup (2 ounces) Swiss cheese, shredded

Combine all ingredients and turn into an ungreased 1½ quart casserole dish with tight-fitting lid. Bake, covered, at 350 degrees for 1½-2 hours, or until lentils and rice are done, stirring twice during this time. Uncover. Top with Swiss cheese. Bake 2-3 minutes more until cheese is melted.

Kathy Fisher, Keosauqua Public Library, Keosauqua, IA

The lentil is most likely the oldest cultivated legume, and is believed to be native to southwestern Asia, perhaps northern Syria. Seeds have been found in Egyptian tombs dating from the 12 Dynasty (2400 B.C.E.), and there is also evidence of their cultivation as early as 6,000 B.C.E.
foodreference.com

641.6565 Beans.

Frontier Beans

3 16-ounce cans pork and beans (tomato based or with brown sugar)
1 can butter beans
1 can kidney beans
½ to 1 pound hamburger
1 or 2 medium onions
½ pound bacon (I use thick sliced)
½ cup ketchup
1 teaspoon dry mustard
½ cup brown sugar

Cut up bacon and fry until crisp. Drain and set aside. Brown hamburger. Drain butter and kidney beans. Put all ingredients in large ovenproof casserole dish and mix to combine. Bake at 350 degrees for 1 hour. I have also put this in my crockpot and let simmer on low all day. Less meat makes this a great side dish, more meat and this can be your main dish. My husband loves onions so I usually add 3 or 4 depending on the size. I also use ground venison.

Lisa Baue, Iola Village Library Iola, WI

"The prepartaion of good food is merely another expression of art, one of the joys of civilized living."
Dione Lucas (1909-1971) Cookbook author

Pattie's Beans

½ cup butter or margarine
2 stalks celery, chopped
1 onion, chopped
½ of a green pepper, chopped
2 cans kidney beans, drained
2 cans butter beans, drained
2 cans pork & beans, partially drained
½ cup ketchup
½ cup brown sugar
½ cup maple syrup
½ cup chili sauce
2 tablespoons regular mustard

Melt the butter and sauté the celery, onion, and green pepper. Add the kidney, butter, and pork and beans to the vegetables and mix. Combine the ketchup, sugar, maple syrup, chili sauce and mustard in a bowl. Add to the bean mixture. Pour into a baking dish. Bake 350 degrees uncovered 1-1½ hours. Serves 6

Louise Fossa, Niagara Falls Public Library, Niagara Falls, NY

Peachy Keen Beans

This is a wonderful side dish that catches people off guard with its combination and good flavor.

1 16-ounce can peach slices in heavy syrup, drained
1 16-ounce can pork & beans in tomato sauce
1 tablespoon maple syrup
½ teaspoon cinnamon
½ teaspoon dry mustard

Preheat oven to 350 degrees. Combine all ingredients in a mixing bowl; stir until blended. Pour into 1 quart casserole dish. Bake for 20 minutes.

Corinne Florin, Greenawalt Library, Northwestern Health Sciences University, Bloomington, MN

641.662 Cookery (Beef)

Picadillo *(Latin American, specifically Cuban)*

1½ pounds ground beef
1½ teaspoon salt
11/8 teaspoon pepper
1 clove garlic, minced
1/3 cup onions, chopped
½ green pepper, chopped
½ cup celery, chopped
4 tablespoons raisins
¼ cup slivered almonds
¼ cup stuffed olives
¼ teaspoon oregano
¼ teaspoon cinnamon
1 8-ounce tomato sauce
½ cup water
¼ cup ketchup

Brown ground beef. Add salt, pepper, garlic, onion, green pepper and celery. Cook slowly 10 minutes. Add raisins, almonds, olives, oregano, cinnamon, tomato sauce, water, and catsup. Mix well and cover. Simmer 20 minutes. Serve over rice, or stir into rice, or pack rice around the sides and bottom of a bowl, leaving a well in the middle. Pack the meat mixture into the center of the well.

Susan Radosti, South O'Brien High School Library, Paullina, IA

"Beef is the soul of cooking."
Marie-Antoine Carême (1784-1833) Founder and architect of French haute cuisine

Slow-roasted Beef Rib Roast (Prime Rib)

Rib roast
1 cup sea salt
2 tablespoons garlic powder
2 tablespoons onion powder
1 tablespoon pepper, coarsely ground
Container of herb seasonings for meat

Purchase a rib roast cut from the "small end" of the rib that is the part nearest the loin. Have the butcher remove the backbone and leave intact the rib bones. The day before roasting, pat the roast dry. With a sharp knife, cut "X"s in the fat at intervals and insert whole cloves of garlic in the openings.

In a large bowl, mix sea salt, garlic powder, onion powder, pepper and 2 small or 1 large containers of herb seasonings for meat. (These can be purchased in the spice section at the grocery store). Mix well. Roll the whole roast in the seasoning including the ends and place in the refrigerator overnight.

To cook the rib roast, heat the oven to 450 degrees. Place the roast rib side down in a roasting pan, insert a meat thermometer in the thickest part of the roast and then roast at 450 degrees for 10 minutes. Turn the oven down after 10 minutes to 250 degrees and roast until desired doneness. Meat thermometer will read 115-125 for rare, 125-130 for medium rare, 135-145 for medium. Estimated time of cooking is around 15-30 minutes per pound depending on desired degree of doneness.

When desired doneness is reached, remove from oven and let stand for 15-30 minutes, covered loosely with foil before carving. This makes the meat juicier. Carve and enjoy.

Linda Mack, Waukee Public Library, Waukee, IA

"Roast Beef, Medium, is not only a food. It is a philosophy. Seated at Life's Dining Table, with the menu of Morals before you, your eye wanders a bit over the entrees, the hors d'oeuvres, and the things a la, though you know that Roast Beef, Medium, is safe and sane, and sure."
Edna Ferber (1887-1968) American novelist

Taco Meat Balls

2 pounds lean ground beef
1 cup onion, chopped
1 cup instant rice, such as Minute Rice
1 egg
Salt
1 15-ounce can tomato sauce
1 package taco seasoning
1 can of cheddar cheese soup

Mix ground beef, onion, minute rice, egg, and salt. Form into balls and place in a casserole. Mix the tomato sauce and taco seasoning mix. Pour over meatballs and bake at 350 degrees for 45 minutes. Top with can of cheddar cheese soup and bake 15 minutes more.

Fran Fessler, State Library of Iowa, Des Moines, IA

"Cut round on the top near to the outer edge with a chisel and hammer."
Directions on a can of roast veal, 1824

Tamale Pie

1½ pounds hamburger
1 medium onion chopped
1 tablespoon butter
2 eggs, lightly beaten
1 can whole kernel corn
2 cans tomato sauce
1 teaspoon salt
1 can of black olives, optional
2 cups milk
2 cups yellow corn meal
2 tablespoons chili powder

Brown ground beef and onion in butter. Add eggs, corn, tomato sauce, salt, and oil and cook over medium/medium high heat for 15 minutes, stirring often. Pour into greased 13"x 9" pan. Mix milk, corn meal and chili powder. Spread over meat mixture. Bake at 350 degrees for 35-40 minutes.

Maybeth Gilliam, Retired, Blairstown Public Library, Blairstown, IA

641.663 Cookery (Lamb and mutton)

Mutton

Preheat oven to 475 degrees.

Take your mutton quarter, sized for the family, and put it in a turkey pan on an oak board. Bake for 4 hours, basting every 20 minutes with a mixture of 4 eggs, one quart of apple brandy and 2 jiggers of good quality vodka. Remove from oven and let sit for 10 minutes. Throw away the mutton and eat the board.

641.664 Cookery (Pork)

Apricot Pork Medallions

1 pound pork tenderloin
1 tablespoon butter
½ cup apricot jam
2 sliced green onions
¼ teaspoon dried mustard
1 tablespoon cider vinegar

Cut pork into 1" slices; flatten each piece slightly. Heat butter over medium-high heat in a skillet. Sauté pork about 2 minutes each side. Remove from pan. Add jam, green onions, dried mustard, and vinegar to juices in the skillet. Cover and simmer for 3-4 minutes. Return pork to skillet and heat through.

Susan Henricks, Carnegie-Stout Public Library, Dubuque, IA

"The greatest animal in creation, the animal who cooks."
Douglas Jerrold (1803-1857) English writer

Calabacita

2 tablespoons shortening
3 pounds pork chops, boned and cubed
3-4 serrano chilies, or more or less to taste
1 large onion
2 teaspoons whole comino
4 cloves garlic
1/3 cup flour
3 pounds squash (yellow or zucchini or Mexican squash) sliced (large slices quartered)
1 can whole kernel corn, including liquid
2 cans Rotel tomatoes, chopped
2 teaspoons salt
1 teaspoon black pepper

Heat shortening in Dutch oven; fry pork cubes in batches until browned. Return all pork to pan. Place chilies and onion in food processor container and process until chopped (or chop together by hand). Slice garlic and place with cominos and salt in a mortar and pestle and grind together. (The garlic and cominos and salt can be chopped in the food processor with the chilies and onion, but grinding it gives it more flavor). Add all vegetables to pan with pork and cook over high heat until onion is transparent. Sprinkle flour over pork and vegetables and stir to combine. Cook a few minutes to remove the raw taste of the flour. Add all remaining ingredients plus about 1 tomato can of water- enough so that pork and vegetables are not quite covered with liquid. Bring to a boil, then reduce to a simmer and cover with a lid. Cook at a simmer for about 2 hours, stirring occasionally, checking periodically and adding more water if necessary. Makes a lot, but it freezes well.

These are both very popular with staff in our library, where food is free flowing and constant.

Susan Buentello, Briscoe Library
University of Texas Health Science Center, San Antonio, TX

"Some people have a foolish way of not minding, or pretending not to mind, what they eat. For my part, I mind my belly very studiously, and very carefully; for I look upon it, that he who does not mind his belly will hardly mind anything else."
Samuel Johnson (1709-1784) In James' Boswell's *The Life of Samuel Johnson*

Green Chile Pork

4-5 pounds pork butt roast or loin
2 cans green chiles, diced
6 cloves of garlic, chopped in half
2 whole onions, chopped
1 quart chicken broth
2 7 ¾ -ounce cans Mexican hot-style tomato sauce

Brown the meat on the stove. Put in the other ingredients, cover and simmer for 6 hours.

Mary Beth Revels, St. Joseph Public Library, St. Joseph, MO

Ham Balls

3 pounds ground ham
1 pound ground beef
1 pound ground pork
3 cups graham crackers crumbs
3 eggs, beaten
1 teaspoon onion salt
1 teaspoon salt
¼ teaspoon pepper
2 cups milk
1 can tomato soup
½ can water
1 cup brown sugar
1 tablespoon dry mustard
¼ cup vinegar

Mix ground meats, cracker crumbs, eggs, onion salt, salt and pepper together until well blended. Roll into balls using approximately ¼ cup of meat mixture per ball. Place balls in a baking pan. Stir together the tomato soup, water, brown sugar, mustard and vinegar. Pour over meatballs and bake 1 hour at 325 degrees. Makes 48 balls

Pat Means, Villisca Public Library, Villisca, IA
Denise S. Crawford, Glenwood Public Library, Glenwood, IA

"If you want a subject, look to pork!"
Charles Dickens (1812-1870) English novelist, *Great Expectations*

Pork and Sauerkraut Supper

2 tablespoons vegetable oil
6 ¾" pork chops
1 medium onion, diced
1 ¾ cups apple juice
2 14-16 ounce bags or cans of sauerkraut
2 medium potatoes, cut into ¼" slices
2 red cooking apples, cut in ½" chunks
2 teaspoons brown sugar
½ teaspoon salt
1/8 teaspoon pepper

About 2 hours before serving, in a 12" skillet over medium high heat in hot oil cook pork chops until browned. Remove. Add onion to drippings and cook until tender. Add ¼ cup apple juice. In a 13" x 9" baking dish, combine onion, sauerkraut, potatoes, apples, sugar and left over apple juice. Tuck in pork chops, sprinkle with salt and pepper. Cover with foil and bake at 350 degrees for 1½ hours or until meat and potatoes are fork tender, basting occasionally.

Susan Henricks, Carnegie-Stout Public Library, Dubuque, IA

Pork Chop Dinner

6 pork chops
1 can creamed corn
1 egg
¼ cup onion, chopped
1 cup stuffing mix
1 tablespoon margarine

Brown chops and season with salt and pepper. Place browned pork chops in a baking dish. Mix other ingredients and spread on top of chops. Cover. Bake at 325 degrees for approximately 1½ hours.

Joan Schultz, Upham Memorial Library, Fredericksburg, IA

He described the pig as "an encyclopedic animal, a meal on legs."
Grimod de la Reynière (1758-1838) Famous critical gastronomist

64

Pork Chops in Grape-Mustard Sauce

4 boneless pork chops, cut ¾" thick
2 teaspoons butter
1 cup seedless grapes, halved
½ cup light cream
1/3 cup parsley, chopped
1 tablespoon Dijon-style mustard
1 tablespoon shallot, chopped
2 cloves garlic, minced
Salt and pepper to taste

Heat butter in skillet over medium-high heat. Cook pork chops for 8-10 minutes, turning occasionally, until evenly browned. Remove; keep warm. Add remaining ingredients to skillet. Cook over medium-high heat stirring constantly, until sauce thickens. Spoon sauce over pork chops.

Susan Henricks, Carnegie-Stout Public Library, Dubuque, IA

Pork Chops with Parmesan Crust

¼ cup dried bread crumbs
2 tablespoons Parmesan cheese, grated
1 teaspoon dried basil leaves
¾ teaspoon salt
¼ teaspoon pepper
1 egg
4 boneless pork loin chops, each 1" thick
2 tablespoons olive oil

On waxed paper, mix bread crumbs, grated Parmesan, basil, salt and pepper. In a shallow dish, beat egg and 1 tablespoon of water. Dip pork chops first in the egg mixture, then in the bread crumb mixture to coat both sides well. In a skillet over medium-high heat, heat olive oil. When hot, add the pork chops and cook for 4 minutes. Carefully turn chops over and cook over a medium heat 5 minutes longer or until coating is golden brown and pork chops are tender and just lose their pink color.

Susan Henricks, Carnegie-Stout Public Library, Dubuque, IA

"That's something I've noticed about food: whenever there's a crisis if you can get people to eating, normally things get better."
Madeleine L'Engle (1918-) American author

Pork Tenderloin with Red Wine Gravy and Roast Red Potatoes

2 pounds pork tenderloin.
2 Granny Smith apples
1 onion
1 head of garlic
Red wine
5 or 6 red potatoes, a bag of little ones will work too
Olive oil
Salt & pepper
1 can chicken broth
2 tablespoons cornstarch

Preheat oven to 375 degrees. Clean and dry the potatoes, cut them into chunks or halve the little ones, toss with oil, salt and pepper. Put into a baking pan large enough so they don't crowd each other and are skin side up. Cover with foil. Place a roast rack in a pan not much larger than the rack. Peel, core and slice apples into rings and line the pan with them. Drizzle with a little oil. Quarter the onion, break the sections apart, and place over the apples. Peel the garlic cloves and throw them in the pan, too. Pour red wine over veggies until the bottom of the pan is covered. Place roast in rack. Place both the potatoes and the roast in the oven. Take foil off potatoes after 30 minutes. Put back in oven for another 20 minutes. Take potatoes out (check roast) and carefully turn them trying not to damage the crust. Turn again in another 10-15 minutes. They are done when the skin gets wrinkly. Take the roast out when it registers 150 degrees with a meat thermometer; let rest for 10 minutes. Strain veggies reserving the pan juices, and set them aside keeping warm. Pour reserved pan juices in a saucepan. Mix cornstarch into ¼ cup chicken broth. Pour remaining broth into the roasting pan to deglaze it. Let that sit for a few minutes to loosen up the bits and scrape with a wooden spoon. When you think you have all the bits, pour the broth and bits into the saucepan with the strained juices. Add cornstarch mixture and bring to a boil. Serve over pork and potatoes.

Katie Mills, Nicholson Memorial Library, Garland, TX

"The true cook is the perfect blend, the only perfect blend, of artist and philosopher. He knows his worth: he holds in his palm the happiness of mankind, the welfare of generations yet unborn."
Norman Douglas (1868-1952) British novelist and essayist

Roast Pork Loin with Apple Topping

2 tablespoons flour
1½ teaspoons salt
1 teaspoon dry mustard
1 teaspoon caraway seeds
½ teaspoon sugar
¼ teaspoon black pepper
¼ teaspoon ground sage
4-5 pound pork loin roast

Mix together flour, salt, mustard, caraway seeds, sugar, pepper and sage. Rub mixture over surface of pork. Set the pork roast, fat side up, in roasting pan. Bake at 325 degrees for 1½ hours. Prepare topping:

Topping

1½ cups applesauce
½ cup brown sugar
¼ teaspoon cinnamon
¼ teaspoon mace
¼ teaspoon salt

Mix all ingredients. Spread over the top of the roast. Bake the roast for 1 hour longer, adding water to the bottom of the pan if necessary.

Susan Henricks, Carnegie-Stout Public Library, Dubuque, IA

"The army from Asia introduced a foreign luxury to Rome; it was then the meals began to require more dishes and more expenditure... the cook, who had up to that time been employed as a slave of low price, became dear: what had been nothing but a métier was elevated to an art."
Livy (Titus Livisu) (59-17 B.C.E.) Roman historian *The Annals of the Roman People*

67

Apricot Chicken

1 teaspoon salt
1/8 teaspoon pepper
½ cup flour
8 boneless, skinless chicken breasts
¼ cup butter
¼ cup dark rum
1 large onion, chopped
Pinch of ginger
½ cup chicken broth
1 cup dried apricots
¼ cup dark rum
1 tablespoon brown sugar
Pinch ginger

Mix salt, pepper and flour. Roll chicken breasts in the seasoned flour. Melt butter in a heavy frying pan and brown the chicken well on both sides. Pour ¼ cup dark rum over the chicken and ignite. When the flame has burned down, add chopped onion and a pinch of ginger. Cook for 5 minutes, then add chicken broth. Cover the pan and cook over a low heat for 40 minutes or until chicken in tender. Meanwhile, cook dried apricots in ½ cup filtered water for 15 minutes or until barely tender. Add to the chicken when it is done along with ¼ cup dark rum, brown sugar and a pinch of ginger. Mix in well, stirring up all the brown particles from the bottom of the pan, and cook 1 minute longer. Serve the chicken and apricots in the sauce.

Jana L. Prock, Bay City Public Library, Bay City, TX

Baked Chicken Breasts with Stuffing and Cheese

8 chicken breasts
1 stick butter or margarine
1 can cream of chicken soup
1 can cream of celery soup
8 slices Swiss cheese
1 package stuffing mix

Melt butter or margarine in a 13" x 9" pan. Place chicken breasts in pan. Top each with a slice of Swiss cheese. Mix cream of chicken soup and cream of celery soup with 1 can of water and stuffing mix. Place over chicken breasts. Bake 1 hour at 350 degrees, covered. Uncover and bake an additional 20 minutes.

Connie Mataloni, Sibley Public Library, Sibley, IA

Chicken and Dumplings

1 10-ounce can chicken
1 can cream of chicken soup
1 cup milk
1 cup water
2 chicken bouillon cubes
2 teaspoons butter or margarine
1¾ cups flour
2½ teaspoons baking powder
¾ teaspoon salt
1/3 cup margarine
1 cup water

Combine chicken, soup, milk, water, bouillon cubes and margarine; mix. Pour into a large pan or skillet. Bring mixture to a boil over medium-high heat. Meanwhile, in a large bowl stir together flour, baking powder, salt, margarine and water. Drop this batter by the spoonful into the boiling chicken mixture. Cover and reduce heat to a simmer for about 10 minutes.

Faith, Jana, Kathi and Wanda, Red Oak Public Library, Red Oak, IA

Chicken Breasts with Pesto

4 chicken breasts
1 cup pesto
1 cup mozzarella cheese
1 jar roasted red peppers
Handful of toothpicks

Preheat the oven to 400 degrees. Use a mallet to tenderize chicken breasts. Spread generous coating of pesto on one side of each chicken breast. Cover pesto with roasted red peppers laid end to end. Cover peppers with cheese. Roll chicken breasts up and secure with toothpicks. Put rolled chicken breasts in casserole dish and sprinkle any remaining cheese over all. Bake for 45 minutes.

Vicki Hibbert, Clive Public Library, Clive, IA

"Poultry is for cookery what canvas is for painting, and the cap of Fortunatus for the charlatans. It is served to us boiled, roast, hot or cold, whole or in portions, with or without sauce, and always with equal success." Jean-Anthelme Brillat-Savarin (1755-1826) Wrote one of the most celebrated works of food, 'Physiologie du gout,' *The Physiology of Taste*

69

Chicken Curry

2 cups uncooked rice
Chicken pieces
3 tablespoons margarine
1 teaspoon curry
1 teaspoon paprika
¼ cup almonds
¼ cup raisins
2 10-ounce cans chicken broth
1 ½ cups water
1 can cream of chicken soup
1 cup plain yogurt
½ teaspoon cumin

Spread rice evenly in baking dish sprayed with cooking spray. Top with chicken pieces and dot with margarine. Sprinkle with spices, almonds, and raisins. Pour broth and water over all. Cover and bake at 375 degrees for 1½ hours. Prepare sauce. Remove chicken from oven and top with sauce. Sauce: In small pan, stir yogurt until creamy. Blend in soup and ½ teaspoon cumin. Heat to serving temperature over medium heat.

Suzanne Pontius, Preble County District Library Eaton, Ohio

Enchilada Chicken

6-8 boneless, skinless chicken breasts (may use bone in pieces if preferred, adjust cooking time)
4-6 tablespoons margarine
1 medium onion, coarsely diced
1 large can mild enchilada sauce
1 can tomato soup
2 cups Mexican cheese or Colby-Monterey Jack mixture, shredded
Tortilla or Dorito chips, crushed

Place 4 tablespoons margarine and onion in a 13"x 9" pan. Heat oven to 375 degrees, letting margarine melt while oven preheats. When margarine has melted, place chicken breasts in pan, coating with melted margarine and onions. Bake for 20 minutes. Mix enchilada sauce and tomato soup and pour over chicken. Bake for 15-20 minutes more. Spread cheese and crushed chips over the top and return to the oven until cheese is melted. Serve with rice or noodles to soak up the sauce.

Natasha Forrester, Winfield Public Library, Winfield, KS

Oven Crusty Chicken

10-12 pieces of chicken
½ cup margarine, melted
½ teaspoon salt
2 cups crushed puffed rice cereal such as Rice Krispies

Wash and drain chicken, set aside. Add salt to melted margarine. Dip chicken pieces into the seasoned margarine, then roll in the crushed puffed rice cereal. Place chicken pieces on an aluminum foil lined cookie sheet. Bake 375 degrees for an hour. Do not turn or cover the chicken while baking.

Joan Schultz, Upham Memorial Library, Fredericksburg, IA

Rotel Chicken

4-6 skinless, boneless, chicken breasts
Cayenne pepper to taste
1 red onion, chopped
2 cans Rotel tomatoes
1 can cream of mushroom soup
1 can cream of chicken soup
½ can chicken broth
2 cups cheese, shredded (choice of flavor)
1 medium or large bag of Doritos, crushed

Boil chicken for 30-35 minutes. Drain and chunk into cubes. Place in bottom of 13" x 9" baking dish. Sprinkle with cayenne pepper to taste. Top with onion. Sprinkle with half the cheese. Add half of the crushed Doritos. Mix soups and Rotel tomatoes in bowl. Pour half of this mixture over entire casserole. Layer again with the cheese, Doritos, and the tomato/soup mixture. Top with remaining Doritos. Bake in 375 degree oven for 30-35 minutes.

*This can also be made in a slow cooker layering everything the same way and just cooking on low for about 4-5 hours.

Shannon Surly, Evansdale Public Library, Evansdale, IA

"Show me another pleasure like dinner which comes every day and lasts an hour."
Talleyrand (1754-1838) French statesman, diplomat, and grand gourmet, called the 'first fork of France." Many culinary preparations have been created or named for him.

71

641.66592 Cookery (Turkey)

Turkey Cutlets with Provolone, Basil, and Roasted Peppers

4 6-ounce turkey cutlets, each ¼" thick
¼ pound (1 cup) provolone or mozzarella cheese, shredded
1/3 7-ounce jar (¼ cup) roasted red peppers, chopped
2 teaspoons dried basil leaves
2 tablespoons Parmesan cheese, grated
1 tablespoon dried parsley flakes
½ teaspoon salt
½ teaspoon pepper
2 tablespoons milk
2 tablespoons olive oil

On half of each turkey cutlet, arrange ¼ each of shredded cheese, chopped roasted peppers, and basil. Fold other half of turkey cutlets over filling. Press edges of turkey cutlets together to seal slightly. On waxed paper, combine bread crumbs, Parmesan cheese, parsley flakes, salt and pepper. Pour milk in pie plate and dip turkey cutlets, one at a time, into milk, then into bread crumb mixture. In a 12" skillet over medium heat, in hot olive oil, cook turkey cutlets about 10 minutes or until golden brown, fork-tender and cheese melts; turn once.

Susan Henricks, Carnegie-Stout Public Library, Dubuque, IA

"I wish the bald eagle had not been chosen as the representative of our country... The turkey is a much more respectable bird, and withal a true original native of America."
Benjamin Franklin (1706-1790) Author, printer, scientist

Turkey and Ham Jambalaya

¼ pound bacon (4-6 slices)
1 medium onion
1 cup uncooked rice
1 28-ounce can tomatoes, whole with their juice
1 cup chicken broth
½ teaspoon thyme
¼ teaspoon black pepper
1 bay leaf
1½ cups (about ½ pound) turkey, cubed and cooked
1½ cups (about ¼ pound) lean ham, cubed and cooked
1 medium red bell pepper
¼ cup parsley, chopped

In a large skillet, cook the bacon over medium heat until crisp; about ten minutes. Reserve the fat in the pan. Drain bacon on paper towels, crumble and set aside. Coarsely chop the onion. Add the onion and rice to the pan and cook, stirring constantly, for 2 minutes. Increase the heat to medium-high and add the tomatoes and their juice, broth, thyme, pepper and bay leaf. Bring the mixture to a boil, breaking up the tomatoes with a spoon. Reduce heat to medium-low, cover the pan and simmer for 15 minutes. Cut the bell pepper into thin slivers. Stir the turkey, ham, and bell pepper into the jambalaya. Cover and cook, stirring occasionally, until the pepper is limp, about 5 minutes. Serve sprinkled with crumbled bacon and parsley.

Susan Henricks, Carnegie-Stout Public Library, Dubuque, IA

"After a good dinner, one can forgive anybody, even one's relatives."
Oscar Wilde (1854-1900) Irish novelist and dramatist

Ground Turkey Loaf with Creole Sauce

Loaf:
1 pound lean ground turkey
½ cup whole-grain bread crumbs
1 small onion, finely chopped
¼ cup carrot, finely chopped
2 eggs, lightly beaten
1 tablespoon fresh parsley, finely chopped
1 clove garlic, finely minced
½ teaspoon dried rosemary, crumbled
¼ teaspoon paprika
Pinch of cayenne pepper
Salt and black pepper to taste

Sauce:
½ cup chicken broth
1 small onion, finely chopped
1 clove garlic, finely minced
½ cup crushed canned tomatoes in puree
8-10 basil leaves, finely chopped
2 tablespoons fresh parsley, finely chopped

Preheat the oven to 375 degrees. Lightly coat a loaf pan with vegetable cooking spray. In a large bowl, combine all the loaf ingredients and mix with your hands until well blended. Press gently into the prepared loaf pan and bake for 40 minutes until the center is firm to touch. Allow loaf to rest at room temperature for 10-15 minutes. In the meantime, prepare the sauce in a nonstick saucepan. Bring the broth, onion and garlic to a boil; cook over medium heat for 7-10 minutes or until the vegetables are softened. Add the tomatoes, basil, parsley, salt and pepper to taste. Bring to a boil, cover, and simmer slowly for 15 minutes. Slice the turkey loaf, arrange on a platter, and top with the sauce. Garnish with Parmesan cheese.

Susan Henricks, Carnegie-Stout Public Library, Dubuque, IA

"Sir, respect your dinner: idolize it, enjoy it properly. You will be many hours in the week, many weeks in the year, and many years in your life happier if you do."
William Makepeace Thackeray (1811-1863) English novelist

Turkey Tetrazzini

8 ounces fusilli or spaghetti
4 tablespoons butter
1 pound mushrooms, thinly sliced
1 small onion, diced
¼ cup all purpose flour
1¼ teaspoons salt
1 teaspoon dried thyme leaves
1 teaspoon chicken-flavor instant bouillon
3 cups milk
¼ cup dry sherry
¼ cup parsley, chopped
3 cups cooked turkey, diced
2 large tomatoes
1 tablespoon Parmesan cheese, grated

Cook fusilli or spaghetti as label directs; drain and return to saucepot; keep warm. Meanwhile, in a 10" skillet over medium-high heat in hot butter, cook mushrooms and onion stirring occasionally until mushrooms and onion are tender and liquid evaporates. Over medium heat stir flour, salt, thyme, and bouillon into mushroom mixture until blended; cook 1 minute. Gradually stir in milk and sherry; cook stirring constantly until mixture boils and thickens slightly. Reserve 1 tablespoon chopped parsley for topping. Stir turkey and remaining chopped parsley into sauce; heat through. Preheat broiler. Cut tomatoes into thin slices. Add the turkey mixture to the fusilli or spaghetti in saucepot; gently toss to mix well. Spoon half of mixture into a shallow 2-quart broiler-safe baking dish (or 12" x 8" baking dish). Arrange half of tomato slices on top of mixture in baking dish; top with remaining turkey mixture, then remaining tomato slices. Sprinkle tomato slices with grated Parmesan and reserved parsley. Broil 5 minutes or until tomatoes are heated through. Serves 6

Susan Henricks, Carnegie-Stout Public Library, Dubuque, IA

"I don't like to say that my kitchen is a religious place, but I would say that if I were a voodoo priestess, I would conduct my rituals here."
Pearl Bailey (1918-1990) *Pearl's Kitchen,* 1973

Rabbit

Marinade

¼ cup vinegar
1 small onion, sliced
1 bay leaf
8 pepper balls
Dash salt
Dash pepper

Mix all ingredients in a large bowl or plastic bag and add rabbit. Marinate over night in refrigerator. Turn the rabbit occasionally.

2 tablespoons butter or margarine, melted
1 small onion, chopped
Dash salt
Dash pepper
1 teaspoon caraway seed
1 large bay leaf
½ cup sour cream
1 tablespoon flour

Coat the bottom of a roasting pan with the melted butter or margarine. Remove the rabbit from the marinade and pat dry. Place the rabbit in the roasting pan. Sprinkle with the onion, salt, pepper, caraway seed and bay leaf. Bake the rabbit at 300 degrees for two hours, or until done. Remove to a warm platter. Place roasting pan with drippings on the stove. In a small bowl, blend the sour cream and flour. Add to the drippings in the roasting pan allowing it to come to a slow boil. Strain and pour over the rabbit. Serve.

Susan Henricks, Carnegie-Stout Public Library, Dubuque, IA

Rabbit was a favorite of French monks, because they considered them fish and could eat them when abstinence from meat was called for.
foodreference.com

📖📖📖📖📖

Mom's Special Cottage Cheese

2 cups cottage cheese
¼ cup sour cream
¼ cup mayonnaise
½ teaspoon Accent brand seasoning
¾ teaspoon seasoned pepper
¾ teaspoon garlic salt
1/8 teaspoon salt
Dash Tabasco sauce
½ tablespoon Worcestershire sauce
¾ tablespoon dried minced onion

Mix all ingredients together until well blended. Refrigerate.
Serve with crackers as hors d'oeuvres, or as an accompaniment to a meal.

Susan Henricks, Carnegie-Stout Public Library, Dubuque, IA

"An egg is always an adventure; the next one may be different."
Oscar Wilde (1854-1900) Irish novelist and dramatist

641.675 Eggs.

Hard-Boiled Egg

Tear out kitchen. Replace with a fabulously designed kitchen by Ralph Lauren, complete with Viking stove and built-in Aga Refrigerators.

Have Mauricio, the ever-so-buff handyman, build a chicken coup. Buy chickens raised on organic feed and massaged daily by underlings with verbana-scented oils. If possible, have underlings dress the chickens in disposable diapers; who wants chicken manure all over the place?

While chickens are maturing, buy Prada aprons; if none is available, substitute with Betsey Johnson, but make sure Paris Hilton never catches you wearing one. Check with Mauricio to see which apron he likes the best.

Hire chef. Make sure he's trained by at least one of the celebrity chefs featured on the Food Network. (Note: Nigella Lawson does _not_ count.)

Have Mauricio gather eggs. Make sure it's a verrry hot day and he's wearing his special tank-top tee.

Give chef eggs. Discuss egg-boiling process for hours, preferably while you're talking to your hair colorist at the same time on your cell phone/PDA combo.

Check eggs to make sure they didn't go bad while sitting on the counter during all those egg-boiling discussions. Make appointment with colorist after deciding upon "Retro Harvest Gold" for the highlights. Tell chef you'll be back in three hours and that egg better be damn well ready.

After the three hours, place yourself daintily at the Michael Graves-designed cafe table. Impatiently wait for eggs to be served. When served, have chef explain to you just what that hard covering is over the egg and force him to take it off. Eat with salt and pepper.

Repeat recipe you want another egg just for Mauricio....

Linda Absher, The Lipstick Librarian http://www.lipsticklibrarian.com

Pickled Eggs

12-16 hard-boiled eggs
2 tablespoons sugar
1 teaspoon salt
1 teaspoon mixed pickling spices
2 cups cider vinegar

Peel eggs and put them in a jar. Pour the brine over them, seal jar, and let stand for 3 days before serving. If you want to serve in 1 day, boil the brine and put it hot on the eggs. Food coloring may be added to color the eggs.

Jean Gullikson, Carnegie-Stout Public Library, Dubuque, IA

Scalloped Eggs

8 eggs, hard boiled and peeled
1 small onion, chopped
8 ounces mushrooms, chopped
6 tablespoons margarine
4 tablespoons flour
2 cups of milk
1 cup of chicken broth
Season with salt and pepper
Dried bread crumbs
4 tablespoons butter

Slice each egg into 8 or so pieces. Arrange in a buttered baking dish. Sauté onion and mushrooms in 2 tablespoons margarine. Remove with slotted spoon to a small bowl.
White sauce: Melt 4 tablespoons margarine in the same pan and add flour. Cook for 1 minute over low heat. Slowly stir in milk and chicken broth. Cook over medium heat until fairly thick. Add mushroom and onion mix. Pour over eggs; top casserole with dry bread crumbs and dot with butter. Bake at 375 degrees for 15 minutes or until hot and browned.

Christine Lind Hage, Clinton-Macomb Public Library, Clinton Township, MI

"I did toy with the idea of doing a cook book ... I think a lot of people who hate literature but love fried eggs would buy it if the price is right."
Groucho Marx (1890-1977) *Groucho and Me*, 1959

Scotch Eggs with Fresh Herbs

1 pound bulk sausage meat
3 tablespoons fresh chives, minced
3 tablespoons fresh parsley, chopped
1 large egg
1 tablespoon Dijon mustard
5 cups fresh bread crumbs, made from crustless French bread
1 cup flour
6 large hard-boiled eggs, peeled
Vegetable oil for deep-frying

Mix sausage, chives, and parsley in medium bowl to blend. Whisk egg and mustard in bowl to blend. Place bread crumbs in large bowl. Place flour in another bowl. Roll 1 hard-boiled egg in flour. Using wet hands, press 1/3 cup sausage mixture around egg to coat. Brush egg with mustard mixture, and then roll in bread crumbs, covering completely and pressing to adhere. Place Scotch egg on a plate. Repeat with remaining eggs. (Can be made one day ahead. Cover and refrigerate.) Add enough oil in heavy large sauce pan to reach depth of 1 ½ inches. Attach deep-frying thermometer and heat oil to 325 degrees. Add 3 prepared eggs to oil; fry until sausage is cooked through and coating is deep brown, about 6 minutes. Using slotted spoon, transfer eggs to paper towels to drain. Repeat with remaining 3 eggs. Serve warm. Makes 6 (one per person is plenty)

Christine Lind Hage, Clinton-Macomb Public Library, Clinton Township, MI

"Put not your Knife to your mouth unless it to be to eat an Egge"
Hannah Wooley, 17th century etiquette expert, *Guide to Ladies, Gentlewoman and Maids*

641.77 Stir frying.

Chicken Asparagus

Marinade:

1 tablespoon vegetable oil
1 teaspoon light soy sauce
1 tablespoon cornstarch
2 cups white chicken meat, uncooked and thinly sliced

Mix oil, soy sauce and cornstarch well. Add chicken. Refrigerate overnight.

2 tablespoons salted black beans, rinsed in cold water
4 tablespoons and ½ teaspoon vegetable oil, divided
3 cloves garlic, peeled and crushed
4 cups fresh asparagus, sliced diagonally
¼ cup chicken broth
1 teaspoon corn starch
½ teaspoon sugar
1 tablespoon dark soy sauce

Mix the black beans, ½ teaspoon oil and garlic. Heat 2 tablespoons oil in a wok; when hot stir-fry the black bean mixture and asparagus. Add 1 teaspoon chicken broth and ½ teaspoon sugar. Stir-fry for about 5 minutes until crisp, but not overdone. Set aside on a platter. Add the cornstarch to the remaining chicken broth and stir until blended.

Heat 2 tablespoons oil in the wok and when hot add the chicken with marinade. Stir-fry approximately 3 minutes. Add the chicken broth mixture and the dark soy sauce. Stir thoroughly, then add the asparagus mixture until heated through. Remove from heat. Serves 4.

Susan Kling, Marion Public Library, Marion, IA

"The pleasures of the table are of all times and all ages, of every country and of every day." ." Jean-Anthelme Brillat-Savarin (1755-1826) wrote one of the most celebrated works of food, 'Physiologie du gout,' *The Physiology of Taste*

81

Garlic Pork with Vegetables

½ pound pork tenderloin, shredded
1 egg
5 tablespoons peanut oil
3 tablespoons dry sherry
¼ teaspoon salt
1 teaspoon garlic, minced
1 teaspoon fresh ginger, minced
2 tablespoons tree ear mushrooms, soaked in warm water for 30 minutes
½ cup fresh snow peas, stems and strings removed, and shredded
½ cup sweet red pepper, shredded
8 canned water chestnuts, sliced
½ cup canned bamboo shoots, shredded
½ cup chicken broth
2 tablespoons dry sherry
3 tablespoons soy sauce
1 teaspoon chili paste with garlic
1 teaspoon sugar
1 tablespoon white rice vinegar
2 teaspoons cornstarch, dissolved in 2 teaspoons cold water
Peanut oil for stir-frying

Mix the egg, 1 tablespoon of peanut oil, 1 tablespoon dry sherry, and salt until smooth. Add the shredded pork and marinate for 30 minutes. Stir the minced garlic and ginger in a cup and set aside. Combine the tree ear mushrooms, snow peas, red pepper, water chestnuts and bamboo shoots together in a bowl. Set aside. Blend the chicken broth, dry sherry, soy sauce, chili paste, sugar and vinegar together until smooth. Set aside.

Heat the wok over high heat. When hot add 2 tablespoons peanut oil. When oil is hot add the pork and marinade and stir-fry 3 minutes until the pork loses its pink color. Remove the pork from the wok and set aside. In the same wok, heat 2 tablespoons peanut oil. Add the garlic and ginger and stir-fry for 30 seconds. Add vegetables and stir-fry 1 minute. Add the sauce and stir until it boils. Return pork to the wok and stir to heat through. Add the cornstarch and water mixture and stir about 1 minute until it is thickened. Remove from heat and serve immediately.

Susan Henricks, Carnegie-Stout Public Library, Dubuque, IA

"One cannot think well, love well, sleep well, if one has not dined well."
Virginia Woolf (1882-1941) English novelist, *A Room of One's Own*

Mongolian Beef

1 pound sirloin tip steak, thinly sliced at a 45 degree angle against the grain, about
¼" thickness x 1 ½" x 2" long
1 egg
¼ teaspoon black pepper
1 teaspoon sugar
2 tablespoons cornstarch
1 tablespoon peanut oil
1 whole scallion, minced
1 teaspoon fresh ginger, minced
1 teaspoon garlic, minced
2 tablespoons soy sauce
3 tablespoons dry sherry
1 tablespoon hoisin sauce
3 tablespoons water
8 whole green onions cut into 2" pieces
Peanut oil for stir-frying
1 teaspoon sesame oil, optional

Mix the egg, pepper, sugar, cornstarch, and peanut oil in a bowl until smooth. Add
the beef slices and set aside uncovered for at least 20 minutes. (Can be marinated
up to 24 hours, covered, in the refrigerator.) Mix the minced scallion, ginger, and
garlic in a small bowl. Set aside. Blend the soy sauce, sherry, hoisin sauce, and
water until smooth.

Heat the wok over high heat; when hot add ¼ cup peanut oil. When oil is hot add
the meat and marinade. Stir-fry for about 2 minutes or until the meat loses its pick
color. Remove meat from wok and set aside in a bowl, uncovered. Add 2
tablespoons peanut oil to the wok. When the oil is hot, add the scallion, ginger and
garlic mixture. Stir a few times and add the sauce mix (soy sauce, sherry, hoisin and
water.) Stir and add the green onion pieces. Stir for ½ minute and return the beef
to the wok. Stir just to heat through. Stir in sesame oil if desired. Remove wok
from heat and serve immediately.

Susan Henricks, Carnegie-Stout Public Library, Dubuque, IA

*"If a man be sensible and one fine morning, while he is lying in bed, count
at the tips of his fingers how many things in this life truly will give him
enjoyment, invariably he will find food is the first one."*
Lin Yutang (1895-1976) Chinese author

Yang Chow Fried Rice

4 cups rice, boiled and cold*
¼ cup cooked shrimp, coarsely chopped
¼ cup ham, diced
6 canned water chestnuts, chopped
½ cup bean sprouts
¼ cup frozen peas, thawed
6 dried Chinese (Shiitake) mushrooms, soaked in warm water 30 minutes then rinsed and diced, discarding tough stems.
¼ cup whole green onion, chopped
2 eggs, scrambled and broken into small pieces
2 tablespoons soy sauce
1 tablespoon dry sherry
1 teaspoon salt
¼ cup chicken broth
Peanut oil for stir-frying

Combine the shrimp, ham, water chestnuts, sprouts, peas, mushrooms, scallions, and egg in a large bowl. Set aside. Blend the soy sauce, sherry, salt and chicken broth until smooth. Set aside.

Heat wok over high heat; when hot add 3 tablespoons peanut oil. When oil is hot, add shrimp, ham, all vegetables and eggs. Stir-fry for 1 minute. Place rice on top of the mixture and cover for 1 minute. Stir thoroughly, add sauce, stir and heat for 3 minutes. Serve immediately.

*For best results the rice should be cooked the day before so it is thoroughly dry when you fry it. Store in the refrigerator until ready to use.

Susan Henricks, Carnegie-Stout Public Library, Dubuque, IA

"Our lives are not in the lap of the gods, but in the lap of our cooks."
Lin Yutang (1895-1976) Chinese author, *The Importance of Living*, 1937

Baked Fish Stroganoff

8 pounds or 25 pieces of fish filet such as flounder, sole
1 cup butter or margarine
1 cup onion, finely chopped
2 pounds fresh mushrooms, sliced
½ cup flour
1 cup dry white wine
1 cup water
¼ cup lemon juice
1 tablespoon salt
½ teaspoon Tabasco
1 quart sour cream

Roll each filet and place in oblong casserole. Set aside. In large frying pan, sauté onions and mushrooms in butter. Sprinkle with flour and blend lightly to mix flour and butter. Gently stir in wine, water and lemon juice. Add salt and Tabasco. Stir in sour cream. Pour mixture over fish. Bake covered at 350 degree for 30 minutes. Serves 24. (Make the same amount of sauce for less fish to use over rice.)

Christine Lind Hage, Clinton-Macomb Public Library, Clinton Township, MI

Cod with Sun-dried Tomatoes

1½ pounds cod fillets about ½" thick, cut into 4 pieces
¼ cup lemon juice
3 tablespoons sun-dried tomatoes, finely chopped
2 teaspoons dried thyme
2 teaspoons garlic, minced
¼ teaspoon salt
1/8 teaspoon pepper

Preheat oven to 400 degrees. Cut four 12" circles from foil or parchment paper. Fold each circle in half. Open circles; place 1 piece of fish on each circle to one side of the fold. Combine lemon juice, tomatoes, thyme, garlic, salt and pepper. Evenly top fish with tomato mixture. Close paper over fish so that the edges meet. Fold edges together around packets to seal. Place on a baking sheet; bake 12-14 minutes until parchment packets are browned, or fish flakes easily with fork.

"Fish is held out to be one of the greatest luxuries of the table and not only necessary, but even indispensable at all dinners where there is any pretense of excellence or fashion." Isabella Beeton (1836-1865) Cookbook writer

Fish "Fry"

1 egg white
1/3 cup dried bread crumbs
2 tablespoons Parmesan cheese, grated
¾ teaspoon dried basil leaves
¼ teaspoon pepper
Salt
4 6-ounce cod fillets
½ cup non-fat mayonnaise dressing
¼ cup dill pickles, finely chopped
1 tablespoon parsley, chopped
2 teaspoons lemon juice
1½ teaspoons hot pepper sauce

Preheat oven to 450 degrees. In pie plate, with fork, beat egg white slightly. On waxed paper mix bread crumbs, cheese, basil, pepper, and ½ teaspoon salt. Dip cod fillets in egg white and then bread crumb mixture to coat. Place fish on ungreased cookie sheet; bake 10-12 minutes, without turning fish, until fish flakes easily when tested with a fork. If you prefer a golden brown crust, finish by broiling close to heat source about 2-3 minutes. Meanwhile, in a small bowl, mix mayonnaise, pickles, parsley, lemon juice, pepper sauce, and ¼ teaspoon salt. To serve, arrange cod fillets on a platter; garnish with basil sprigs and lemon wedges. Serve with the sauce.

Susan Henricks, Carnegie-Stout Public Library, Dubuque, IA

Pêches à tonne (Peaches with Tuna)

1 large ripe peach
1 single serving can of tuna packed in water
1 tablespoon mayonnaise (or to taste)
Dash of salt dash of pepper

Cut peach in half, remove pit and scoop out enough flesh to make a bowl. Drain the tuna. Mix with mayonnaise, salt and pepper. Spoon tuna into peach bowls.

Jesse Lewis, Palm Beach County Library System, West Palm Beach, FL.

"Soup and fish explain half the emotions of human life."
Sydney Smith (1771-1845) English essayist

Salmon Burgers

2 cans (14 ¾ ounces each) red salmon, drained; skin and larger bones discarded
1 onion, grated
1 cup dry bread crumbs
¼ cup mayonnaise
1 egg
1 tablespoon lime juice
¼ teaspoon salt
¼ teaspoon pepper
¼ cup fresh parsley, chopped
1/3 cup yellow cornmeal
¼ cup oil

Combine salmon, onion, bread crumbs, mayonnaise, egg, lime juice, salt, pepper, and parsley. Shape into 6 burgers. Coat in cornmeal. In a large skillet, heat oil over medium-high heat. Cook burgers until done, about 5 minutes per side. Serve on buns with lettuce, tomato, and mayonnaise if desired.

Susan Henricks, Carnegie-Stout Public Library, Dubuque, IA

"Why does Sea World have a seafood restaurant? I'm halfway through my fish burger and I realize, Oh my God ... I could be eating a slow learner."
Lyndon Johnson (1908-1973) President of the United States

Salmon, Pea Pod, and New Potato Casserole

4 salmon fillets, approximately 6 ounces each
2 tablespoons margarine, softened
1 tablespoon dried tarragon
1 small lemon, thinly sliced
8 ounces pea pods (if frozen, thaw and drain)
12 baby new potatoes, halved
½ teaspoon pepper
1/3 cup apple cider

Preheat oven to 325 degrees. Lightly coat a 13" x 9" baking pan with cooking spray. Place salmon fillets in the dish and spread each fillet with ½ tablespoon margarine. Sprinkle fillets with tarragon and cover with lemon slices. Place potatoes randomly around fillets, wherever there is space; sprinkle with pepper. Pour cider over the entire dish. Cover and back for 35-40 minutes, or until fish flakes and potatoes are soft. During the last 10 minutes of cooking time, place pea pods randomly around the dish.

Susan Henricks, Carnegie-Stout Public Library, Dubuque, IA

Salmon with Peach Chutney

2 pounds salmon fillet, cut into 6 equal pieces
1¼ teaspoon salt
1 medium-size red onion, diced
1 jalapeño chile, seeded and diced
4 scallions, sliced
2 tablespoons vegetable oil
1 teaspoon curry powder
¼ teaspoon ground red pepper
1 12-ounce jar peach preserves
1 mango, peeled, pitted and diced

Heat oven to 450 degrees. Coat 13" x 9" baking dish with cooking spray. Place salmon in dish. Season with ¼ teaspoon salt. Roast for 13 minutes or until fish flakes when touched with fork. Meanwhile, sauté onion, chile, half the scallions in oil in saucepan 3 minutes. Add curry and pepper; cook 1 minute. Add preserves, remaining salt, and mango; cook 5 minutes. Remove chutney from heat. Serve chutney on top of salmon with scallions sprinkled on top.

Megan VanderHart, Rock Island Public Library, Rock Island, IL

Swordfish Teriyaki

1 garlic clove, minced
1 teaspoon fresh gingerroot, minced
2 tablespoons soy sauce
1 tablespoon dry sherry
4 4-6-ounce swordfish steaks (or tuna steaks)
1 large green onion, thinly sliced
2 teaspoons orange marmalade

In 11" x 7" baking dish, combine garlic, gingerroot, soy sauce and sherry. Place swordfish steaks in dish, turning to coat with soy mixture; arrange with pointed ends toward center of dish. Cook, covered with waxed paper, in the microwave on high for 5-7 minutes until fish turns opaque; turn fish over and rearrange halfway through cooking. Let stand covered for 2 minutes. Stir green onion and orange marmalade into cooking liquid; spoon liquid over fish. Serves 4

Susan Henricks, Carnegie-Stout Public Library, Dubuque, IA

Barbecue Shrimp

1 stick butter
½ cup olive oil
¼ cup chili sauce
2 tablespoons Worcestershire sauce
1 lemon sliced paper-thin
2 cloves of garlic, minced
2 tablespoons fresh lemon juice
1½ teaspoons of fresh parsley, minced
1 teaspoon Hungarian paprika
1 teaspoon fresh oregano
1 ½ teaspoon of red cayenne pepper
½ teaspoon of Tabasco sauce
1 teaspoon liquid smoke
4 pounds of shrimp

Mix the above ingredients and pour over shrimp. Marinate 2-3 hours. Baste and turn. Bake for 30 minutes at 300 degrees.

Jana L. Prock, Bay City Public Library, Bay City, TX

"Everything is done at dinner in the century in which we live, and it is by these dinners that men are governed."
Charles Pierre Monselet (1825-1888) French author

Butterflied Shrimp in Wine

1/3 cup dry vermouth
1 teaspoon instant chicken-flavor bouillon
¼ teaspoon salt
1/8 teaspoon pepper
1 pound large shrimp
1 egg
About ½ cup all-purpose flour
3 tablespoons butter
2 tablespoons salad or olive oil
Lemon slices for garnish

In a measuring cup mix vermouth, bouillon, salt, pepper, and ½ cup of water; set aside. Butterfly shrimp: Remove shells from shrimp; with knife cut each shrimp ¾ of the way through along center back; spread each shrimp open. Rinse shrimp under running water to remove vein; pat dry with paper towels. In pie plate, with a fork, beat egg. Measure flour on to waxed paper. Dip shrimp in egg, then coat with flour. In a 12" skillet over medium heat, heat butter and oil until hot and bubbly. Cook shrimp, half at a time, until lightly browned on both sides (about 1-2 minutes on each side), removing shrimp to plate as they brown. Return shrimp to skillet; stir in vermouth mixture. Over medium-high heat, heat to boiling; cook about 1 minutes to blend flavors, stirring occasionally. Spoon shrimp and sauce onto platter; garnish with lemon slices. Makes 4 main-dish servings

Susan Henricks, Carnegie-Stout Public Library, Dubuque, IA

"Happy and successful cooking doesn't rely only on know-how; it comes from the heart, makes great demands on the palate and needs enthusiasm and a deep love of food to bring it to life."
George Blanc (1943-) French Chef, *Ma Cuisine des Saisons,* 1997

Cajun Shrimp

Don't let the ingredients fool you; this is hot!

1 teaspoon paprika
½ teaspoon dried thyme leaves
¼ teaspoon salt
¼ teaspoon ground red pepper
1/8 teaspoon ground nutmeg
2 teaspoons olive oil
1 clove garlic, crushed
12 extra-large shrimp (about ½ pound), shelled and deveined

In a cup, combine paprika, salt, pepper, and nutmeg. In a nonstick 10" skillet, heat olive oil over medium-high heat until hot. Add garlic; cook 1 minute. Discard garlic. Add spice mixture and cook 30 seconds, stirring constantly. Add shrimp, stirring to coat evenly with spices and cook 2-3 minutes until shrimp turn opaque throughout, stirring frequently. Makes 2 main-dish servings

Susan Henricks, Carnegie-Stout Public Library, Dubuque, IA

Captain's Stew with Rice

1 cup parboiled rice
¼ teaspoon turmeric
1 ½ pounds sea scallops
2 tablespoons olive oil
1 teaspoon salt
1 large onion, diced
1 8-ounce bag of carrots, diced
1 14 ½-16-ounce can stewed tomatoes
1 tablespoon parsley, chopped
1 teaspoon fresh thyme leaves, or ¼ teaspoon dried thyme leaves

Prepare rice as label directs, adding turmeric. Meanwhile, rinse scallops to remove any sand from crevices. Pat dry with paper towels. In a 12" skillet over medium-high heat, in hot olive oil, cook scallops with salt until lightly browned. Remove with a slotted spoon to a bowl. In the drippings cook onion and carrots until browned and tender, about 10 minutes. Stir in stewed tomatoes, parsley, thyme, scallops and any liquid in bowl and ¼ cup water. Over a high heat, heat until boiling. Reduce heat to low; simmer 2 minutes or until scallops turn opaque throughout. To serve, arrange yellow rice and scallop stew on a large platter; garnish with fresh thyme sprigs.

Susan Henricks, Carnegie-Stout Public Library, Dubuque, IA

Crab in Cream Sauce au Gratin

1 pound fresh crab meat, preferably lump
2 tablespoons butter
2 tablespoons flour
1½ cups milk
Pinch of cayenne pepper
1/8 teaspoon nutmeg
Salt and pepper to taste
½ cup heavy cream
4 tablespoons dry sherry
1 egg yolk
2 tablespoons shallots, finely chopped
4 hard-cooked eggs, cut into quarters
2 tablespoons Parmesan cheese

Preheat broiler to high. Pick over crab meat to remove any bits of shell and cartilage. Leave in as large lumps as possible. Heat 1 tablespoon butter in saucepan and add flour, stirring. Add milk, shirring rapidly with a whisk. When blended and smooth, add cayenne pepper, nutmeg, salt and pepper. Add cream and bring to boil. Let simmer briefly and add half of sherry. Beat in egg yolk and remove pan from heat.
Heat remaining butter in skillet and add shallots. Cook briefly and add crab meat. Cook just to heat through, stirring gently so as not to break up crab. Sprinkle with remaining sherry. Spoon crab meat into baking dish and smooth over. Arrange egg quarters on top, cut side down. Spoon on hot cream sauce and smooth it. Sprinkle with cheese. Place dish under the broiler until golden brown and bubbling on top. Serves 4

Christine Lind Hage, Clinton-Macomb Public Library, Clinton Township, MI

"Scallops are expensive, so they should be treated with some class. But then, I suppose that every creature that gives his life for our table should be treated with class."
Jeff Smith (1939-2004) The Frugal Gourmet

Ritzo's Scalloped Oysters

1 pint oysters
2 cups cracker crumbs
½ teaspoon salt
1/8 teaspoon pepper
½ cups butter melted
¼ teaspoon Worcestershire sauce
1 cup of milk

Drain oysters, set aside. Mix crumbs, salt, pepper, and butter. Place 1/3 of the crumb mixture into a buttered casserole dish. Cover with ½ of oysters, then the rest of the crumb mix and top with a layer of the remaining oysters. Mix milk and sauce, pour over dish. Bake at 350 degrees for 30 minutes.

Linda Magley, patron, Mesa Family History Center Library, Mesa, AZ

"As I ate the oysters with their strong taste of the sea and their faint metallic taste that the cold wine washed away, leaving only the sea taste and the succulent texture, and as I drank their cold liquid from each shell and washed it down with the crisp taste of the wine, I lost the empty feeling and began to be happy and to make plans."
Ernest Hemingway (1899-1961) *A Moveable Feast,* 1964

Seafood and Lemon Risotto

1 medium leek, sliced
2 cloves garlic, minced
1 cup Arborio rice
2 cups low-sodium chicken broth, divided
1 cup dry white wine
8 ounces bay scallops, rinsed
8 ounces medium shrimp in shells, rinsed, peeled and deveined
3 ounces fresh snow pea pods trimmed and halved crosswise
½ medium red bell pepper, chopped
3 tablespoons shredded Parmesan cheese
2 tablespoons fresh basil, chopped (or 2 teaspoons dried, crumbled basil)
1½-2 tablespoons finely shredded lemon rind
Parmesan cheese, shredded, optional

Spray medium saucepan with cooking spray. Cook leek and garlic over medium heat until leek is tender, about 5 minutes. Add rice; mix. Cook for 5 minutes stirring often. Add 1½ cups broth. Bring to a boil over high heat, stirring occasionally. Reduce heat and simmer, uncovered, 5 minutes, stirring occasionally. Add remaining broth and wine. Increase heat to medium and cook 5-8 minutes, stirring constantly. Add scallops, shrimp, pea pods, and bell pepper. Cook, stirring until liquid is almost absorbed, about 5 minutes (rice should be just tender and slightly creamy). Stir in basil and lemon rind. Heat through. Sprinkle with additional Parmesan if desired.

Susan Henricks, Carnegie-Stout Public Library, Dubuque, IA

"A little garlic, judiciously used, won't seriously affect your social life and will tone up more dull dishes than any commodity discovered to date." Alexander Wright *How to Live Without a Woman,* 1937

Shrimp Stroganoff

1 pound large shrimp
3 tablespoons butter or margarine
½ pound mushrooms
2 tablespoons dry sherry
2 tablespoons all-purpose flour
1/8 teaspoon pepper
1 envelope chicken-flavor bouillon
1 8-ounce container sour cream (light or fat free can be substituted)
2 teaspoons parsley, minced, for garnish

Shell and devein shrimp; rinse and pat dry with paper towels. In a 10" skillet over medium-high heat, in 2 tablespoons hot butter, cook shrimp stirring frequently, until shrimp turn pink and are tender, about 5 minutes. With slotted spoon, move shrimp to a bowl. Add 1 more tablespoon of butter to drippings in skillet, the mushrooms and sherry; cook stirring frequently, until mushrooms are tender. In cup, stir flour, pepper, bouillon, and 1 cup of water until blended; stir into mushrooms. Cook mushroom mixture, stirring constantly, until sauce boils and thickens slightly. Reduce heat to low; stir in sour cream until blended. Return shrimp to skillet and cook over low heat, stirring until shrimp are hot. Do not boil. Pour into serving bowl and garnish with parsley. Fluffy rice and pea pods are the perfect complement to this dish!

Susan Henricks, Carnegie-Stout Public Library, Dubuque, IA

"Those who have a profound indifference to the pleasures of the table are generally gloomy, charmless and unamiable."
Lucien Tendret (1825-1896) Author of *La Table au Pays de Brillat-Savarin,* 1892

641.812 Appetizers.

4-3-2-1 Dip

4 8-ounce packages cream cheese
3 medium tomatoes, diced
2 cans crab meat
2 cans mild green chilies, chopped
1 small red onion, chopped

Mix all ingredients. Put in shallow baking dish such as a quiche pan. Bake at 350 degrees for 25 minutes. Serve warm with tortilla chips.

Susan Elgin, Waukee Public Library, Waukee, IA

Artichoke Dip

2 cans artichoke hearts, (not marinated) drained and chopped into small pieces
1 cup mayonnaise
1 cup Parmesan cheese, freshly grated
1 teaspoon lemon juice
Garlic salt

Preheat oven to 350 degrees. Combine all ingredients in a bowl, then spread into a shallow baking dish. Bake for about 30 minutes or until the top layer is slightly brown and bubbly. Serve with any kind of hearty cracker or bread and enjoy!

Kelly Chambala, Huntington Memorial Library, Oneonta, NY
Charlotte Rabbitt, Peterborough Town Library, Peterborough, NH

"Every investigation which is guided by principles of nature fixes its ultimate aim entirely on gratifying the stomach."
Athenaeus, A.D. 200. Athenaeus, a Greek gourmet, wrote *Deipnosophistai* ('The Learned Banquet'). It is a dialogue between two banqueters who discuss food and recipes over a period of several days.

Cheese Ball

2 8-ounce packages of cream cheese
1 glass jar of sharp cheese, such as Old English
1 small triangle of blue cheese
1 cup pecans, chopped
1 cup parsley, finely cut
Clove of garlic

Rub clove of garlic on cover and inside of bowl. Mix the cheeses; add ½ of the nuts and parsley; form into a ball. Roll in remaining nuts and parsley; store in covered bowl. Refrigerate.

Ann Straley, Carnegie-Stout Public Library, Dubuque, IA

Cheese Spread

1 tablespoon dried, minced onion flakes
2 tablespoons red wine vinegar
1 jar Roka cheese, such as Kraft
2 jars Old English cheese, such as Kraft
2 8-ounces packages cream cheese
Garlic to taste

Soak dried onion in red wine vinegar in large mixing bowl. Beat in cheeses, cream cheese, and garlic. Refrigerate until ready to serve on crackers. Tasty cheese snack that keeps well for up to 10 days. 15 servings

Marge Helsell, Nixon IMC, Hiawatha, Iowa

"Many's the long night I've dreamed of cheese --- toasted, mostly."
Robert Louis Stevenson (1850-1894) Scottish poet and novelist

Chicken Liver Pâte

1 pound chicken livers
3 tablespoons mayonnaise
2 tablespoons lemon juice
2 tablespoons butter, softened
1 tablespoon onion, chopped
8-10 drops of hot sauce
½ teaspoon salt
½ teaspoon dry mustard
Dash pepper

Cook the chicken livers, covered, in a small amount of butter over a low heat so as to not allow them to get brown and crispy. When cooked, place in a food processor and process just until broken up. Add the mayonnaise, lemon juice, butter, onion, hot sauce, salt, dry mustard and pepper. Process until smooth. Chill in a mold for several hours before serving.

Kim Byers, patron, Hiawatha Public Library, Hiawatha, IA

"My idea of heaven is eating pates de foie gras to the sound of trumpets."
Sydney Smith (1771-1845) English writer

Crab Rangoon

1 8-ounce package cream cheese
½ small onion, finely chopped
2 pieces celery hearts, finely chopped
6 ounces crab meat
Dash lemon juice
Garlic salt to taste
Pepper to taste
2 teaspoons cornstarch mixed with 2 teaspoons water
Wonton wrappers

In a non-stick pan, cook onions until light brown. Add celery to onions; cook until translucent. Remove from heat. Add cream cheese, crabmeat, lemon juice, garlic salt and pepper, mixing well. Spoon small amounts of mixture in the middle of wonton wrappers; seal edges of wraps by brushing with cornstarch and water mixture. Deep fat fry the wonton wrappers until golden brown. Serve with hot plum sauce or sweet and sour sauce.

Denise S. Crawford, Glenwood Public Library, Glenwood, IA

Crabbies

1 6-ounce jar Old English Cheese
½ cup butter, softened
¼ teaspoon garlic powder
1 tablespoon mayonnaise
1 6-ounce can crab meat, drained
English muffins

Blend the first four ingredients. Stir in crab. Spread on English muffins. Cut each muffin into 6 pieces. Bake at 400 degrees for 10 minutes.

Shirley L. Headlee, Van Meter Public Library, Van Meter, IA

Cucumber Cooler

1 cup sour cream
1 ½ cup cucumber, peeled, grated, and squeezed dry
½ teaspoon lemon juice
½ teaspoon salt
1 tablespoon green onion, finely sliced

Combine all ingredients and refrigerate until ready to serve. Serve with wheat crackers or vegetable dippers. Makes about 1½ cups dip.

Kathy Fisher, Keosauqua Public Library, Keosauqua, IA

Fresh Vegetable Dip

2 cups salad dressing
4 tablespoons instant minced onion
2 teaspoons garlic salt
2 teaspoons tarragon vinegar
2 teaspoons prepared horseradish
2 teaspoons curry powder

Mix all ingredients well. Serve with fresh raw vegetables such as cauliflower, broccoli, celery and carrots.

Cheryl Boothe, Newton Public Library, Newton, IA

Liver Sausage Pâte

1 package unflavored gelatin
1 10-ounce can beef broth
12 ounces packaged liver sausage
1 cup sour cream
1 tablespoon parsley, chopped
2 teaspoons lemon juice
½ teaspoon salt
½ teaspoon pepper
4½ ounce can chopped ripe olives

Dissolve gelatin in ¼ cup beef broth. Heat remaining broth; add gelatin and stir until dissolved. Stir sausage in a large bowl until it is soft and creamy. Add remaining ingredients and blend. Place in a 3½ cup mold and chill overnight. Unmold and serve with French bread or crackers.

Kathy Fisher, Keosauqua Public Library, Keosauqua, IA

Mexican Cheese and Jalapeño Spread

5 fresh jalapeño peppers, minced
3 green onions, minced
8 ounces pepper cheese, shredded
½ cup sour cream
¼ cup mayonnaise
1/8 teaspoon of white pepper
1/8 teaspoon of salt
Tabasco sauce to taste

Place minced jalapeños in two quart or larger bowl and add green onions. Add remaining ingredients to the bowl, except Tabasco, and stir until smooth. Cover and refrigerate 2-48 hours. Stir well, taste, and add Tabasco if desired. Preheat oven to 350 degrees. Put spread in oven proof dish and bake 20 minutes or until heated through and bubbly along the edges. Makes two cups.

Annette Wetteland, State Library of Iowa, Des Moines, IA

"The way to a man's heart is through his stomach."
Fanny Fern (1811-1872) American journalist

100

Olive Cheese Melts

1 cup green olives, stuffed with pimento, (i.e., manzanilla olives), chopped
1/3 cup scallions, chopped
1½ cups cheddar cheese, grated
½ teaspoon curry powder
½ cup mayonnaise
6 English muffins

Combine the olives, scallions, cheese, curry powder and mayonnaise; mix well. Split the muffins in half so that there are 12 halves. Spread the mix onto each muffin half, and cut into 4 pieces. Bake at 400 degrees for 10 minutes.

Maureen O'Connor, Brampton Library, Brampton, ON, Canada

Olive Nut Spread

8 ounces cream cheese, softened
½ cup mayonnaise
1 tablespoon juice from olives
½ cup green olives, chopped
½ cup ripe black olives, chopped
½ cup pecans, chopped
Dash of pepper

Mix all together and let sit 24 hours. It will be "mushy" at first, but will thicken as it sits.

Dee Davisson, Waukee Public Library, Waukee, IA

"The olive tree is surely the richest gift of Heaven, I can scarcely expect bread."
Thomas Jefferson (1743-1826) 3rd President of the United States

Shrimp and Crab Loaf

2 oval sourdough loaves, unsliced
3 8-ounce blocks of cream cheese
2 cans of shrimp (reserving the liquid from one can, drain the other can)
1 can of crab meat
½ cup green onions, chopped
1½ teaspoon garlic salt

Cut a lid out of the top of the whole loaf and set aside. Dig out the inside of the loaf to form a hollow bowl. Combine cream cheese, shrimp, liquid from one of the shrimp cans, crab meat, onions and garlic salt; mix until smooth. Stuff the loaf and bake for 1 hour at 350 degrees uncovered. Put the bread lid on and cook for ½ hour more.

Linda Magley, patron, Mesa Family History Center Library, Mesa, AZ

Spinach and Artichoke Casserole/Dip

2 10-ounce packages of frozen chopped spinach, thawed and drained
1 13.75-ounce can quartered artichokes, drained
2 cups cream-style cottage cheese
½ cup butter, cut into pieces
1½ cups cheddar cheese, cubed
3 large eggs, beaten
¼ cup flour
1 teaspoon seasoned salt

Thoroughly combine all ingredients in mixing bowl. Pour into greased slow cooker. (I use part of the ½ cup of butter to do this.) Cover and cook on high for 1 hour; stir and turn to low for 4-5 hours. Serve with crudités, nacho chips, and/or crackers. This recipe may be doubled.

Note: If you serve it more than 4 times a year, I can give you the name of a good cardiologist.

J.A.E.Kiszewski, Parsippany-Troy Hills Public Library, Parsippany NJ

"Everything I eat has proved by some doctor or other to be a deadly poison, and everything I don't eat has been proved to be indispensable to life..... But I go marching on."
George Bernard Shaw (1856-1950) Irish playwright

Swiss Cheese Spread

2 cups Swiss cheese, finely grated
¼ cup (or one 4-ounce can) finely chopped black olives
¼ green pepper, finely chopped
½ teaspoon garlic powder
½ cup mayonnaise, or salad dressing

Mix all with a fork. Chill. Makes just over 2 cups. Serve with crackers (especially good on Triscuits!) This will freeze if Miracle Whip is used.

Judy Havlik, Algona Community Schools, Algona, IA

Four tablespoonfuls of onions, fried with pork. One quart of boiled potatoes, well mashed. One and a half pounds sea-biscuit, broken. One teaspoonful of thyme, mixed with one of summer savory. Half-bottle of mushroom catsup. One bottle of port or claret. Half of a nutmeg, grated. A few cloves, mace, and allspice. Six pounds of fish, sea-bass or cod, cut in slices. Twenty five oysters, a little black pepper, and a few slices of lemon. The whole put in a pot, covered with an inch of water, boiled for an hour, and gently stirred."
Daniel Webster's Chowder Recipe, from *The Cook*, 1885

*From the archives of the Carnegie-Stout Public Library,
Dubuque, Iowa*

641.813 Soups.

Baked Potato Soup ...in 30 minutes or less!

1 tablespoon butter
1 small onion, chopped
1 clove garlic, minced
3 tablespoons flour
½ teaspoon basil
½ teaspoon pepper
3 cups chicken broth
2 large baked potatoes (about 2 cups) peeled and cubed, (microwave to quickly bake)
1 cup half and half cream
Shredded cheese
Fresh parsley
Diced bacon bits

Melt butter in a large saucepan. Sauté onion and garlic. Stir in flour, salt, basil, and pepper. Add broth. Bring to a boil and stir for 2 minutes. Add the potatoes and cream. Heat through being careful not to boil. Garnish with cheese, parsley, and bacon bits.

Bette Jollifee, Marathon Public Library, Marathon, IA

Broccoli Cheese Soup

1 can cream of potato soup
1 soup can of milk
4-6 slices American cheese (shredded cheddar cheese doesn't melt easily; but you could use Velveeta)
½ pound broccoli florets

Cut broccoli florets into small pieces. Steam until tender but not soggy. Set aside. Break pieces of cheese up so they will be ready to stir into hot soup. Make cream of potato soup with can of milk. Stir constantly until warmed. (The milk can lead to burning the bottom of the pot.) Stir cheese into soup until melted. Add more cheese if desired. Once cheese is all melted stir in the steamed broccoli and you're done.

This recipe makes 2-3 servings. Just increase ingredients for more soup. To fill a regular size crockpot about 2/3 full you would use 3 cans soup, etc.

Valerie Smith, Lorain Public Library System, Lorain, OH

Cheese Soup

1 quart water
4 chicken bouillon cubes
1 large onion, chopped
1 cup celery, chopped
1 pound American cheese, shredded
1 cup carrot, chopped
2½ cups potatoes, diced
2½ cups mixed vegetables
2 cans cream of chicken soup

Combine water, bouillon, onion, celery, carrot and potatoes in a 4-quart saucepan. Cover and simmer 20 minutes. Add mixed vegetables and soup. Continue to simmer until the vegetables are done and the soup is heated through. Add cheese, stirring occasionally, until cheese is melted. Season to taste.

Variations: cauliflower and bacon bits; potatoes and ham, corn, hamburger and red pepper flakes for a Mexican style cheese soup.

Deb Anderson, Estherville Public Library, Estherville, IA

"It [soup] breathes reassurance, it offers consolation; after a weary day it promotes sociability...There is nothing like a bowl of hot soup, it's wisp of aromatic steam teasing the nostrils into quivering anticipation."
Louis P. DeGouy, Waldorf-Astoria chef, *The Soup Book,* 1949

Chicken Stew with Tortellini

2 cups water
1 14½-ounce can reduced-sodium chicken broth
1 medium yellow summer squash
6 cups torn beet greens, turnip greens, or spinach
1 green sweet pepper, coarsely chopped
1 cup dried cheese-filled tortellini pasta
1 medium onion, cut into thin wedges
1 medium carrot, sliced
1½ teaspoons fresh rosemary, snipped
½ teaspoon salt-free seasoning blend
¼ teaspoon pepper
2 cups cooked chicken, chopped
1 tablespoon fresh basil, snipped

In a Dutch oven bring water and chicken broth to a boil. Meanwhile, halve summer squash lengthwise and cut into ½ inch slices. Add squash, greens, sweet pepper, pasta, onion, carrot, rosemary, seasoning blend, and pepper to Dutch oven. Return heat to boiling; reduce heat. Simmer, covered, about 15 minutes or until pasta and vegetables are nearly tender. Stir in chicken. Cook, covered, about 5 minutes more or until pasta and vegetables are tender. Stir fresh basil in soup.

Susan Henricks, Carnegie-Stout Public Library, Dubuque, IA

"And Tom brought him chicken soup until he wanted to kill him. The lore has not died out of the world, and you will still find people who believe that soup will cure any hurt or illness and is no bad thing to have for the funeral either." John Steinbeck (1902-1968) American author, *East of Eden*, 1952

Cream of Squash Soup

1 large onion, diced
2 tablespoons olive oil
1½ teaspoons mild curry powder
2 small butternut squash, about 1¼ pounds each
2 medium-size Rome Beauty apples, peeled, cored, and diced
1 14 ½-ounce can chicken broth
1 ¼ teaspoon salt
1/8 teaspoon white pepper
1½ cups half-and-half
Fresh chives for garnish, chopped

Heat olive oil in a 4-quart saucepan over medium heat. Add the diced onion and cook until tender, about 15 minutes. Stir in curry powder; cook for 1 minute. Meanwhile, peel and cut butternut squash into 1" chunks. To saucepan add squash, apples, chicken broth, salt, pepper, and 1 ½ cups water. Over a high heat, heat until boiling. Reduce heat to low; cover and simmer 10-15 minutes until squash is very tender, stirring frequently. Spoon 1/3 of the squash mixture into a blender or food processor. Cover and blend on low speed until smooth. Repeat with remaining squash mixture. Return squash mixture to saucepan, add half-and-half; cook over a medium heat stirring occasionally until heated through. Garnish with chives.

Susan Henricks, Carnegie-Stout Public Library, Dubuque, IA

"Every investigation which is guided by principles of nature fixes its ultimate aim entirely on gratifying the stomach."
Athenaeus, A.D. 200. Athenaeus, a Greek gourmet, wrote *Deipnosophistai* ('The Learned Banquet'). It is a dialogue between two banqueters who discuss food and recipes over a period of several days.

Erwtensoep ("*Snert*")
(Dutch Split Pea Soup)

1½ pounds dried split peas
2 cups carrots, sliced
2 quarts water
1 cup onion, diced
1 quart chicken broth
1 cup heavy cream
1 large ham bone
½ pound smoked ham, diced
1 cup celery, diced
Salt and fresh ground pepper

Wash peas. Place in bowl and cover with water. Soak for 8 hours.
Drain and rinse. Place peas into a slow cooker. Add water, chicken broth
and ham bone. Cover and cook on low 4 hours. Remove ham bone.
Add celery, carrots, onion and diced ham. Add salt and pepper to taste. Cook
on low another four hours. Add heavy cream 15 minutes before serving.

Sharon Luttikhuizen Warne, General Dynamics, AIS, Buffalo, NY

Garden Patch Soup

2 ½ quarts chicken broth
1 bay leaf
6 peppercorns
1 clove garlic, cut in half
2 carrots, (1 cup) thinly sliced
2 celery stalks, (1 cup) sliced
1 onion, sliced
¼ cup parsley, chopped
8 ounces uncooked Vermicelli, broken in pieces
2 tomatoes, peeled and cut into wedges
Salt and pepper to taste

Tie bay leaf, peppercorns and garlic into a cheesecloth bag. Heat chicken broth,
bay leaf, peppercorns and garlic to boiling; remove seasonings and add vegetables
and parsley. Simmer 20 minutes; add Vermicelli and tomatoes. Add salt and
pepper to taste. Simmer 8-10 minutes or until Vermicelli is done. Serves 8

Ann Straley, Carnegie-Stout Public Library, Dubuque, IA

"Soup of the evening, beautiful..."
Lewis Carroll (1832-1898) English author

Hamburger Tomato Soup

2 large potatoes, peeled and cut in cubes
3 carrots, cut small
½ cup onion, chopped
1 can tomato soup
1 soup can milk
1 6-ounce can tomato paste
¾ pound ground beef

Cook potatoes, carrots, and onions in 1½ cups water until tender, approximately 15 minutes. Drain. Meanwhile, cook ground beef until no pink remains, drain. In large saucepan stir potatoes, carrots, onion and ground beef together. Add soup, milk, and tomato paste. Stir until mixed. Simmer until ready to serve. Garnish with green olives if desired.

Susan Simmon, Volunteer, Glenwood Public Library, Glenwood, IA

Mama Graziana's Golden Vegetable Soup

For each person use:
One potato, peeled
One carrot, scraped
¼ cup of frozen corn kernels
2 cups chicken broth
One jalapeño pepper per two or three people, depending on fire level
Scallions, chopped

This is an entirely expandable recipe. Chop the peeled potatoes, peppers, and carrots into small pieces; sauté them in olive oil over medium high heat until they brown a bit on the edges. Bring the broth to a boil, toss in the veggies with any remaining olive oil. Simmer for 25-30 minutes. Add salt and red pepper to taste, remembering how powerful your jalapeño is. Top with the sweet green scallions and serve.

GraceAnne Andreassi DeCandido, Blue Roses Consulting, NY, NY

I live on good soup, not on fine words."
Molière (1622-1673) French playwright

Mongolian Oxtail Soup

1 package oxtails
4 beef bouillon cubes
1 head purple cabbage
1 small can tomato sauce
Water to cover plus 1-2 inches

Combine oxtails, bouillon and water. Bring to boil, skimming off scum. Simmer until meat is very tender, about to fall off bones. Add tomato sauce. Chop and add cabbage. Cook until cabbage is tender. Salt and pepper to taste.

Johanna Hause Lo, Palisades Free Library, Palisades, New York.

Southwestern Vegetable Soup

1 can chili, with or without meat
1 8-ounce can corn, drained
1 8-ounce can green beans, drained
1 16-ounce can kidney beans, drained
½ cup onion, chopped
½ cup green pepper, chopped
2 cups tomato juice
1 teaspoon chili powder, hot sauce or hot pepper, chopped, optional

Mix all the ingredients in a large saucepan and simmer for 30 minutes.

Karen Keller, Johnston Middle School Library, Johnston, IA

Super Easy Corn Chowder

2 cups water
1 envelope dry chicken noodle soup mix
1 can cream style corn
½ cup milk

Bring the water to a boil in a saucepan. Add the dry soup mix and simmer for 10 minutes. Add the corn and milk. Heat through and serve. Serves 2-3

Susan Simmon, Volunteer, Glenwood Public Library, Glenwood, IA

"Only the pure of heart can make good soup"
Ludwig van Beethoven (1727-1880) Musician and composer

Taco Soup

2 pounds ground beef
1 onion, chopped
2 cans chili beans (or use kidney or black beans)
2 cans whole corn, drained
2 cups water
1 8-ounce can tomato sauce
1 15-ounce can tomatoes, chopped
1 package dry ranch dressing mix, such as Hidden Valley
1 package taco seasoning mix

Brown ground beef and onion; drain. In a large saucepan combine the cooked beef with all other ingredients and simmer approximately 30 minutes. Serve with taco chips, shredded cheese, and sour cream if desired.

Kathy Hembry, Newton Public Library, Newton, IA

Wild Rice Soup

½ cup wild rice
1 small onion, chopped
2 cups chicken broth
1 cup mushrooms, sliced
1 cup broccoli, chopped
3 tablespoons flour
2 cups low-fat milk
1½ cups American cheese
Salt and pepper to taste

Cook the wild rice, onion, and chicken broth in a saucepan for 35 minutes. Add mushrooms and broccoli and cook for 10 minutes. Sprinkle flour over the rice and vegetables and stir in gradually. Slowly add the milk. Cook over a medium heat until the mixture thickens and boils. Add the cheese, stir until melted. Add salt and pepper to taste.

Denise S. Crawford, Glenwood Public Library, Glenwood, IA

641.814 Ketchup

Homemade Ketchup

1 tablespoon olive oil
4 shallots, minced
1 tablespoon fresh ginger, grated
6 plum tomatoes, peeled, seeded, and diced
2 tablespoons cider vinegar
2 tablespoons honey
½ teaspoon ground cloves, or to taste
¼ teaspoon cinnamon
1 teaspoon each salt and pepper, freshly ground
Pickle juice, optional, to taste

Heat oil in medium saucepan over medium-high heat. Sauté shallots and ginger until soft, about 4 minutes. Add remaining ingredients. Bring to a boil, reduce to a simmer, and cook, stirring frequently, until thickened, twenty minutes. Puree in blender or mash with potato masher. Chill and serve. Yields 1 cup

Barbara Feist Stienstra, Middletown Thrall Library, Middletown, NY

"Shake and shake
The catsup bottle,
None will come,
And then a lot'll."

Ogden Nash (1902-1971) American poet

113

641.814 Salsas (Cookery)

Black Bean Salsa

2 15-ounce cans black beans, rinsed and drained
1 15-ounce can whole kernel corn, drained
6 tablespoons olive oil
6 tablespoons fresh lime juice
½ cup green pepper, minced
½ cup red pepper, minced
3 jalapeño peppers, minced (may use pickled jalapeño pepper rings)
1 teaspoon cumin, ground
Fresh cilantro, snipped

Mix all ingredients and refrigerate for several hours. Stir again before serving with taco chips.

Sandy Dixon, State Library of Iowa, Des Moines, IA

Quick Fresh Salsa

2 cans petite diced tomatoes with zesty jalapeño, such as Del Monte
1 can petite diced tomatoes with garlic and olive oil, such as Del Monte
1 white, sweet onion, diced
1 clove garlic, minced
Cilantro
Juice of ½ lime

Drain tomatoes. In a mixing bowl mix tomatoes, onion, garlic, cilantro to taste and lime juice. Stir until well mixed. Serve with tortilla chips and enjoy!

Denise S. Crawford, Glenwood Public Library, Glenwood, IA

Salsa vs. Relish

The only difference is that the word 'relish' is of French origin, and the word 'salsa' is of Spanish origin. They are both condiments intended to add flavor to other foods, and both can be either raw or cooked. foodreference.com

Salsa

2 cups fresh tomatoes, chopped
1 8-ounce can tomato sauce
1 small can green chilies, diced and drained
1 small bunch green onions, chopped (use green part, too)
1 golf-ball sized onion, chopped (Vadalia if possible)
1 tablespoon salt
½ rib celery, chopped
1 jalapeño pepper, diced (use seeds also)
1 tablespoon oil, optional

Mix all ingredients well and chill at least 2 hours before serving.

Judy Snetselaar, Webster City High School Library, Webster City, IA

"Condiments are like old friends -- highly thought of, but often taken for granted."
Marilyn Kaytor, *Condiments: "The Tastemakers,"*
Look Magazine, January 29, 1963

641.814 Sauces.

Bee Keeper's Sundae Sauce

¾ cup slivered, blanched almonds
1 cup honey
2 tablespoons instant coffee crystals

Toast almonds in a 350 degree oven until golden brown. Cool. Combine honey and instant coffee and cook over medium heat stirring occasionally until coffee dissolves and mixture is heated. Stir in almonds. Cool slightly and serve over ice cream.

Kathy Fisher, Keosauqua Public Library, Keosauqua, IA

Chocolate Sauce

¼ cup unsalted butter
1 cup sugar
½ cup good quality cocoa
1 cup milk
1 tablespoon cornstarch
¼ cup cold water
½ cup chocolate syrup (Hershey's brand recommended)
¼ cup brandy

In a very heavy saucepan, melt the butter with the sugar and cocoa until the mixture starts to caramelize. Immediately add the milk, stirring constantly. The hard lumps will dissolve as the liquid comes to a boil. Dilute the cornstarch with the water. Pour this in a slow stream into the boiling syrup, stirring constantly. Remove from heat and cool to room temperature. Add the chocolate syrup and brandy. Refrigerate.

This recipe came from the "Bakery", a restaurant owned and run by Louis Szathmary in Chicago circa 1980's. No question, this chocolate sauce IS the best.

Susan Henricks, Carnegie-Stout Public Library, Dubuque, IA

Dutch Honey

1 cup brown sugar
1 cup cream
1 cup Karo syrup
1 teaspoon vanilla

Mix all ingredients together in a saucepan and boil about 1 minute. Remove from burner. Cool thoroughly, then beat until honey-colored and creamy (about 5 minutes).

Jean Gullikson, Carnegie-Stout Public Library, Dubuque, IA

Kathy's Mom's Spaghetti Sauce

1 pound ground beef
2 tablespoons parsley
4 medium onions, chopped
4 cloves garlic, chopped
¼ teaspoon pepper
1 teaspoon salt
½ teaspoon chili pepper
½ teaspoon Tabasco sauce
½ teaspoon oregano
2 teaspoons Worcestershire sauce
1 6-ounce can tomato paste
1 small can mushrooms
1 can cream of mushroom soup
1 can cream of tomato soup

Brown ground beef in a heavy pan, drain fat. To the ground beef add parsley, onions, garlic, pepper and salt, Tabasco sauce, oregano, Worcestershire sauce, tomato paste, mushrooms, and both soups. Simmer for about 45 minutes stirring frequently. Serve over cooked spaghetti. Top with grated Parmesan cheese (*if you don't forget! – my mother's note.*)

Mother's recipe card continues with the following note: "First tried on March 29, 1956. Kathy home from SUI. Easter. Dick's birthday. Cold, snowy and so windy we had to turn off oil burner!"

Kathy Fisher, Keosauqua Public Library, Keosauqua, IA

"Everything you see I owe to spaghetti."
Sophia Loren (1934-) Italian actress

641.815 Bread.

Asiago Bread

7-8 cups of bread flour
1/3 cup sugar
1 tablespoon salt
2/3 cup milk
2 cups water
2 packages of dry yeast
¾ pound of Asiago cheese, shredded

In a large bowl, mix 2 ½ cups of flour, sugar, salt and dry yeast. Combine water and milk and heat to 120-130 degrees. Gradually add to the dry mixture. Beat two minutes on medium speed of mixer, scraping bowl often. Add cheese and ½ cup flour and beat on high speed for 2 minutes, scraping bowl often. Stir in additional flour to make a stiff dough.

Turn on to a lightly floured board and knead until bread becomes smooth and elastic, about 8-10 minutes. Place in a large greased bowl, turning to grease top of dough. Cover and let rise until double in bulk about 1 hour. Punch dough down, turn onto floured board and let rest for 15 minutes. Divide dough in half. Roll each half in a 14" x 9" rectangle. Shape into loaves, or into French bread style, and place on baking sheet. Cover and let rise until double in bulk about 1 hour. Bake on lowest rack in oven at 350 degrees for about 40 minutes or until done. Remove from pan and cool and cool on wire racks. Brush tops with melted butter or margarine.

Ann Garas, patron, Rockford Public Library, Rockford, IL

"Without bread all is misery."
William Cobbett (1763?-1835) British journalist

118

Beau Monde Bread

1 loaf sandwich bread, unsliced
8 ounces Swiss cheese, sliced
½ pound margarine (soft tub is good)
2 tablespoons onion, grated
1 tablespoon mustard
½ teaspoon Beau Monde seasoning
2 tablespoons lemon juice
1 tablespoon poppy seeds

Cut the top and side crusts off the bread. Cut X's ¾ of the way through the bread top. Stuff all the X's with the cheese. Blend margarine, onion, mustard, Beau Monde seasoning, lemon juice and poppy seeds. Place the loaf on foil. Frost the loaf with the margarine mix. Bake 30 minutes at 350 degrees. Watch that it doesn't get too brown. It will hold in the warm oven quite awhile. This can be made up and frozen to bake later.

Nancy Voltmer, Hiatt Middle School Library, Des Moines, IA

Beer Bread

3 cups of flour
3 tablespoons of sugar
3 ¾ teaspoons of baking powder
Pinch of salt
1 12-ounce bottle of lager, such as Yuengling, or your favorite beer
1 tablespoon of butter, optional

Mix the flour, sugar, baking powder, salt, and beer together. Do not over mix. Place batter in a greased bread pan. Melt butter and pour over batter. Bake at 375 degrees for 45-60 minutes until golden brown. Cool for ½ hour before slicing.

Variations: Instead of beer, use 12 ounces of cranberry juice, orange juice, cola, or any beverage you like.

Tom Meyer, Lansdale Public Library, Lansdale, PA

"If thou tastest a crust of bread, thou tastest all the stars and all the heavens."
Robert Browning (1812-1889) English poet

Beer Bread

3 cups self-rising flour
1/3 cup sugar
12 ounce can of beer (heavy Irish)

Mix all ingredients; put in greased loaf pan. Bake at 350 degrees for 50-60 minutes

Jean Gullikson, Carnegie-Stout Public Library, Dubuque, IA

Bentonsport Bread

Although this recipe has no eggs or shortening, it is very tasty.

1 cup all purpose unbleached flour
2 cups whole wheat flour
1 tablespoon baking powder
½ teaspoon baking soda
1 teaspoon salt
1 cup dark brown sugar
1½ cup milk
1 cup walnuts, coarsely chopped

Combine the flours, baking powder and soda and salt in a large bowl. Set aside. Stir brown sugar into milk until it is dissolved. Stir milk mixture into dry ingredients just until mixed. Add walnuts. Turn into 2 greased medium 8 ½"x 4 ½" loaf pans and bake at 300 degrees for about 1 hour. Turn onto wire racks and cool completely.

Kathy Fisher, Keosauqua Public Library, Keosauqua, IA

"Acorns were good till bread was found."
Francis Bacon (1561-1626) English philosopher, statesman

Cheddar Cheese Bread

1 cup warm water (100-115 degrees)
1 package dry yeast
½ teaspoon sugar
3½-4 cups flour
2 teaspoon salt
1½ cups cheddar cheese, grated
3 eggs
2 tablespoons milk

Proof yeast in water and sugar, about 6 minutes. Combine flour, salt, cheese and two eggs then add yeast. Knead for 10 minutes, or until smooth. Set in a warm place to rise for about 1 hour or until doubled in bulk. Knead again. Shape into loaf and let rise in a buttered bread pan. Brush with remaining egg and 2 tablespoons milk. Bake 375 degrees for 45 minutes or until internal temperature reaches 190 degrees.

Christine Lind Hage, Clinton-Macomb Public Library, Clinton Township, MI

Cinnamon Marshmallow Rolls

1 stick butter
1 package crescent refrigerator rolls
1 large marshmallow for each roll
Cinnamon and sugar mixture

Melt the butter. Roll a marshmallow in the butter; then dip it in the cinnamon and sugar mixture. Roll the marshmallow up inside a crescent roll. Pinch the crescent roll to seal it. Roll the crescent roll in butter and then in the cinnamon/sugar mixture. Place roll in a well-greased muffin tin. Repeat for all rolls. Preheat oven to 375 degrees. Bake rolls for 11-13 minutes. Remove from oven and from tins; place on wax paper as they are sticky.

Decadent but fun.

Ann Straley, Carnegie-Stout Public Library, Dubuque, IA

"God made yeast, as well as dough, and loves fermentation just as dearly as he loves vegetation."
Ralph Waldo Emerson (1803-1882) American poet, essayist

Dilly Bread

1 package yeast
¼ cup warm water (105-115 degrees)
1 cup cottage cheese
2 tablespoons sugar
1 tablespoon minced onion
1 tablespoon butter
2 teaspoons dill seed
1 teaspoon salt
¼ teaspoon baking soda
1 egg
2¼ cups -2 ½ cups flour

Dissolve the yeast in warm water. Heat the cottage cheese until it is lukewarm. Combine the yeast, cottage cheese, sugar, onion, butter, dill seed, salt, soda and egg in a mixing bowl. Beat until mixed. Add flour to form stiff dough. Turn into a well greased 8" round casserole dish and let rise until light and doubled in size. Bake at 350 degrees for 40-45 minutes until golden brown.

Susan Henricks, Carnegie-Stout Public Library, Dubuque, IA

English Muffin Loaves

5½ to 6 cups flour
2 packages dry yeast
1 tablespoon sugar
2 teaspoon salt
¼ teaspoon baking soda
2 cups milk
½ cup water
Cornmeal

In a large mixing bowl, combine 3 cups flour, yeast, sugar, salt and baking soda; set aside. In saucepan, combine water and milk and heat to 125 degrees. Add to flour mixture. Gradually add enough of the remaining flour to make a stiff dough. Set aside. Prepare two 8 ½" x 4 ½" loaf pans by greasing lightly and sprinkle with cornmeal. Pour half the batter in each pan; sprinkle tops with cornmeal. Cover pans with slightly damp cloth; let stand in a warm place until doubled in bulk 1½ hours. Bake at 400 degrees for 25 minutes and until light brown. Take out of pans to cool.

Christine Lind Hage, Clinton-Macomb Public Library, Clinton Township, MI

Irish Soda Bread (County Cork)

3½ cups sifted flour
2/3 cup sugar
1 teaspoon salt
1 teaspoon baking soda
1 tablespoon baking powder
1½ cups raisins
1 tablespoon caraway seeds, optional
2 eggs, lightly beaten
1½ cups buttermilk
2 tablespoons butter, melted

Grease a round cake pan. Heat oven to 375 degrees.
Sift dry ingredients into bowl. Add raisins, caraway, eggs, buttermilk, and butter and blend. Pour into greased round pan (batter will be soft.) Cut a cross on top of the dough with a knife. Pat on a little dry flour. Bake 1 hour. Test for doneness by inserting a toothpick in the middle of the loaf. Brush melted butter on the loaf while cooling.

Katherine Mazzella, Tappan Library, Tappan, NY

"Bachelor's fare: bread and cheese, and kisses."
Jonathan Swift (1667-1745) Irish author and satirist

Julekake (Norwegian Christmas bread)

2 cups milk
1 cup butter, melted
2 teaspoons salt
1 cup sugar
2 packages yeast
½ cup water
8-9 cups flour
1 tablespoon cardamom
½ cup almonds, chopped
½ cup candied cherries, sliced
1 cup raisins
½ cup citron, chopped

Dissolve yeast in lukewarm water. Scald milk and add butter, salt, and sugar. When lukewarm, stir in yeast and water. Stir in 4 cups flour. Set in a warm place to rise until doubled, about 2 hours. Punch down and stir in remaining ingredients. Work in the remaining flour until dough is as soft as can be conveniently handled. Let rise in warm place 2-3 hours, or until doubled. Knead slightly and form into loaves and place into 2 greased loaf pans. Let rise 1-2 hours until doubled. Bake in 350 degree oven 45-55 minutes. Glaze top with powdered sugar frosting and serve with butter.

LeAnn Rugland Watson , Montgomery County Public Library - South Regional Branch, The Woodlands, TX

"The smell of good bread baking, like the sound of lightly flowing water, is indescribable in its evocation of innocence and delight."
M. F. K. Fisher (1908-1992) American food critic and writer

Kringla (Norwegian sweet bread)

1 cup sugar
½ cup butter or stick margarine
1 egg
1 teaspoon vanilla
1 cup buttermilk
1 teaspoon baking soda
3 cups flour
2 teaspoons baking powder

Cream together sugar and butter. Add egg and vanilla; mix well. Add buttermilk and baking soda, blending thoroughly. Add flour and baking powder and mix slowly. Cover and refrigerate dough overnight. The dough is tacky, so keep it chilled. Roll the dough out forming 5-6" snakes. It helps to use as little flour as possible in rolling the dough. (Too much flour will toughen dough.) Put 2 ends of each snake together and twist, placing ends on opposite side of circle. (Resembles a pretzel). Bake at 450 degrees on the lowest oven rack until the Kringla spreads out. Then move to the top shelf to finish baking. Bake until it barely shows a brown color; less than 10 minutes.

Joyce Kreitlow, Lake View Public Library Lake View, IA

Mustard and Caraway Seed Bread

3 cups flour
¼ cup sugar
2 tablespoons baking powder
1 tablespoon caraway seeds
1 tablespoon mustard seed
2 teaspoons salt
3 eggs, beaten
1 ¾ cups milk
¼ cup oil

Combine flour, sugar, baking powder, caraway and mustard seeds. Stir in beaten eggs, milk, and oil mixing only enough to moisten flour. Bake in a 9" greased loaf pan at 350 degrees about 65-70 minutes. Cool 15 minutes before removing from pan.

Kathy Fisher, Keosauqua Public Library, Keosauqua, IA

New Orleans Beignets

1 cup whole milk, scalded
2 tablespoons unsalted butter
1 tablespoon brown sugar
1 tablespoons white sugar
3 cups enriched bread flour
1 teaspoon nutmeg
1 egg
1 teaspoon salt
1 package granulated yeast
Peanut oil for deep frying
Powdered sugar for dusting

Heat milk in saucepan to scalding stage. Do not let it scorch. Stir often. Place butter in a mixing bowl and add sugar. Pour in the scalded milk and stir until ingredients are melted. Cool to lukewarm stage. Add yeast. Stir until yeast is dissolved. Sift dry ingredients together. Gradually add approximately half of flour mixture to milk mixture to form batter. Add whole egg. Beat thoroughly. Stir in remaining flour mixture. Cover. Set aside to allow to double in bulk, approximately 1 hour. Knead gently. Roll out on floured board to ¼" thickness. Cut into diamond shapes. Cover. Let rise in warm place from ½ to 1 hour. Fry in hot peanut oil (385 degrees), turning only once. Drain and dust with powdered sugar. Serve warm.

Marsha Valance, Wisconsin Regional Library f/t Blind & Physically Handicapped, Milwaukee, WI

"Without wishing in the slightest degree to disparage the skill and labour of breadmakers by trade, truth compels us to assert our conviction of the superior wholesomeness of bread made in our own homes."
Eliza Acton, *Modern Cookery for Private Families,* 1845

Oat Bran Banana Bread

1 cup bananas, mashed
½ cup sugar
1/3 cup vegetable oil
1 egg, or 2 egg whites or ¼ cup egg substitute such as Egg Beaters
1/3 cup skim milk (or soy milk)
1¼ cup flour (or ½ whole wheat flour)
1 cup oat bran
2 teaspoons baking powder
½ teaspoon baking soda
½ teaspoon salt
Nuts to taste

Mix all ingredients in food processor. If mixing by hand, mix dry ingredients together before adding to wet ingredients (mix together first.) Bake in 9"x 3" greased loaf pan at 350 degrees approximately 40 minutes or until tooth pick inserted comes out clean. Before baking, you may sprinkle loaf with raw cane sugar and chopped nuts.

Mary Rose Corrigan, patron, Carnegie-Stout Public Library, Dubuque, IA

Olive Bread

2¼ cups flour
4 teaspoons baking powder
¼ cup sugar
¼ teaspoon salt
¾ cup pimento stuffed green olives, chopped
1 egg, beaten
1¼ cup milk
2 tablespoons butter, melted

Sift together the flour, baking powder, sugar and salt; set aside. Combine the olives, egg, milk and butter. Add to the flour mixture; stir only until moistened. Pour into a loaf pan. Bake at 350 degrees for about 1 hour.

Kathy Fisher, Keosauqua Public Library, Keosauqua, IA

"Bread is the king of the table and all else is merely the court that surrounds the king. The countries are the soup, the meat, the vegetables, the salad, but bread is king."
Louis Bromfield (1896-1956) American novelist

Orange Bread

This quick bread, which I remember my mother baking when I was a little girl (60-some years ago!) is very moist. The opening procedure removes the bitterness from the orange peel.

2 large orange peels (about ¾ cup), grated
½ cup water
½ teaspoon salt
½ cup sugar
1 cup sugar
2 cups flour
3 teaspoons baking powder
1 teaspoon salt
2 eggs
1 cup milk

Place grated orange peel in a small pan. Cover with water and ½ teaspoon salt. Simmer 10 minutes. Discard liquid. Add ½ cup water and ½ cup sugar. Simmer until thickened. Sift together 1 cup sugar, flour, baking powder and 1 teaspoon salt. Set aside. Beat two eggs and 1 cup milk. Add egg/milk mixture and orange mixture to the dry ingredients. Stir; do not beat. Pour into a greased loaf pan and bake at 350 degrees for about 50 minutes.

Kathy Fisher, Keosauqua Public Library, Keosauqua, IA

Overnight Sticky Rolls

24 frozen dinner rolls
½ cups nuts
1 small package butterscotch pudding mix (not instant)
1 tablespoon cinnamon
½ cup brown sugar
½ cup butter

Generously butter a 13"x 9" baking pan. Place frozen rolls in a single layer in the pan. Mix nuts, pudding, and cinnamon together; sprinkle on and around rolls. In a small saucepan mix the butter and brown sugar; bring to a boil. Drizzle over the rolls. Cover with foil and a towel and set on a table to rise. Leave overnight. Bake in the morning, at 350 degrees for 25-30 minutes. Invert at once on tray or foil.

Karen Keller, Johnston Middle School Library Johnston, IA

Pear Bread

½ cup butter or margarine
1 cup sugar
2 eggs beaten
2 cups flour
½ teaspoon salt
½ teaspoon baking soda
1 teaspoon baking powder
1/8 teaspoon nutmeg
¼ cup yogurt or buttermilk
1 cup pears, cored and coarsely chopped
1 teaspoon vanilla

Cream butter, sugar and eggs. Combine dry ingredients and add to egg mixture alternately with yogurt. Stir in pears and vanilla. Pour into buttered 9"x 5"x 3" loaf pan. Bake at 350 degrees for 1 hour

Linda Magley, Mesa Family History Center Library patron, Mesa, AZ

Poppy Seed Bread

3 cups flour
1½ teaspoon baking powder
1½ cups milk
1½ teaspoons poppy seeds
1½ teaspoons vanilla
1½ teaspoons salt
2½ cups sugar
1 cup, plus 1 tablespoon vegetable oil
3 eggs
1½ teaspoon almond flavoring

Combine all ingredients and beat for 2 minutes. Pour into 2 greased loaf pans. Bake 350 degrees for 1 hour and 15 minutes. While bread is still warm, remove from pans and pour glaze over.

Glaze

¾ cup sugar
2 tablespoons melted margarine
½ teaspoon almond extract
¼ cup orange juice
½ teaspoon vanilla

Kristel Mayberry, Library Trustee, Glenwood Public Library, Glenwood, IA

Potato Rolls

1 cup boiling potato water
¼ cup butter
¼ cup lard
1 tablespoon warm water
2 eggs, beaten
½ teaspoon sugar
1 teaspoon salt
1/3 cup sugar
1 package dry yeast
4 cups flour

Mix boiling potato water, 1/3 cup sugar, salt, butter and lard together and cool to lukewarm. Soften yeast in warm water (approximately 120 degrees) and ½ teaspoon sugar. Add yeast mixture to the water, sugar, butter and lard mixture. Beat in 2 eggs and 2 cups flour. Add remaining flour. Do not knead. Chill dough overnight.

Form dough into rolls. Allow to rise in a warm place until doubled in size. Bake at 375 degrees for 10 to 15 minutes until golden brown.

This dough can be used for almost any type of dinner roll such as Parker House, clover leaf, or rolled out for cinnamon rolls. This dough can be kept covered in the refrigerator for up to one week.

Cheryl Boothe, Newton Public Library, Newton, IA

"I am going to learn to make bread to-morrow. So you may imagine me with my sleeves rolled up, mixing flour, milk, saleratus, etc., with a deal of grace. I advise you if you don't know how to make the staff of life to learn with dispatch."
Emily Dickinson (1830 – 1886) American poet

Pumpkin Cranberry Bread

3½ cups flour
2 teaspoons cinnamon
1 teaspoon salt
1 teaspoon baking soda
½ teaspoon baking powder
2 teaspoons orange zest or orange juice
¾ cup low calorie margarine, softened
1½ cups sugar
3 large eggs
1 16-ounce can pumpkin
1 cup cranberries, fresh or thawed frozen, chopped

Combine the first 6 ingredients in a medium bowl and set aside. In a large mixing bowl cream margarine and sugar for 3 minutes. Add eggs one at a time beating for 1 minute after each addition. Add pumpkin and dry ingredients alternately until just blended. Stir in cranberries. Spoon batter into lightly greased bread pans. Smooth surfaces with spatula. Drop pans from 6" height 3 times to get rid of air bubbles. Bake 60- 65 minutes at 350 degrees. Check with toothpick. Cool completely before cutting.

Alyssa Bruecken, Waukee Public Library, Waukee, IA

Pumpkin Bread

3½ cups unsifted all-purpose flour
3 cups sugar
2 teaspoons baking soda
1½ teaspoons salt
1 teaspoon cinnamon
2 cups cooked or canned pumpkin
1 cup vegetable oil
⅔ cup water
4 eggs
2 cups (12-ounce package) peanut butter chips
1 cup chopped nuts
1 cup raisins, optional

Preheat oven to 350 degrees. Grease and flour three 8 ½ x 4 ½ x 2 ½ " loaf pans. In large mixing bowl, combine flour, sugar, soda, salt, cinnamon; set aside. In large bowl blend pumpkin, oil, water, eggs. Gradually add dry ingredients until well blended. Stir in peanut butter chips, nuts, raisins. Pour into pans; bake 50-60 minutes. Cool in pans 10 minutes. Remove from pans and cool completely.

Candice Michalik, Lynchburg Public Library Lynchburg, VA

Rhubarb Bread

1½ cups brown sugar
1/3 cup salad oil
1 egg
1 teaspoon vanilla
2½ cups flour
1 teaspoon salt
1 teaspoon baking soda
1 cup sour milk
2 cups rhubarb
½ cup nuts

Preheat oven to 325 degrees. Grease and flour two 8½" x 4½" x 2½" loaf pans. In large bowl blend sugar, oil, egg and vanilla. In large mixing bowl, combine flour, salt, and soda; set aside. Alternately add the flour mixture and the sour milk to the sugar and egg mixture until well blended. Stir in rhubarb and nuts. Pour into pans; bake for one hour.

Rosanne Krubsack, J. B. Young Intermediate School, Davenport, IA

Rye-Graham Bread

2 cups milk, scalded
1 cake yeast
½ cup lukewarm water (110-115 degrees)
1 tablespoon sugar
½ cup shortening
½ cup brown sugar
1 ½ teaspoon salt
½ cup mild molasses
2/3 cup rye flour
11/3 cup graham (whole wheat) flour
5 cups white flour

Dissolve yeast in lukewarm water to which the granulated sugar has been added and let stand for about ¾ of an hour. Scald milk and cool. Cream shortening, brown sugar and salt. Add molasses, milk and yeast. Mix in the flours to make a stiff dough. Knead until smooth. Set in a warm place to rise for about 1 hour or until doubled in bulk. Knead again. Shape into two loaves and let rise. Bake 50-60 minutes in a pre-heated over at 350 degrees or until internal temperature reaches 190 degrees. To freeze, wrap well in foil and then in a plastic bag.

Christine Lind Hage, Clinton-Macomb Public Library, Clinton Township, MI

Sour Cream and Chive Batter Buns

1 package dry yeast
¼ cup warm water (between 105-115 degrees)
2 tablespoons sugar
1 teaspoon salt
2 tablespoons vegetable oil
1 egg, room temperature
1 tablespoon dried chopped chives
¾ cup sour cream, room temperature
2¼ cups unsifted flour

Dissolve yeast in warm water in a large bowl. Add sugar, salt, oil, eggs, chives, sour cream and flour. Beat until smooth. Cover bowl; let rise until doubled in size, about 35 minutes. Stir down the batter, spoon into greased muffin tins. Cover, let rise until doubled in size, about 45 minutes. Bake at 400 degrees for 15 minutes, or until done. Remove from cups and cool on wire racks. Serve warm.

Susan Henricks, Carnegie-Stout Public Library, Dubuque, IA

"In Paris today millions of pounds of bread are sold daily, made during the previous night by those strange, half-naked beings one glimpses through cellar windows, whose wild-seeming cries floating out of those depths always makes a painful impression. In the morning, one sees these pale men, still white with flour, carrying a loaf under one arm, going off to rest and gather new strength to renew their hard and useful labor when night comes again. I have always highly esteemed the brave and humble workers who labor all night to produce those soft but crusty loaves that look more like cake than bread."
Alexandre Dumas, (1802-1870) French author and playwright

Stuffed Vienna Bread

1 loaf bread (French or Italian)
2 sticks butter, melted
2 tablespoons poppy seeds
1 teaspoon seasoned salt
1 teaspoon dry mustard
½ teaspoon lemon juice
8 ounces shredded (not grated) Parmesan cheese
2 tablespoons onion, chopped
1 large can mushrooms, or 1 package fresh

Mix melted butter, poppy seeds, seasoned salt, dry mustard, and lemon juice in glass measuring cup. Cut bread almost in half horizontally, open and distribute onions and mushrooms on bottom half. Close loaf. Cut 1" slices almost to the bottom, place loaf on aluminum foil, sprinkle top with Parmesan cheese, and pour butter mixture over top. Close aluminum foil around loaf. Bake at 350 for 30 minutes.

Meagan VanderHart, Rock Island Public Library, Rock Island, IL

"Recipes are like poems; they keep what kept us. And good cooks are like poets; they know how to count."
Henri Coulette (1927-1988) American poet

Whole Cranberry Bread

4 cups flour
2 cups sugar
1 teaspoon salt
1 teaspoon baking soda
1 tablespoon baking powder
2 cups coarsely chopped walnuts or pecans, optional
1 ½ cups whole cranberries
¼ cup vegetable oil
1¼ cup hot water
1 cup orange juice
2 tablespoons grated orange peel, optional
2 eggs, slightly beaten

Preheat oven to 325 degrees. Grease two 8" or 9" bread pans. (You can also use 3 mini pans instead of one large.) Line pans with waxed paper. In a large bowl, stir together flour, sugar, salt, baking soda, and baking powder. Set aside. In a small bowl, combine nuts, cranberries and ½ cup of the flour mixture. Put the vegetable oil in a two-cup measure. Add water and orange juice. Stir slightly. Add liquid, eggs, and orange peel to the flour mixture, stirring just enough to moisten. Fold in the cranberry and nut mixture. Pour into baking pans; bake 1 hour or until toothpick stuck in the middle comes out clean. Cool slightly, remove from pans and cool completely. Wrap and keep in the refrigerator, or freeze.

Notes: The cranberries mix in better if they are used frozen. This also makes great toast!

Gretchen Taft, Memorial Library of Little Valley, Little Valley, NY

Good ripe cranberries will bounce. Bounceberry is another name for them. There are several theories as to the origin of the name 'cranberry.' One is that the open flowers look like the head of a crane; another is that cranes like to eat these sour berries. foodreference.com

641.815 Muffins.

Eggnog Muffins

2 cups flour
2/3 cups sugar
1 tablespoon baking powder
½ teaspoon salt
¾ cup prepared eggnog
½ cup dark rum
5 tablespoons butter, melted
1 egg, beaten to blend
½ teaspoon freshly grated nutmeg

Preheat oven to 400 degrees. Grease one 12-cup muffin tin. Sift flour, sugar, baking powder and salt into large bowl. Stir in eggnog, rum, butter, egg and nutmeg. Spoon into prepared tin. Bake until tester inserted in center comes out clean, about 20 minutes. Cool muffins completely before serving. Makes 1 dozen

Christine Lind Hage, Clinton-Macomb Public Library, Clinton Township, MI

Muffins in Cinnamon

2 tablespoons shortening
1 egg
½ cup milk
2 cups flour
1 tablespoon baking powder
½ teaspoon salt
½ teaspoon nutmeg
¾ cup margarine, melted
2/3 cup sugar and 1 tablespoon cinnamon, blended

Mix shortening, egg and milk with flour, baking powder, salt and nutmeg. Spoon into well greased small muffin tins. Fill until 2/3 full. Bake at 400 degrees for 15 minutes or until golden brown. Cool. Dip in melted margarine, roll in sugar cinnamon mixture. Makes 3 dozen

Christine Lind Hage, Clinton-Macomb Public Library, Clinton Township, MI

Pecan Muffins

1¾ cups sifted all-purpose flour
½ cup sugar
1 teaspoon baking powder
½ teaspoon baking soda
½ teaspoon salt
½ cup sour cream
½ cup peach preserves
1 egg
1 teaspoon vanilla extract
2/3 cup pecans chopped and toasted

Position rack in center of oven and preheat to 400 degrees. Line 10 muffin cups with muffin papers. Sift first 5 ingredients into large bowl. Whisk sour cream, preserves, egg and vanilla to blend in medium bowl. Add sour cream mixture and pecans to dry ingredients and stir just until combined; do not over mix. Divide batter among muffin cups. Bake until tester inserted into center of muffins comes out clean, about 20 minutes. Cool 15 minutes before serving. 10 Servings

Christine Lind Hage, Clinton-Macomb Public Library, Clinton Township, MI

Refrigerator Muffins

2 cups boiling water
1 cup lard, or shortening
2 cups Bran Buds
4 eggs, beaten
1 quart buttermilk
4 cups All-Bran cereal
5 cups flour
3 cups sugar
5 teaspoons baking soda
1¼ teaspoon salt

Pour boiling water over the lard or shortening. Add Bran Buds cereal and stir well. Add the eggs and buttermilk. Sift together the flour, sugar, soda and salt; stir in All Bran. Stir into the shortening, eggs and buttermilk mixture. Mix only until flour is moistened. Do not beat. Store in a covered container in the refrigerator and use as needed. Do not stir the batter down. Pour into muffin cups and bake at about 400 degrees until a toothpick inserted comes out clean. Note: You can substitute 4 cups of 40% bran cereal and 2 cups of quick oatmeal in place of the All Bran.

Kathy Fisher, Keosauqua Public Library, Keosauqua, IA

Streusel Raspberry Muffins

¼ cup brown sugar
¼ cup flour
¼ cup pecans, chopped
2 tablespoons margarine or butter, melted
½ cup milk
½ cup margarine or butter, melted
1 egg, beaten
1½ cups flour
½ cup sugar
2 teaspoons baking powder
1 cup fresh or frozen raspberries

Preheat oven to 375 degrees. Place paper liners in 12 muffin cups.
Combine brown sugar, flour, and chopped pecans in a bowl. Stir in 2 tablespoons
melted butter until mixture resembles moist crumbs. Set aside. In large bowl,
combine milk, ½ cup melted butter or margarine, and egg until well blended.
Combine flour, sugar, and baking powder and stir in the milk, egg and butter
mixture just until moistened. Spoon half of the batter into the muffin cups. Place 4
–5 raspberries in each muffin cup, then top with remaining batter. Sprinkle muffin
tops with the reserved pecan streusel topping. Bake 15-20 minutes or until a
toothpick inserted in the center of muffins comes out clean. Remove from pan.

Karen Ransom, Marion Public Library, Marion, IA

641.815 Pancakes, waffles, etc.

Batty Cakes

*These simple (but delicious) cornmeal griddle cakes are great with soups, stews, a
big pot of green beans, or any simple country dish.*

1 cup white cornmeal
½ teaspoon baking soda
½ teaspoon salt
1¼ cup buttermilk
1 egg
1 tablespoon oil or bacon fat

Combine all ingredients. Drop by tablespoonful on hot griddle. Turn once when
edges begin to cook – just like pancakes. No need to oil or grease the griddle.

Kathy Fisher, Keosauqua Public Library, Keosauqua, IA

DrWeb's Spicy Crab-Potato Pancakes

1½ cups leftover mashed potatoes
1 sweet onion, such as Vadalia, grated,
1 small scallions, (about 1/2 cup), chopped
¼ cup garlic, chopped
1 to 2 cloves Italian or curly parsley, chopped
2 tablespoons crab, fresh backfin and/or claw
1 cup flour
¼ cup sea salt
1 teaspoon pepper, fresh ground, or to taste
½ teaspoon Tabasco sauce or to taste
Paprika (sprinkling)
1 egg
½ cup whole milk
1 tablespoon lemon or lime juice
Clarified butter or olive oil

In a medium bowl, combine the potatoes, onions, scallions, garlic, herbs and crab.
Sift in the flour, salt and pepper. In a small bowl, combine the egg and milk gently.
Fold into the crab cake mixture and add the lemon or lime juice. Adjust seasonings
if necessary. Add the Tabasco sauce and mix lightly. Coat the bottom of a non-stick
sauté pan with clarified butter or olive oil. Heat until moderately hot. By hand,
mold small balls of the crab-potato mixture into 2" circles for each pancake, and pat
into cakes for frying. Sauté each cake about 2 minutes in a hot sauté pan with light
oil, about 3 minutes each side or until golden brown. Drain on paper towel,
salt/season, top with a sprinkling of paprika, and serve hot. You may wish to serve
cocktail sauce on the "side" for the "Southern" touch. Serves: 8

*Latkes are wonderful and a great treat anytime. From our years in Maryland, we
discovered there's nothing like their crab cakes --real backfin and claw crab, not
too much filling, and great spices. Combining these seemed a natural great dish, so
I tried it out. Everyone has "leftover" mashed potatoes, so this recipe makes great
use of the leftovers and adds the right crab, spices, and "love" to make them to-die-
for! DrWeb is my nickname from my Internet life as a librarian, and Webmaster --
thus, the name for this dish. I've made these cakes for friends and family, and they
love 'em!*

DrWeb a.k.a. Michael McCulley, San Diego Public Library, San Diego, CA

Hootenanny Pancakes

6 eggs
1 cup flour
1 cup milk
1 stick margarine

Melt margarine in a 13" x 9" pan. Beat eggs, milk, and flour in a bowl. Add to melted margarine. Bake at 425 degrees for 25 minutes. Serve with syrup, jam, or fresh fruit. Serves 6.

Tory Rose, Glenwood Public Library, Glenwood, IA

Mini Dutch Apple Pancakes

3 tablespoons unsalted butter
1 large Granny Smith apple, peeled, cored and cut into ½" slices
½ teaspoon ground cinnamon
3 eggs
¾ cup flour
¾ milk
1 tablespoon sour cream
1/8 teaspoon salt
1 teaspoon grated lemon zest
Confectioners' sugar for dusting

Preheat oven to 400 degrees. Spray two 6 ½ inch tapas (small skillets) pans with nonstick cooking spray. In a nonstick sauté pan over medium heat, melt butter. Add apple, granulated sugar and cinnamon and sauté, stirring constantly, until apple begins to soften and brown lightly, 3-5 minutes. Remove from heat and set aside. In a large bowl, whisk eggs until lightly frothy. Add flour, milk, sour cream, salt and lemon zest and whisk just until a smooth batter forms. Immediately divide batter between prepared pans. Divide apple mixture between pans, trying to keep apple pieces on top of batter. Bake until pancakes are puffed and golden brown. 15- 20 minutes. Dust with confectioners' sugar and serve immediately. Serves 2

Christine Lind Hage, Clinton-Macomb Public Library, Clinton Township, MI

"Liza poured thick batter from a pitcher onto a soapstone griddle. The hot cakes rose like little hassocks, and small volcanoes formed and erupted on them until they were ready to be turned. A cheerful brown they were, with tracings of darker brown. And the kitchen was full of the good sweet smell of them." John Steinbeck (1902-1968) American novelist, *East of Eden*

641.815 Scones.

Scones

2 cups flour
1 stick butter, refrigerated
5½ tablespoons sugar
1½ teaspoons baking powder
Dash salt
¾ cup dried fruit, chopped (we like dried apricots or cranberries)
¼ teaspoon orange or lemon peel
2/3 cup milk
1 egg

Thoroughly mix dry ingredients. Cut butter into dry ingredients. Lightly whip egg, then mix with dried fruit, peel and milk. Make a well in center and add milk mixture all at once. Should look and feel like making biscuits. Kneed lightly in the bowl then roll out into a circle approximately 8" around and ¾" thick. Cut into eight pie shaped wedges, place on ungreased cookie sheet and bake at 425 degrees until just brown.

Devon Murphy-Petersen, Waukee Public Library, Waukee, IA

Scones

1¾ cups sifted flour
2½ teaspoon baking powder
½ teaspoon salt
1 tablespoon sugar
5 tablespoons butter
2 eggs, slightly beaten
1/3 cup milk or heavy cream
1 cup chocolate chips or ½ cup raisins, optional

Into large bowl, sift together flour, baking powder, salt and 1 tablespoon sugar. With pastry blender, cut in butter until coarse crumbs form. Reserve 2 tablespoons beaten egg. In small bowl, mix remaining eggs and milk until well-blended. Add milk mixture to butter-flour mixture; with fork, stir until mixture forms a soft dough that leaves side of bowl. Add chocolate chips or raisins, if desired. On lightly floured surface with floured rolling pin, roll out dough into a 15"x 3" rectangle. Cut rectangle into 5 (3") squares; then diagonally cut each square in half. Place triangles 1 inch apart, on greased baking sheet; brush each one with reserved beaten egg and sprinkle with sugar. Bake in 425 oven 10-12 minutes or until golden brown. Serve immediately with lemon curd or jam and clotted cream. Makes 10

Megan VanderHart, Rock Island Public Library, Rock Island, IL

From the archives of the Carnegie-Stout Public Library,
Dubuque, Iowa

Carrot Soufflé

2 cups carrots, cooked
3 eggs
2 tablespoons flour
½ cup sugar
1 cup milk
1 stick margarine
¼ teaspoon cinnamon
1 teaspoon baking powder

Place all in blender and mix. Put in a casserole and bake at 350 degrees for 30 minutes until crust is brown. If made ahead and refrigerated, bake 10-15 minutes longer.

Ann Straley, Carnegie-Stout Public Library, Dubuque, IA

Supposedly, the first recipe for soufflé appeared in Vincent La Chapelle's "Le Cuisinier Moderne" (1742) foodreference.com

Cheese Soufflé

¾ cup butter
3/8 cup flour
1½ cups milk
1½ cups sharp cheese
6 eggs, separated
1½ teaspoons salt
3/8 teaspoon dry mustard
Dash paprika

In a 2-quart saucepan over medium heat, melt butter. Stir in flour until blended and gradually add milk, stirring until thick. Remove from heat. Add cheese and seasonings. Stir until cheese is melted. Add well-beaten egg yolks. Stiffly beat egg whites, and fold into the cheese mixture. Pour into a 1½-quart baking dish. Fill a separate baking dish with enough of hot water to measure about half way up the soufflé dish and place in the oven, baking at 350 degrees for 1 hour. Serve immediately.

Robert L. Manning, Atlanta-Fulton County Library System, Fairburn Branch, Fairburn, GA

Salmon Soufflé

Vegetable cooking spray
1 small red bell pepper, coarsely chopped
1 small green bell pepper, coarsely chopped
1 10-ounce package frozen corn
2 tablespoons margarine
¼ cup flour
¾ teaspoon dried dill weed
¼ teaspoon salt
1/8 teaspoon white pepper
1 ½ cups skim milk
4 egg yolks, lightly beaten
1 6 ½ ounce can boneless, skinless salmon, drained
5 egg whites
Pinch of cream of tartar

Preheat oven to 350 degrees. Coat a 2-quart soufflé dish with cooking spray; set aside. In a medium mixing bowl, combine green and red peppers, corn and margarine. Cover with plastic wrap and microwave on high for 4 -6 minutes, or until vegetables are tender. Stir in flour, dill weed, salt and pepper. Gradually blend in milk. Microwave on high, uncovered, for 7- 8 minutes or until mixture thickens and bubbles, stirring every 2 minutes. Gradually stir in small amount of hot vegetable mixture into egg yolks; blend yolks back into bowl of vegetable mixture. Add salmon and mix well. Set aside. In a large mixing bowl, using an electric beater, beat egg whites. Add a pinch of cream of tartar, and continue beating until stiff peaks form. Gradually fold the egg whites into the salmon mixture. Pour all into the coated soufflé dish. Bake, uncovered, for 45-50 minutes of until a toothpick inserted in the center of the soufflé comes out clean.

Susan Henricks, Carnegie-Stout Public Library, Dubuque, IA

"The only thing that will make a soufflé fall is if it knows you are afraid of it."
James Beard (1903-1985) often hailed as "The Father of American Cooking"

144

Crustless Ham Quiche

½ pound fresh mushrooms, sliced
2 tablespoons butter, melted
1 cup sour cream
1 cup small curd cottage cheese
½ cup Parmesan cheese
4 eggs
¼ cup flour
2 cups (8 ounces) Monterey Jack cheese, shredded
½ cup ham, chopped

In a skillet, sauté mushrooms in butter. Drain well; set aside. Combine remaining ingredients and blend well. Pour into a 10" greased dish. Bake at 350 degrees for approximately 45 minutes, or until quiche is puffed and golden brown. Let stand for 10 minutes before slicing.

Beth Kimm, patron, Blairstown Public Library, Blairstown, IA

"Gastronomers of the year 1825, who find satiety in the lap of abundance, and dream of some newly-made dishes, you will not enjoy the discoveries which science has in store for the year 1900, such as foods drawn from the mineral kingdom, liqueurs produced by the pressure of a hundred atmospheres; you will never see the importations which travelers yet unborn will bring to you from that half of the globe which has still to be discovered or explored. How I pity you!"
Jean-Anthelme Brillat-Savarin (1755-1826) wrote one of the most celebrated works on food, 'Physiologie du gout', *The Physiology of Taste*

Hashed Brown Quiche

1 package hashed browns, shredded, thawed and blotted dry on paper towels
1 stick of butter or margarine, melted
1 small onion, chopped
½ cup green pepper, chopped
½ cup red pepper, chopped
½ cup tomatoes, chopped
1 package boiled ham, chopped
1 cup cheddar cheese, shredded
1 cup Swiss cheese, shredded
2 tablespoons flour
4 eggs, slightly beaten
3 cups half and half

Place the hashed browns in the bottom of a 13" x 9" baking pan. Drizzle the melted butter over the potatoes. Bake for 25 minutes at 400 degrees. Meanwhile, sauté chopped onion until tender. In a large bowl combine the onion, peppers, tomatoes, ham, cheeses and flour. In a separate bowl beat the eggs and half and half. When the hashed browns are removed from the oven, put the vegetable mixture over the top of the potatoes. Pour the egg mixture evenly over the top. Bake at 350 degrees for 45 minutes, or until set.

Kay K. Runge, Des Moines Public Library, Des Moines, IA

Spinach Quiche

2 frozen deep dish pie pan crusts
2 small boxes of frozen chopped or whole-leaf spinach, thawed and drained
1 cup (or more) smoked Gouda cheese, grated
6-7 eggs, beaten
1 cup milk (at least 1% milkfat)
2 teaspoons salt
Black pepper to taste

Pre-heat oven to 375 degrees.
Put thawed, drained spinach in large mixing bowl; add cheese, eggs, milk, salt and black pepper to taste. Optional additions to taste: chopped onion or onion flakes, red pepper flakes, parsley, oregano, bacon bits, nutmeg, etc. Mix all ingredients in the large bowl. Pour mixture into the 2 frozen pie pans; bake at 375 degrees for at least 40 minutes, or until custard is set. Cool both quiches, and if you don't need one, wrap in foil and put it in the freezer until you do!

Robin K. Blum, In My Book ®, Brooklyn, NY

641.821 Casserole cookery.

Corn Casserole

1 can corn, drained
1 can creamed style corn
1 box corn muffin mix, such as Jiffy
1 8-ounce container sour cream
1 stick margarine
2 large eggs, beaten
8 ounces cheddar cheese, shredded

Combine all ingredients except cheddar cheese; mix well. Spread in a rectangular baking dish; sprinkle with cheese. Bake 350 degrees for 35-45 minutes.

Cheryl Boothe, Newton Public Library, Newton, IA

"The most remarkable thing about my mother is that for 30 years she served the family nothing but leftovers. The original meal has never been found." Calvin Trillin (1935-) American author and journalist.

Farmer's Casserole

3 cups frozen shredded hash brown potatoes
¾ cup Monterey Jack cheese with jalapeño peppers (3 ounces) or shredded cheddar cheese, shredded
1 cup fully cooked ham or Canadian bacon, diced
¼ cup green onion, sliced
4 eggs beaten or 1 cup frozen egg product
1 12-ounce can evaporated milk or evaporated skim milk
¼ teaspoon pepper
1/8 teaspoon salt

Grease a 2-quart square baking dish. Arrange potatoes evenly in the bottom of the dish. Sprinkle with cheese, ham and green onion. In a medium bowl combine eggs, milk, pepper and salt. Pour egg mixture over potato mixture in dish. The dish may be covered and refrigerated for several hours or overnight. Bake uncovered in a 350 degree oven for 40-45 minutes (55-60 minutes if made ahead and chilled) or until center appears set. Let stand 5 minutes before serving. Serves 6

Sarah Kennedy, Waukee Public Library, Waukee, IA

Greek Potato and Meat Bake

2 eggs
¼ cup minced parsley
½ teaspoon salt
¼ teaspoon pepper
1 32-ounce bag frozen hash brown potatoes, thawed
1½ pounds ground beef
1 cup onion, chopped
1 garlic clove, minced
1 15-ounce can tomato sauce
½ teaspoon dried basil
¼ teaspoon cinnamon
Parmesan cheese

In a large bowl, with a fork, mix eggs, parsley, salt and pepper. Stir in potatoes and set aside. In a 12"skillet, cook ground beef, onion and garlic until the meat is browned and the onion is tender, about 10 minutes, stirring occasionally. Stir in tomato sauce, basil and cinnamon; heat to boiling. Grease a 13" x 9" inch baking dish. Spoon potato mixture evenly in bottom of dish. Pour meat sauce over potatoes. Sprinkle on Parmesan cheese. Bake at 350 degrees 30 mixture or until mixture is heated through.

Ann Straley, Carnegie-Stout Public Library, Dubuque, IA

Hamburger Rice Dish

1 pound ground beef
½ cup onion, chopped
2 cups water
2/3 cup ketchup
2 teaspoon prepared mustard
1 teaspoon salt
¼ teaspoon pepper
2 cups uncooked instant rice

In skillet, brown beef and onion; drain. In a bowl, mix water, ketchup, mustard, salt, and pepper; add to beef/onion mixture in skillet. Bring to a boil. Stir in rice. Cover and remove from heat; let stand for 5 minutes until rice is cooked.

Jean Gullikson, Carnegie-Stout Public Library, Dubuque, IA

"I refuse to believe that trading recipes is silly. Tunafish casserole is at least as real as corporate stock."
Barbara Grissuti Harrison (1934-2002) American author and essayist

Kitchen Sink Casserole

A very quick supper .... usually 20 minutes/half an hour from beginning to end.

1 pound ground beef
2 medium-sized peppers, green, red, or yellow
1 large (or two small) onions
3 cloves garlic
Olive oil
Salt
Red pepper flakes
Wine, broth, or water

Cut up the garlic, onions, and peppers. Cover the bottom of a large frying pan (do not use teflon) with olive oil, and throw in all the veggies over medium-high heat. Toss and stir until they are soft and a bit golden. Crumble the chopped meat and toss in, cooking only until all the red is gone from the meat. Add salt and red pepper flakes to taste, and a quarter of a cup of liquid: wine, broth, or water. Cook a few more minutes or until the liquid is reduced a bit. Serve in a big bowl mixed with rice or pastina. NOTES: Sometimes I add half a bag of frozen organic corn kernels (defrosted) to this when the meat is done, or add jalapeños with the regular peppers, or Carolina rice, following the directions on the box , or 1 cup of pastina, cooked.

GraceAnne Andreassi DeCandido, Blue Roses Consulting, NY, NY

"Serve this dish with much too much wine for your guests, along with some cooked green vegetables and a huge salad. You will be famous in about half an hour."
Jeff Smith (1939-2004) The Frugal Gourmet

Mac and Corn Casserole

This is a recipe my husband's family introduced to me...

1 can whole kernal corn
1 can cream style corn
1 cup cubed Velveeta type cheese
1 cup dry elbow macaroni

Mix together all ingredients. Bake in a buttered casserole dish at 350 degrees for approximately 1 hour (Check periodically; casserole is done when cheese is melted and macaroni is tender. If your oven runs hot, the recipe may take less time, and you may want to reduce the heat to 325 degrees.)

Darlene Richardson, Leon Public Library, Leon, IA

Quick Macaroni & Cheese

1 8-ounce package elbow macaroni
1 can cream of chicken or mushroom soup
1½ cups cheese, cheddar or Swiss, shredded
½ cup mayonnaise
1 teaspoon dry mustard
¼ teaspoon cayenne or black pepper (go easy if you use cayenne)
1 10-ounce pkg. frozen vegetables (peas, corn, broccoli, etc.) cooked, well drained
1 cup chicken or turkey, cooked and diced
Bread crumbs

Cook macaroni, drain and keep hot. Combine soup, cheese, mayonnaise, dry mustard, and pepper in a large bowl. Add macaroni and stir. Lightly butter (or use cooking spray) a 2 quart casserole dish. Spoon vegetables over the bottom. Top with chicken; spoon macaroni mixture over chicken. Sprinkle some shredded cheese and bread crumbs on the top. Bake in a 375 degree oven for 40 minutes until bubbly hot. Let stand 15 minutes before serving. Serves 4 (or 3 if they are very hungry!)

Jeanne Heuer, Brown County Library Green Bay, WI

"It is odd how all men develop the notion, as they grow older, that their mothers were wonderful cooks. I have yet to meet a man who will admit that his mother was a kitchen assassin and nearly poisoned him."
Robertson Davies (1913-1995) Canadian author

Scalloped Pineapple Casserole

1 20-ounce can of chunk pineapple, drained
1 8-ounce can of crushed pineapple with juice
2 tablespoons flour
1 cup sugar
1½ cups cheddar cheese, shredded
1½ -2 cups of crushed crackers (Ritz or Saltines, as you prefer)
3 tablespoons butter, melted

Directions: Preheat oven to 350 degrees. Pour both cans of pineapple into bottom of 2 quart baking dish. Mix sugar and flour, sprinkle over pineapple. Layer cheese evenly over sugar mixture. Add the crackers, and drizzle all layers with melted butter. Bake at 350 for 25 minutes. Allow to cool for about 10 minutes. Can be served as a side dish with ham or as a dessert with ice cream.

Jo Cronk, Toledo Public Library, Toledo, IA

150

Taco Casserole

2 pounds ground beef
1 onion, finely chopped
2 15-ounce cans chili beans, undrained
1 bag Frito Corn Chips
1 1-¼ ounce Taco Seasoning Mix
1 8-ounce package cheddar cheese, shredded

Brown hamburger and onion. Add chili beans and taco seasoning. Let simmer a short time. Grease a 13" x 9" pan. Put crumbled layer of Frito chips in bottom. Follow with half of hamburger mixture; then layer of cheddar cheese; remaining hamburger mixture; sprinkle on rest of cheddar cheese. Add layer of crumbled corn chips. Bake at 350 degrees 20-30 minutes or until cheese melts and mixture is hot. Serve on plate topped with shredded lettuce and diced tomatoes. Add hot sauce or salsa, if desired.

Jan Behrens, Knoxville Public Library, Knoxville, IA

641.822 Cookery (Pasta)

Cavatini

2 pounds ground beef
½ cup onions, chopped
½ cup green peppers, chopped
1 20-ounce can pizza sauce
4 cups cooked macaroni (shell, elbow or mixed)
1 pound mozzarella cheese, grated
6 ounces pepperoni, thinly sliced
½ stick margarine

Cook macaroni 8-10 minutes. Drain and rinse. Add margarine and toss gently until margarine melts. Brown beef until crumbly; add onions and peppers and cook until tender. Mix together macaroni, beef mixture, and pizza sauce. Mixture should be very moist. If not add more sauce or hot water. (Mixture dries out in baking.) Layer in a 13" x 9" pan: meat mixture, pepperoni slices, and mozzarella cheese. Repeat. End with cheese. Bake at 350 degrees for 35-40 minutes.

Ann Straley, Carnegie-Stout Public Library, Dubuque, IA

"One can say everything best over a meal."
George Eliot (1819-1880) English author

Creamy Spaghetti and Ham Fiorentina

1 10-ounce package frozen chopped spinach
1 8-ounce package spaghetti
¼ cup butter or margarine
1¼ cups milk, heavy, or whipping cream
½ cup ricotta cheese
¼ teaspoon basil
1 4-ounce package sliced cooked ham, cut into ¼" wide strips

Prepare spinach as label directs; drain. Set aside. Prepare spaghetti in saucepan; drain and return to saucepan. Cut butter or margarine into small pieces and add to the spaghetti with the spinach, milk, ricotta, and basil. Over a medium-low heat, heat until the mixture is hot, tossing gently to mix well. Stir in ham; heat through. Serve immediately. Makes 4 servings.

Susan Henricks, Carnegie-Stout Public Library, Dubuque, IA

Curt's Spinach Spaghetti

1 10-ounce package frozen spinach, chopped
3-4 fresh sprigs parsley, chopped
1 medium onion, sliced thinly
1-4 cloves garlic, to taste, minced
1 tablespoon basil
3 tablespoon olive oil
2 tablespoon margarine
Salt & pepper to taste
8 ounces button mushrooms, sliced
Spaghetti for 3 or 4, cooked
¼ cup Parmesan or Romano, grated

Defrost and drain spinach. Squeeze out excess moisture. In a skillet, sauté the onions and garlic in the olive oil till soft. Add spinach, parsley, basil, salt and pepper. Mix and sauté 5 minutes. (Do not overcook spinach). In another pan, sauté the mushrooms in 2 tablespoons margarine. Put the spinach sauce mixture on top of the cooked spaghetti. Toss lightly. Top with the cheese and the sautéed mushrooms. Serve.

Jeanne Heuer, Brown County Library, Green Bay, WI

Fresh Tomato and Brie Pasta

1 pound plum tomatoes, chopped
3 tablespoons red wine vinegar
2 tablespoons freshly chopped, or 1 teaspoon dried oregano
1 clove garlic, finely minced
1 teaspoon salt
12 ounce radiatore pasta
8 ounces Brie cheese, rind removed, cut into bite size pieces.
1 tablespoon olive oil
2 tablespoons Parmesan cheese, freshly grated

In a large bowl, combine tomatoes, vinegar, oregano, garlic and salt. Let stand for 30 minutes. Cook pasta according to package directions; drain. Immediately return pasta to the pot; toss with Brie cheese and oil until cheese is melted. Add pasta mixture to marinated tomato mixture. Toss well. Sprinkle with Parmesan cheese and serve immediately.

Susan Henricks, Carnegie-Stout Public Library, Dubuque, IA

Pasta with Chicken, Raisins, and Pistachios

½ pound spaghetti
3 tablespoons olive oil
1½ pounds boneless, skinless chicken breasts cut into 1" cubes
3 cloves garlic, minced
½ teaspoon salt
¼ teaspoon pepper
1½ cups low-salt chicken broth
½ cup white wine
4 medium plum tomatoes, peeled, seeded and chopped
1/3 cup raisins
1/3 cup pistachios
1/3 cup olives, chopped
½ cup parsley, minced

Prepare spaghetti as label directs. In a large sauté pan, heat oil over high heat. Add chicken and sauté 3 minutes. Add garlic and sauté for 2 minutes more. Add salt and pepper. Remove chicken-garlic mixture to a bowl, return pan to high heat. Add chicken broth, wine and tomatoes and boil 5 minutes until liquid is reduced by half. Add raisins, pistachios, olives, and parsley. Cook 3 minutes. Return chicken to pan and heat through. Serve over hot pasta. Serves 4

Susan Henricks, Carnegie-Stout Public Library, Dubuque, IA

Penne with Yellow Peppers and Sweet Onion

1 16-ounce package penne rigate pasta
2 tablespoons olive oil
2 medium yellow peppers, thinly sliced
1 jumbo (12-ounces) sweet onion such as Vadalia, thinly sliced
¼ teaspoon coarsely ground black pepper
1 tablespoon balsamic vinegar
½ cup fresh basil leaves, chopped

In a large saucepot prepare pasta as label directs. Meanwhile in a 12" skillet, heat olive oil over medium heat until hot. Add yellow peppers, onion, black pepper, and ½ teaspoon salt and cook until vegetables are tender and golden, about 15 minutes, stirring frequently. Remove skillet from heat; stir in balsamic vinegar and chopped basil. When pasta has cooked to desired doneness, remove ½ cup of the pasta cooking water and set aside. Drain pasta and return to saucepot. Add the reserved water and the yellow pepper mixture. Toss well. Serves 4

Susan Henricks, Carnegie-Stout Public Library, Dubuque, IA

Sarah's Rigatoni con Balsamica

7 tablespoons salted butter
6 cloves garlic, slivered
1 bunch peeled and seeded cherry tomatoes (or 2 large peeled and seeded beefsteak tomatoes)
½ bunch fresh basil, chopped
1 tablespoons salt
1 teaspoons pepper
1 tablespoons balsamic vinegar
12 ounces rigatoni
Parmesan cheese, shaved for garnish

In a medium saucepan over medium-high heat, brown the garlic in 1 tablespoon of butter. Add the tomatoes. Smash ½ of the tomatoes to thicken the sauce. Add the basil, salt, pepper, and balsamic vinegar. Continue to warm over low heat. Cook rigatoni, drain, and stir in remaining 6 tablespoons of butter. Stir in remaining sauce and dish onto plates, garnishing with shaved Parmesan cheese.

Sarah Houghton, Marin County Free Library, San Rafael, CA

"Life is a combination of magic and pasta."
Fellini (1920-1993) Italian movie director

641.824 Meat loaf.

Ann Landers' Meat Loaf

2 pounds of ground round steak
1½ cups bread crumbs
¾ cup ketchup
1 teaspoon Accent
½ cup warm water
1 package dry onion soup mix
3 bacon strips
1 8-ounce can tomato sauce

Mix together the ground round steak, bread crumbs, ketchup, Accent, water and onion soup mix. Mix thoroughly. Place in a loaf pan; 1 hour.

Jim Lander, Pfohl Health Science Library, Mercy Hospital, Dubuque, IA

Del's Meat Loaf

1½ pounds ground chuck
½ cup fresh bread crumbs
2 eggs beaten
½ cup Swiss cheese, grated
Salt and pepper
5 tablespoons olive oil
2 cups onion, chopped
Flour
¼ teaspoon dried thyme
¼ cup snipped parsley
3 medium tomatoes, chopped

In a large bowl place bread crumbs, ground chuck, beaten eggs, cheese. 1¾ teaspoon salt, ½ teaspoon pepper. In a medium skillet, heat olive oil. Sauté ½ cup chopped onions until golden. Add to the meat loaf mixture and mix well. Shape meat loaf and put in a loaf pan. In the same skillet, in 3 tablespoons olive oil, sauté 1 ½ cups onion till golden. Stir in 1 teaspoon salt, ¼ teaspoon pepper, thyme, parsley and tomatoes. Cook for about 10 minutes over medium heat.   Pour this mixture over the meat loaf. Bake 50 minutes or until done at 375 degrees.

Susan Henricks, Carnegie-Stout Public Library, Dubuque, IA

155

641.824 Pizza.

Aunt Rosie's Spinach Pizza

5 pounds flour
6 eggs
1 cup Crisco
Add enough water as needed to make dough roll into a large square (12")
8 10-ounce bags of spinach
1 pound of raisins
3 large onions
3 1-pint bottles of green olives with pimento peppers
3 tablespoons olive oil

Cut the spinach into small pieces. Do the same with the onions and olives. Mix them all together and mix in the raisins. Season with salt, black pepper, dry hot pepper (optional) and about 3 tablespoons of olive oil. Spread the mixture on the dough then cover that with dough and pinch the edges closed. It looks like a two crusted pizza with filling or a very thin pie. If you don't want to make the dough, you can buy ready-made dough in the freezer section of the grocery store.
Bake at 350 degrees for 30 minutes. This is a large recipe and makes about 8 pizzas that are 12" square. Can be eaten hot or cold.

Michele Farrell

641.83 Salads.

Autumn Apple Salad

1 20-ounce can crushed pineapple, undrained
2/3 cup sugar
1 3-ounce package lemon Jell-O
1 8-ounce package cream cheese, softened
1 cup diced, unpeeled apples
½-1 cup nuts, chopped
1 cup celery, diced
1 cup whipped topping

Combine pineapple and sugar in a saucepan. Boil 3 minutes. Add Jell-O; stir until dissolved. Add cream cheese; stir until melted. Cool; fold in nuts, celery, apples and whipped topping. Pour into a 9" square pan or bowl. Chill. Serve on a lettuce.

Judi Tjepkes, Gowrie Public Library, Gowrie, IA

Big Apple Salad

3 large apples, finely chopped
2 tablespoons honey
1 tablespoon lemon juice
½ cup dates, chopped
½ cup walnuts, chopped
½ cup shredded coconut
1 cup plain yogurt

Mix honey, lemon, dates, and nuts. Fold in apples, coconut, and yogurt. Serve chilled.

Margaret McCoy, Cordova District Library, Cordova IL

Broccoli Salad

1-2 heads of broccoli, cut in small pieces
8-10 bacon strips, fried crisp and crumbled
1 cup sunflower seeds
1 cup raisins
1 cup shredded cheddar cheese
½ cup chopped onion
1 cup mayonnaise
2 tablespoons vinegar
1/3 cup sugar

Mix the broccoli, sunflower seeds, raisins, cheese and onion together, set aside. Blend the mayonnaise, vinegar and sugar until well mixed. Stir into broccoli mix. Top with crumbled bacon before serving.

Carol Clemens, Ventura Public Library, Ventura, IA

"An apple is an excellent thing -- until you have tried a peach."
George du Maurier (1834-1896) British writer

Caramel Apple Salad

6 Granny Smith apples, peeled and cubed
2 3.4-ounce boxes instant vanilla pudding mix
2 cups milk
6 Snicker bars, cubed
12 ounces whipped topping

Pour milk into bowl. Add pudding mix. Stir until well blended. Add whipped topping, apples, and Snickers. Mix all together. Chill 1 hour, then serve. (This can be served as dessert as it is very sweet.)

Fran Fessler, State Library of Iowa, Des Moines, IA

Cherry Pie Salad

2 3-ounce packages cherry Jell-O
1¾ cups boiling water
1 cup cold water
1 can cherry pie filling
1 cup miniature marshmallows
2 teaspoons hot milk
1 3-ounce package cream cheese, softened
1 container frozen whipped topping, thawed

Combine Jell-O, boiling water, cold water and cherry pie filling and mix well. Pour into 11" x 7" pan and refrigerate until firm. Cook marshmallows in milk over low heat until melted. Stir in cream cheese. Add the whipped topping. Spread topping on Jell-O and refrigerate until ready to serve.

Lisa Torgerson, Waukee Public Library, Waukee, IA

Chinese Cabbage Salad

1 bag shredded cabbage
1 package chicken flavored Raman noodles
1 small package slivered almonds
½ cup sunflower seeds
½ cup vegetable oil
½ cup sugar
½ cup onion, chopped

Break up the Raman noodles and toast with almonds. Mix the oil, sugar, and Raman noodles flavor packet. Mix the cabbage, noodles, almonds, sunflower seeds, and oil mixture just before serving.

Cheryl Boothe, Newton Public Library, Newton, IA
Karen Keller, Johnston Middle School Library, Johnston, IA

Chunky Chicken Salad

1 cup raisins
1 cup celery, diced
2 cups apples, cut in chunks
2 cups chicken or turkey, cut in cubes
1 cup salad dressing
2 tablespoons milk
1 tablespoon sugar
¼ cup walnuts, chopped

Combine raisins, celery, apples and chicken in a mixing bowl. In a separate bowl, blend salad dressing, milk, and sugar. Stir into chicken mixture. Top with nuts.

Karen Keller, Johnston Middle School Library, Johnston, IA

"When men reach their sixties and retire, they go to pieces. Women go right on cooking."
Gail Sheehy (1937 -) American author

Colorful Vegetable Salad

6 cups broccoli florets
6 cups cauliflowerets
2 cups cherry tomatoes, halved
1 large red onion, sliced
1 6-ounce can pitted ripped black olives, drained and sliced.
1 envelope ranch salad dressing mix
2/3 cup vegetable oil
¼ cup vinegar

In a large bowl, toss the broccoli, cauliflower, tomatoes, onion and olives. In a jar with a tight fitting lid, combine dressing mix, oil and vinegar; shake well. Pour dressing over salad and toss. Refrigerate for at least 3 hours. Serves 20

Judy J. Grienke-Miller, Cherokee Public Library, Cherokee, IA

Cranberry Waldorf Salad

1½ cups cranberries, chopped (a food processor works well)
1 cup red apple, chopped
1 cup celery, chopped
1 cup seedless green grapes, halved
¼ cup walnuts, chopped
2 tablespoons sugar
1 8-ounce container vanilla yogurt

Combine cranberries, apples, celery, grapes, walnuts, sugar and yogurt. Toss to coat. Cover and chill 2 hours.

Sarah Kennedy, Waukee Public Library, Waukee, IA

"A number of rare or newly experienced foods have been claimed to be aphrodisiacs. At one time this quality was even ascribed to the tomato. Reflect on that when you are next preparing the family salad."
Jane Grigson (-1990) English Cookbook Author

Del's Antipasto Bean Salad

1/3 cup olive oil
2 tablespoons red wine vinegar
½ teaspoon salt
½ teaspoon crushed tarragon
½ teaspoon onion powder
½ teaspoon garlic powder
Pinch black pepper
¾ cup roasted sweet red peppers (1 jar)
2 ounces salami cut in ¼" strips
2 ounces ham cut in ¼" strips
1 20-ounce can drained kidney beans
1 20-ounce can drained chick peas (garbanzo beans)

In a medium bowl, combine oil, vinegar, salt, tarragon, onion, garlic powder, and pepper. Add red peppers, salami, ham, kidney beans and chick peas. Mix well. Cover and refrigerate overnight. Serve at room temperature on a large lettuce leaf.

Susan Henricks, Carnegie-Stout Public Library, Dubuque, IA

Festive Tossed Salad

1 head Romaine lettuce, torn
1 cup (4 ounces) Swiss cheese, shredded
1 medium apple, cored and cubed
1 medium pear, cored and cubed
¼ cup dried cranberries
2 tablespoons onion, finely chopped
½ -1 cup chopped cashews

Poppy Seed Dressing

½ cup sugar (Splenda can be used in place of sugar)
1/3 cup red wine vinegar
2 tablespoons lemon juice
½ teaspoon salt
2/3 cup vegetable oil
2 -3 teaspoons poppy seeds

In a blender, combine sugar, vinegar, lemon juice, onion and salt. Cover and process until blended. With blender running, gradually add oil. Add poppy seeds last and blend. Combine salad ingredients in a bowl and drizzle with desired amount of poppy seed dressing:

Kalla C. Kalloway, Dakota County Inver Glen Library, Inver Grove Heights, MN

Fresh Apple Salad

Pineapple juice from a 20-ounce can of pineapple (reserve pineapple)
¼ cup margarine
¼ cup sugar
1 tablespoon lemon juice
2 tablespoons cornstarch
2 tablespoons water
1 cup plain yogurt
1/3 cup light salad dressing such as Miracle Whip
8 cups chopped tart red apples, unpeeled
1 20-ounce can pineapple chucks, drained
2 cups seedless green grapes
1-2 teaspoons poppy seeds
1½ cups pecans, toasted

Prepare dressing by combining the pineapple juice, margarine, sugar and lemon juice in a small saucepan. Heat to boiling. Combine the cornstarch and water to make a smooth paste; add to the hot mixture. Cook until thick and smooth. Chill completely. When chilled, stir in yogurt and salad dressing. Combine apples, pineapple chunks, grapes and poppy seeds. Add chilled dressing: refrigerate until time to serve. Stir in pecans just before serving. Serves 16

Judy J. Grienke-Miller, Cherokee Public Library, Cherokee, IA

"Give me book, fruit, French wine, and fine weather and a little music out of doors played by someone I do not know."
John Keats (1795-1871) English poet

Garfield Salad

4 cups tri-colored pasta, cooked and chilled
½ cup red sweet pepper, diced
½ cup black olives, sliced
½ cup scallions, diced
½ cup sundried tomatoes, chopped
¼ cup pine nuts, roasted
1 cup feta cheese, crumbled

Toss salad ingredients and prepare dressing:

¼ cup balsamic vinegar
¼ cup lime or lemon juice
¼ cup olive oil
1 tablespoon garlic, minced

Whisk dressing ingredients.
Pour the dressing over the salad and mix thoroughly. Chill overnight.

Mary Beth Revels, St. Joseph Public Library, St. Joseph, MO

Great-Grandmother's Christmas Salad

4 egg yolks, beaten slightly
2 tablespoons sugar
1 can white cherries, drained
1 can crushed pineapple, drained
1 can pears, drained
1 pound marshmallows
Juice of one lemon
1 pint whipping cream

Combine sugar and egg yolks in a double boiler and cook to form a thin custard. Cool. Combine cherries, pineapple, pears, and marshmallows. Stir in the lemon juice. Add the egg-sugar mixture and stir until blended. Whip the cream. Fold into the fruit and custard mixture. Refrigerate 24 hours; garnish with additional white cherries.

This recipe was adapted from a family recipe, circa 1880s.

Jim Lander, Pfohl Health Science Library, Mercy Hospital, Dubuque, IA

"A good cook is like a sorceress who dispenses happiness."
Elsa Schiaparelli (1890-1973) *Shocking Life,* 1954

Green Stuff

1 16-ounce container small curd cottage cheese
1 3-ounce package lime Jell-O
1 20-ounce can crushed pineapple
1 8-ounce container frozen, thawed, whipped topping such as Cool Whip
Miniature marshmallows, optional

Drain the cottage cheese and place in large bowl. Add the package of dry Jell-O powder and stir. Drain the pineapple. Add the drained pineapple and stir. Stir or fold in the whipped topping. Add marshmallows, if desired. Refrigerate before serving.

Note: The salad will set up faster if the can of pineapple is cold (put in the refrigerator the night before making). Some people use the orange gelatin and also add Mandarin oranges.

This is the only way I will eat cottage cheese!

Luann Elvey, East Tawas Library, East Tawas, MI

Macaroni Salad

1 pound macaroni
½ package frozen peas
¾ pound ham
½ cup celery, diced
¼ cup onion,, diced
½ pound cheese, optional
½ cup sugar
1 teaspoon vinegar
1 tablespoon prepared mustard
½-¾ quart salad dressing such as Miracle Whip (depending on how moist you want it.)

Cook macaroni and peas together; drain well. When cool, add ham, celery, onion and green pepper. Set aside. Mix sugar, vinegar, mustard and salad dressing in a bowl until well blended. Add to the macaroni mixture, stirring well. Refrigerate.

Fran Fessler, State Library of Iowa, Des Moines, IA

Mandarin Orange Salad

Romaine or spinach leaves, cleaned and torn
¼ cup almonds
2 tablespoons sugar
½ teaspoon salt, optional
2 tablespoons white vinegar
¼ cup salad oil
1 small can Mandarin oranges, drained
Green onions, sliced, to taste

Toast almonds over medium heat until browned. Mix sugar, salt, vinegar and salad oil together; shake, or whisk until well blended. Combine romaine lettuce or spinach with toasted almonds, green onions and mandarin oranges. Toss with dressing.

Sarah Kennedy, Waukee Public Library,Waukee, IA

"Talking of Pleasure, this moment I was writing with one hand, and with the other holding to my Mouth a Nectarine -- how good how fine. It went down all pulpy, slushy, oozy, all its delicious embonpoint melted down my throat like a large, beatified Strawberry."
John Keats (1795-1821) English Poet

Mrs. Petersen's Salad

1 can pineapple, drained
1 can fruit cocktail, drained or 1 cup halved seedless grapes
1 large can mandarin oranges, drained
1 small container sour cream
Shredded coconut
Miniature marshmallows

Mix together pineapple, fruit cocktail, and Mandarin oranges. Add sour cream and stir gently until mixed. Add coconut and marshmallows to taste.

Devon Murphy-Petersen, Waukee Public Library, Waukee, IA

Pink Champagne Salad

1 8-ounce package cream cheese, softened
¾ cup sugar
1 large can crushed pineapple, drained
1 10-ounce package frozen, sliced strawberries with juice
1 banana, quartered and sliced
1 8-ounce carton whipped topping such as Cool Whip

Mix cream cheese and sugar. Add remaining ingredients. Pour into a 13" x 9" pan and freeze. Let stand at room temperature a few minutes before serving.

Laurie Hews, Iowa Library Association, West Des Moines, IA
Judy J. Grienke-Miller, Cherokee Public Library, Cherokee, IA

"A woman should never be seen eating or drinking, unless it be lobster, salad and champagne. The only true feminine and becoming viands"
Lord Byron (1788-1824) Poet

Seashell Salad

1 8-ounce package of small seashell macaroni
3 cups seedless green grapes, halved
1 8-ounce can pitted ripe olives, drained and halved
¾ cup green onions, chopped
3 ounces bleu cheese, crumbled
Salt and pepper to taste
¼ teaspoon garlic powder
3 tablespoons fresh or bottled lemon juice
1 cup mayonnaise

Cook shells according to the directions on the package. Drain. Combine hot shells with all other ingredients. Mix well. Cover and refrigerate several hours or overnight. Serves 8-12

Katy Obringer, Palo Alto Children's Library, Palo Alto, CA

Taco Pasta Salad

1 16-ounce package spiral pasta
1 pound ground beef
¾ cup water
1 envelope taco seasoning
2 cups (8 ounces) cheddar cheese, shredded
1 large green pepper, chopped
1 medium sweet onion, chopped
2 2-ounce cans sliced ripe olives, drained
1 16-ounce bottle Catalina dressing

Cook pasta according to package directions. Meanwhile, in a skillet, cook beef over medium heat until no longer pink, drain. Add water and taco seasoning; simmer, uncovered for 15 minutes. Rinse pasta in cold water and drain; place in a large bowl. Add beef mixture, cheese, green pepper, onion, tomato and olives; mix well. Add the dressing and toss to coat. Cover and refrigerate for at least 1 hour. Serves 10.

Denise Crawford, Glenwood Public Library, Glenwood, IA

Tortellini Bean Salad

1 10-ounce package refrigerated spinach tortellini (or other type of tortellini)
2 cups broccoli florets
1 cup canned garbanzo beans or chickpeas, rinsed and drained
1 cup canned red kidney beans, rinsed and drained
1 cup canned white kidney or cannellini beans, rinsed and drained
1 8-ounce bottle fat free Italian Caesar salad dressing
24 cherry tomatoes, halved
Parmesan cheese to taste

Prepare tortellini according to the package. Drain and place in a large bowl. Add broccoli and beans. Pour salad dressing over the mixture. Toss minimally. Cover and refrigerate overnight. Just before serving, stir in cherry tomatoes and sprinkle Parmesan cheese on top.

Margaret McCoy, Cordova District Library, Cordova, IL

Unbelievable Salad

1 15 ½ -ounce can crushed pineapple
1 3-ounce package cherry gelatin
1 11-ounce can mandarin oranges, drained
1 8-ounce carton creamed cottage cheese
1 cup whipping cream, whipped

Pour the pineapple with its juice in to a glass measure (4 cup measure) Microwave on high for about 3 minutes, until boiling. Remove from microwave. Add gelatin; stir with a wooden spoon until dissolved. Chill in refrigerator until it is cool and begins to thicken, about 1 hour. Remove from refrigerator and stir in oranges, cottage cheese and whipped topping. Pour into a 9" square dish and refrigerate until firm.

This is as good as dessert too!

Jo Tresnak, Kenwood Elementary School Media Center, Cedar Rapids, IA

Winter Fruit Salad

Sometimes I find myself with a fruit bowl full of apples and oranges a little past their prime, so I have figured out a way to use them happily.

Squeeze and strain the juice of two oranges into a pan. Peel and slice four or five apples of any kind (it's most fun when you have a variety of apples; today I used Galas, Fujis, and Macs) and toss in that pan with the juice. Throw in a few big tablespoonfuls of currants or raisins and a heaping tablespoonful of candied ginger (powdered ginger will do in a pinch, but you won't get those lovely bits of ginger to bite into then. Use about a quarter teaspoon of powdered ginger). Sprinkle it all with two teaspoons of brown sugar. Cover, turn the heat up high, and when it starts to bubble and sizzle stir and lower the heat. Once the apples are nearly dry and getting soft, take the lid off the pan and cook a few minutes longer until nearly all the liquid is gone. The whole cooking process probably won't take more than ten minutes. Serve with yogurt, on top of cold cereal or oatmeal, or even on buttered toast. Yum!

GraceAnne Andreassi DeCandido, Blue Roses Consulting, NY, NY

"A thriving household depends on the use of seasonal produce and the application of common sense."
Olivier de Serres (1539-1619) French agronomist

641.84 Sandwiches.

Beef Burgers

1 pound ground beef
½ cup onion, chopped
1 can chicken gumbo soup
2 tablespoons ketchup
1 teaspoon prepared mustard
¼ teaspoon black pepper

Brown and drain ground beef. Add the onion, soup, catsup, mustard, and pepper. Simmer for five minutes. To serve, spoon on buns.

Carol Clemens, Ventura Public Library, Ventura, IA

Jambon Beurre (Ham and Butter Sandwich)

1 baguette
2-3 thick-cut slices of ham
Butter

Cut a sandwich length off the baguette. Slice in half lengthwise. Liberally butter both halves, place ham on baguette and close around the ham.

Jesse Lewis, Palm Beach County Library System, West Palm Beach, FL

The simple ham sandwich is still the most popular sandwich in the U.S., and in second place is the BLT. foodreference.com

Hot Ham for Sandwiches

1 tablespoon butter
1 tablespoon flour
1 teaspoon dry mustard
2 tablespoons sugar
¼ teaspoon salt
¼ cup boiling water
¼ cup vinegar
¼ cup mayonnaise
2 tablespoons sweet relish
1½ cups cooked ham, chopped or ground

Melt butter, add flour, mustard, sugar and salt, and blend. Remove from heat. Slowly stir in boiling water and vinegar. Return to heat and cook, stirring constantly until thick and smooth. Gradually stir in mayonnaise, relish, and ham. Heat through.

Christine A. Cowles, Fort Madison Public Libraries, Fort Madison, IA

Peanut Butter and Onion Sandwich

1 onion
Vinegar and water
Peanut butter
2 slices bread

Slice the onion and soak the slices in a bowl of vinegar water for 4-6 hours or overnight. (This takes some of the sharpness out of the onion.) Spread peanut butter on one slice of bread. Cover with onion slices. Top with the other slice of bread.

This is the sandwich my mother used to fix for herself to eat while she was reading when she was a child in Nebraska in the 1920s and 30s.

Susan Radosti, South O'Brien High School Library, Paullina, IA

"My favorite sandwich is peanut butter, baloney, cheddar cheese, lettuce, and mayonnaise on toasted bread with catsup on the side"
Hubert Humphrey (1911-1978) Vice President, 1964-1968

Quick-Fix Sandwiches

1 tube of refrigerated French Bread
Spread: baba ganouche, jam, etc. as desired
Lunch Meat: ham, turkey, chicken, vegetables, etc. as desired
Cheese

Grease cookie sheet. Preheat oven to 350 degrees. Unroll bread dough. Put choice of spread on one side of the dough. Follow with a layer of meat, cheese, and vegetables. Roll up. Pinch seams. Cut slits in sandwich.
Bake for 26-30 minutes until golden brown.

(Suggestion: Spread: Blackberry Jam and Cranberries, with Turkey and Cheddar Cheese.)

Erin Zolotukhin-Ridgway, Saint Paul Public Library, St. Paul, MN

Sloppy Joes

1½-2 pounds ground beef
2 tablespoons sugar
1 small onion, chopped
2 tablespoons regular mustard
¼ teaspoon salt
2 tablespoons vinegar
¾ cup ketchup
2 tablespoons Worcestershire sauce

Brown meat slowly in skillet with onion and salt. Meanwhile, make sauce by mixing together the other ingredients and cooking slowly over low heat for 15 minutes. Add meat to sauce and stir. Let simmer 30 minutes or longer before serving so that the meat absorbs the sauce. Serves 6-8

Susan Sterling, Dimmick Memorial Library, Jim Thorpe, PA

"I dined at the Cocoa Tree ... That respectable body affords every evening a sight truly English. Twenty or thirty of the first men in the kingdom ... supping at little tables ... upon a bit of cold meat, or a Sandwich."
Edward Gibbon, Historian. The first written record of the word 'sandwich', from Edward Gibbons Journal, November 24, 1762

Stromboli

2 packages/boxes of pizza crust mix, such as Jiffy
2 cups mozzarella cheese, shredded
2 cups of cheddar cheese, shredded
1 jar mild or hot peppers, sliced
1 package of thinly sliced ham
1 package of sliced pepperoni

Mix pizza crust dough as directed. Roll out on floured 9" x 15" board. Cover with ham slices, then cheddar cheese, pepperoni, mozzarella cheese and ½ to all of the sliced peppers. Roll into a loaf and put on greased cookie sheet. Cook at 425 degrees for 30 minutes. Spread butter on loaf when out of oven. Let cool slightly and slice.

Annette Wetteland, State Library of Iowa, Des Moines, IA

641.853 Candy

Caramels

1 cup butter or margarine
2¼ cups brown sugar
Dash salt
1 15-ounce can sweetened condensed milk
1 teaspoon vanilla
1 cup light corn syrup

Melt butter in a heavy 3-quart saucepan. Add sugar and salt. Stir thoroughly. Stir in corn syrup; mix well. Gradually add milk, stirring occasionally. Cook and stir over medium heat to firm ball stage (245 degrees), 12-15 minutes. Remove from heat; stir in vanilla. Pour into a 9" x 9" x 2" pan. Cook and cut into squares.

Deb Morrow, Harris-Lake Middle/High School Library, Lake Park, IA

"Once in a young lifetime one should be allowed to have as much sweetness as one can possibly want and hold."
Judith Olney, American journalist and cookbook author

Cranberry Kisses

2 cups fresh or frozen cranberries
¾ cup light corn syrup
3 cups sugar
1 tablespoon butter or margarine
½ cup walnuts, chopped
1 cup flaked coconut
1 teaspoon vanilla extract

Cut cranberries in half. Add syrup, sugar and butter. Cook over low heat stirring until mixture starts to come to a boil. Add nuts, coconut, and vanilla. Cook at a boil until temperature on a candy thermometer registers 238 degrees or until soft ball forms when a small amount of the syrup is dropped into cold water. Remove from heat and pour mixture into a shallow buttered pan or platter. Cool until candy is just lukewarm. With buttered fingers shape candy into small 1" balls. Wrap in waxed paper or plastic wrap. Store in a cool dry place. Makes 2½ pounds

Susan Radosti , South O'Brien High School Library, Paullina, IA

Mabel Prock's Divinity

2 cups sugar
½ cup corn syrup
½ teaspoon salt
2 egg whites, stiffly beaten
1 teaspoon vanilla
1 teaspoon powdered sugar
1 cup walnuts

Cook sugar, corn syrup, and salt over low heat stirring to dissolve. When it begins to boil, cover. Stir no more. Place a candy thermometer in the pan but leave it sticking out from the cover. Cook until it reaches 260-265 degrees. Remove from heat and pour gradually over the stiffly beaten egg whites beating continuously. Add vanilla and powdered sugar, blend; add walnuts. When it will hold its shape drop on sheets of waxed paper. Dry out overnight.

Jana L. Prock, Bay City Public Library, Bay City, TX

Microwave Fudge

1 12-ounce package milk chocolate chips
1 stick real butter
1 8-ounce can sweetened condensed milk
1 teaspoon vanilla

Place all ingredients in glass bowl. Microwave mixture, stirring every 90 seconds until melted and blended well. Optional: Fold in chopped nuts (walnuts or pecans) after mixture is melted. Pour into a buttered 8"x 8" glass pan and set in refrigerator to harden. After two to three hours, cut into small pieces and serve.

Judy J. Grienke-Miller, Cherokee Public Library, Cherokee, IA

Mints

3 ounces cream cheese
1½ cups powdered sugar
½ teaspoon mint flavor

Mix with mixer, it will be very thick. Roll in balls, then roll in sugar. Press in rubber mint molds and push out onto a cookie sheet to let them get a dry outer shell. Put them on wax paper to separate the layers so they will not stick. Freezes well.

Eileen Robinson, Marion Public Library, Marion, IA

Mrs. See's Fudge

4½ cups sugar
1 can evaporated milk
2 12-ounce bags chocolate chips
½ pound butter
1 teaspoon vanilla
2 cups nuts, if desired

In a large saucepan stir sugar and milk until well blended. Bring to a boil and let boil 7 minutes. Add chocolate chips, butter, vanilla, and nuts. Mix until well blended. Pour in jellyroll pan lined with wax paper. Leave at room temperature until firm. Cut into small squares, then refrigerate.

Susan Elgin, Waukee Public Library, Waukee, IA

"Look, there's no metaphysics on earth like chocolates."
Fernando Pessoa (1888-1935) Portuguese poet

Peanut Brittle

1 cup raw peanuts
1 cup sugar
½ cup light corn syrup
Dash of salt
1 teaspoon vanilla
1 teaspoon butter
1 teaspoon baking soda

Stir together peanuts, sugar, corn syrup and salt in a 2-quart bowl. Cook on high in the microwave for 7-8 minutes stirring once. Add vanilla and butter; blend well and cook for 1-2 minutes more. Add baking soda. Gently stir until foamy. Pour onto a buttered cookie sheet and let cool for ½ hour. Break into pieces.

Maybeth Gilliam, Retired, Blairstown Public Library, Blairstown, IA

641.8653 Cheesecake (Cookery)

Individual Cherry Cheesecakes

1 box vanilla wafers
1 cup sugar
1 teaspoons vanilla
2 8-ounce packages cream cheese
1 egg
1 can cherry pie filling
Cupcake papers

Put one wafer in paper cup. Beat cream cheese, sugar, egg and vanilla. Spoon mixture on wafer and bake at 350 degrees for 20 minutes. Add topping.

Michelle Minerd, Kent District Library, East Grand Rapids Branch, East Grand Rapids, MI

Cheesecake may be considered an American classic, but they have been popular throughout the ages. Cheesecakes of differing types were popular in ancient Greece. foodreference.com

175

Irish Creme Cheesecake

1 cup vanilla wafer crumbs
½ cup nuts, chopped
3 tablespoons granulated sugar
¼ cup margarine, melted
2 8-ounce packages cream cheese
½ cup brown sugar, packed
2 eggs
1 6-ounce package semi-sweet chocolate pieces, melted
2 tablespoons Bailey's Irish Cream liquor
2 cups sour cream
2 tablespoons granulated sugar

Prepare crust. Combine crumbs, pecans, sugar and margarine. Press into the bottom of a 9" springform pan. Bake at 325 degrees 10 minutes. Meanwhile, combine cream cheese and brown sugar, mixing at medium speed of an electric mixer until well blended. Add eggs one at a time, mixing well after each addition. Blend in chocolate and Bailey's. Pour over crust. Bake at 325 degrees for 35 minutes.
Increase oven temperature to 425 degrees. Combine sour cream and granulated sugar. Carefully spread over cheesecake. Bake at 425 degrees for 10 minutes. Loosen cake from rim of pan; cool before removing rim of pan. Chill before serving.

Deb Tully, Carnegie-Stout Public Library, Dubuque, IA

"Never hesitate to take the last piece of bread or the last cake; there are probably more."
Hills Manual of Social and Business Forms: Etiquette of the Table, 1880

Margarita Cheesecake

½ cup lime juice, fresh or bottled
¼ cup orange liqueur such as Triple Sec or Cointreau
¼ cup tequila
1 cup sugar
2 tablespoons cornstarch
½ cup orange juice
Green food coloring
1 cup crushed graham cracker crumbs
¼ cup margarine or butter, melted
2 8-ounce packages of cream cheese, regular or low-fat
1 14-ounce sweetened condensed milk (not evaporated milk)
3 eggs
¼ teaspoon salt

Mix juices and liquors in a small saucepan, reserving 3 tablespoons of juice for later. Add ¾ cup sugar, and heat juice mixture to just simmering, stirring to dissolve sugar completely. Mix cornstarch with reserved juices and stir into saucepan, continuing to heat and whisk until it begins to boil and thicken. Remove from heat and stir in enough green food color to look appropriate for St. Patrick's Day. Cool.

Mix graham cracker crumbs, margarine, and sugar. Add margarine and ¼ cup sugar and mix well. Reserve 2 tablespoons of crumb mixture for garnish later. Pour into 9" or 9-1/2" springform pan and press firmly on bottom and about 1" up the sides. Bake at 375 degrees for 6-8 minutes, or until firm but not toasty. Remove and cool crust. Turn oven down to 300 degrees.

Beat cream cheese until fluffy. Beat in condensed milk, salt, and then eggs one at a time. Scrape mixing bowl and beaters to incorporate lumps of cheese and beat until smooth. Set aside 2 tablespoons of the Margarita syrup and stir the remaining syrup into cheese mixture. Pour into the cooled crust, smoothing top. Drizzle reserved syrup on top of cheesecake, then gently draw a knife blade through to marble. Sprinkle reserved crust crumbs on edges. Bake at 300 degrees for 50-60 minutes, or until surface of cheesecake (not a syrup spot) springs back lightly from touch 1" from center. (The middle will still jiggle slightly when pan is gently shaken.) Turn oven off and leave cheesecake in for 1 hour. Remove from oven and draw a thin knife blade around the outside edge to release from sides of pan. Cool. Cover to refrigerate after completely cool.

Margaret Vande Kamp, retired, Clinton High School Library, Clinton, IA

From the archives of the Carnegie-Stout Public Library,
Dubuque, Iowa

Apple Crisp

5 large, tart apples, peeled, cored, and sliced
½ cup brown sugar
½ cup quick cooking oatmeal
½ cup flour
1 teaspoon cinnamon
1/3 cup butter

Place apples in a baking dish. Mix brown sugar, oatmeal, flour, cinnamon and butter until crumbly. Pour over the apples. Bake at 350 degrees until apples are tender; approximately 1 hour.

Carol Clemens, Ventura Public Library, Ventura, IA

Better Than Pumpkin Pie Dessert

1 yellow cake mix
½ cup margarine, melted
3 eggs, divided
3 cups (29-ounce can) pumpkin
¾ cup sugar
1 teaspoon cloves
1 teaspoon ginger
Pinch of salt
¾ cup milk
¼ cup sugar
1 teaspoon cinnamon
¼ cup margarine

Grease a 13" x 9" baking pan. Set aside 1 cup of the yellow cake mix for later use. Mix together the remaining cake mix, margarine and 1 egg. Press mixture into the bottom of the baking pan. Using an electric mixer, mix the pumpkin, sugar, cinnamon, cloves, ginger, salt, milk and 2 eggs together. Pour over crust mixture in pan. In a small bowl place the 1cup of reserved cake mix, ¼ cup sugar, 1 teaspoon cinnamon, and ¼ cup margarine. Mix. The mixture should be crumbly. Sprinkle over the filling mixture. Bake in a 350 degree oven for 45-50 minutes.

Denise S. Crawford, Glenwood Public Library, Glenwood, IA

Cherries Jubilee

1 16-ounce can dark sweet pitted cherries
¼ cup sugar
2 tablespoons corn starch
¼ cup brandy

Drain cherries; reserve syrup. In a saucepan, blend sugar and cornstarch. Gradually stir in saved cherry juice, mixing well. Cook and stir over medium heat until mixture thickens and bubbles. Remove from heat. Stir in cherries. Turn into a chafing dish. Pour brandy over the cherries and ignite to serve.

Susan Henricks, Carnegie-Stout Public Library, Dubuque, IA

Cherries Jubilee is a dessert created by Auguste Escoffier in honor of Queen Victoria's Diamond Jubille. It consists of cherries flamed tableside with sugar and Kirsch (cherry brandy) spooned over vanilla ice cream.
foodreference.com

Cherry Blossoms

2 8-ounce packages cream cheese, softened (light or fat free should not be substituted)
¾ cup sugar
2 eggs
2 teaspoons vanilla
16 vanilla wafers

Beat the eggs slightly. Add sugar, vanilla and cream cheese. Mix until smooth. Place 1 vanilla wafer in the bottom of 16 muffin cups. Fill each cup 2/3 full with cream cheese mixture. Bake 10-12 minutes at 375 degrees. When cool, top with cherry pie filling. (You could also use blueberry or strawberry.)

Carol Hoke, Cedar Rapids Public Library, Cedar Rapids IA

"Men become passionately attached to women who know how to cosset them with delicate tidbits." Honoré de Balzac (1799-1859) French novelist

Christmas Dessert

1 package Oreo cookies, crushed
1 stick margarine, melted
½ gallon peppermint stick ice cream
1 jar chocolate fudge topping
Whipped cream

Mix the crushed cookies and margarine and press evenly into the bottom of a 13" x 9" pan. Reserve 1 cup of the cookie mixture for topping. Layer on top of Oreo crust the ice cream and chocolate fudge topping. Top with whipped cream and garnish with the last cup of cookies. Freeze.

Susan Elgin, Waukee Public Library, Waukee, IA

English Trifle (easy version)

2 16-ounce pound cakes
Raspberry jam
1 large package vanilla instan*t* pudding and pie filling mix
3 cups half and half
3 cans apricots, drained
Brandy
Whipped cream and sliced almonds, if desired

Slice pound cake. Spread half the slices thickly with raspberry jam. Top with remaining slices. Cut each "sandwich" into three pieces. Cover bottom of a clear glass bowl with half the sandwiches. Sprinkle with half the brandy. Place apricots in blender or food processor and chop into chunks (or chop by hand). Spread half the apricots over the sandwiches in bowl. Prepare instant pudding using the half and half. Pour half over apricots. Repeat with remaining sandwiches, brandy, apricots, and pudding. Refrigerate until serving time; top with whipped cream and sliced almonds if desired.

These are both very popular with staff in our library, where food is free-flowing and constant.

Susan Buentello, Briscoe Library University of Texas, Health Science Center at San Antonio, TX

Frozen Strawberry Dessert

1 cup flour
¼ cup brown sugar
½ cup nuts
½ cup margarine
2 egg whites
1 cup sugar (or 2/3 cup if frozen strawberries used)
2 cups fresh strawberries (if frozen, 10 ounces partially thawed)
2 tablespoons lemon juice
2 cups whipped cream

Combine flour, brown sugar, nuts and margarine. Spread in a shallow baking pan. Bake at 350 degrees for 20 minutes. Sprinkle 2/3 of the crumbs in a 11" x 8" pan reserving the remainder for a garnish. Combine egg whites, sugar, strawberries and lemon juice. Beat to stiff peaks, about 10 minutes. Fold in whipping cream. Spoon over crumbs. Top with reserved crumbs. Freeze 6 hours or overnight. Trim with whole berries and whipped cream if desired.

Linda Magley, patron, Mesa Family History Center Library, Mesa, AZ

"No diet will remove all the fat from your body because the brain is entirely fat. Without a brain, you might look good, but all you could do is run for public office."
George Bernard Shaw (1856-1950) Irish playwright

Hershey's Double Chocolate Mint Dessert

1 cup all-purpose flour
1 cup sugar
½ cup butter or margarine, softened
4 eggs
1 ½ cups chocolate syrup such as Hershey's
2 cups confectioners sugar,
½ cup butter or margarine, softened
1 tablespoon water
½ teaspoon mint extract
3 drops green food coloring, optional
6 tablespoons butter or margarine
1 cup mint chocolate chips or semi-sweet chocolate chips, such as Hershey's

Heat oven to 350 degrees. Grease a 13" x 9" pan. In large mixer bowl beat flour, ½ cup sugar, ½ cup butter, eggs and syrup until smooth. Pour into prepared pan; bake 25-30 minutes or until top springs back when lightly touched. (Top may still appear wet.) Cool completely in pan. Meanwhile, prepare mint cream layer. In small mixer bowl combine confectioners sugar, ½ cup butter or margarine, water, mint extract and food color; beat until smooth. Spread mint cream layer on cooled cake; chill. Prepare chocolate topping. Place butter or margarine in small microwave proof bowl and microwave at high power for 1-1 ½ minutes, or just until chips are melted and mixture is smooth when stirred. Pour chocolate topping over dessert. Cover; chill.

Fran Fessler, State Library of Iowa, Des Moines, IA

"If you are not feeling well, if you have not slept, chocolate will revive you. But you have no chocolate! I think of that again and again! My dear, how will you ever manage?"
Marquise de Sévigné, French writer and lady of fashion, February 11, 1677

Love Notes

1 cup flour
¼ pound margarine
½ cup pecans
1 8-ounce cream cheese
1 cup powdered sugar
1 large carton frozen whipped topping such as Cool Whip, thawed
2 packages instant pudding, any flavor
3 cups cold milk

Mix together flour, margarine and pecans. Press into bottom of a 13" x 9" pan.
Bake at 350 degrees for 15 minutes. Cool. Mix together cream cheese, powdered
sugar and half of the whipped topping. Put on top of crust. Let cool in refrigerator
for at least 2 hours. Mix together the pudding and milk. Put mixture on top of cream
cheese layer. Let set. Spread remaining whipped topping on top. Keep refrigerated
until ready to serve.

Laurie Hews, Iowa Library Association, West Des Moines, IA

Pistachio Dessert

30-40 Ritz crackers, finely crushed
¾ stick margarine, melted
2 small packages instant pistachio pudding
1½ cup milk.
1 quart vanilla ice cream, softened
1 9-ounce container of frozen whipped topping such as Cool Whip, thawed
3 Heath bars, crushed

Mix crushed cracker and margarine and press evenly into a 13" x 9" pan. Bake10
minutes at 350 degrees. Cool. Combine pudding mix and milk. Beat until thick.
Add vanilla ice cream. Fold in whipped topping. Pour into crust. Sprinkle crushed
Heath Bars on top; freeze.

Kim Robinson, Waukee Public Library, Waukee, IA

"Pistachio nuts, the red ones, cure any problem."
Paula Danziger (1944-2004) American children's author

Strawberry Apple Cobbler

1/3 cup granulated sugar
3 tablespoon all-purpose flour
2 teaspoon grated lemon rind
1 teaspoon cinnamon
2 cups apples, peeled and chopped
2 packages (each 300 g) frozen unsweetened strawberries
2 tablespoons lemon juice
1 cup all-purpose flour
3 tablespoons granulated sugar
1 teaspoons baking powder
¼ teaspoon baking soda
¼ teaspoon salt
4 tablespoons cold butter
2/3 cup buttermilk

Combine sugar, flour, lemon rind and cinnamon. Stir in apples, strawberries and lemon juice. Spread mixture in 8-inch square baking dish and bake in 400-degree oven for 10 minutes. Mix together the flour, 3 tablespoons sugar, baking powder, baking soda and salt. Cut in butter until crumbly. With fork, stir in buttermilk until soft dough forms. Drop by spoonfuls onto fruit. Bake 35-40 minutes or until top is golden and biscuits are cooked through. Serves 6

Denette Kellogg, Carnegie-Stout Public Library, Dubuque, IA

"A fruit is a vegetable with looks and money. Plus, if you let fruit rot, it turns into wine, something Brussels sprouts never do."
P. J. O'Rourke (1947 -) American political satirist

Strawberries Romanoff

½ cup sour cream
3 tablespoons brown sugar
1 tablespoon Cognac (rum or vanilla may be substituted)
½ cup heavy cream
3 tablespoons granulated sugar
2 pints fresh strawberries

Mix the sour cream, brown sugar and Cognac together in a medium bowl.
In a separate bowl whip the cream with a whisk or an electric mixer until it starts to thicken. Add the granulated sugar and whip until thick. Using a rubber spatula, fold the cream carefully into the sour cream mixture until well blended. Just before serving, rinse the berries and trim off the green stems with a sharp paring knife. Put the berries into stemmed wineglasses and top with the Romanoff sauce. Serves 4

Megan VanderHart, Rock Island Public Library, Rock Island, IL

"In our opinion food should be sniffed lustily at table, both as a matter of precaution and as a matter of enjoyment, the sniffing of it to be regarded in the same light as the tasting of it."
E.B. White (1899-1985) American author and poet

641.862 Ice cream, ices, etc.

Vanilla Ice Cream (without an ice cream maker)

2 cups milk
1 vanilla bean, split
4 egg yolks
½ cup sugar
4 tablespoons whipped cream
1 egg white, whipped until fluffy

Bring milk and the vanilla bean to boil in a medium size saucepan. Meanwhile, whisk the egg yolks and sugar in a mixing bowl until the yolks become pale yellow. Remove the vanilla bean from the hot milk. Begin to whisk the egg yolks again. Add the boiled milk little by little, to the egg yolk mixture and blend well. Pour the mixture into a saucepan. Over a medium flame, with a wooden spoon, stir back and forth continuously while the cream sauce thickens; do not allow it to boil. Test readiness by dipping the wooden spoon into the sauce and running your finger across the back of the spoon. If the cream sauce runs back into the finger trace, it needs more cooking. If the finger trace stays clean, it has cooked enough. Pour the cream sauce through a fine sieve into a bowl. Set aside to cool, stirring occasionally. When cooled, fold in the whipped cream and the beaten egg white. Place it in the freezer, stirring occasionally until it begins to freeze. After about 4 hours, when completely frozen, serve the glace using a large spoon.

Note: When overcooked, this sauce becomes grainy. To recover it, pour the mixture into bottle or jar. Add 2 tablespoons of mild or heavy cream and shake for 20 seconds. Pour into a large bowl, stirring to cool it so it doesn't continue to cook. Serves 4-6 (For best results, use a metal "ice tray.")

Barbara Feist Stienstra, Middletown Thrall Library, Middletown, NY

"My advice to you is not to inquire why or whither, but just enjoy your ice cream while it's on your plate—that's my philosophy."
Thornton Wilder (1897-1975) American novelist and playwright

187

Black Bottom Pie

14 graham crackers
5 tablespoons butter, melted
1 tablespoon unflavored gelatin, such as Knox
4 tablespoons cold water
4 eggs, separated
2 cups milk, scalded
1 cup sugar, divided
1½ tablespoons corn starch
1½ squares chocolate
2 teaspoons vanilla extract, divided
½ teaspoon cream of tartar
½ cup sugar

Roll the graham crackers to a fine mix; add the melted butter. Pat into a 9"square pan. Bake 10 minutes at 300 degrees.

Dissolve gelatin in the cold water; set aside. Beat egg yolks in the top of a double boiler. Add the scalded milk. Combine ½ cup sugar and cornstarch, then add to the egg and milk mixture. Stir and cook until this becomes a thick custard. Remove from heat. Reserve one cup of the custard mix and set aside.

Melt the chocolate; add the reserved cup of custard mix. Add 1 teaspoon vanilla and beat well. Cool. Pour over the graham cracker crust and chill.

While the reserved custard is still hot, add dissolved gelatin; cool, but do not allow to stiffen. Beat the egg whites until frothy. Add the cream of tartar and continue beating until stiff to form a meringue. Add ½ cup sugar and 1 teaspoon vanilla. Beat again. Fold the meringue into the reserved custard/gelatin mix. Pour over the cool chocolate layer. Top with whipped cream and serve.

Jim Lander, Pfohl Health Science Library, Mercy Hospital, Dubuque, IA

Deep Dish Apple Pie

6-8 apples (about 4 cups) peeled, cored, and sliced
1 tablespoon sugar
1 teaspoon cinnamon
1 stick of butter or margarine, softened
1 cup sugar
1 egg
Pinch salt
1 cup flour
¼ cup nuts, chopped

Place sliced apples in a butter 10" pie plate. Mix 1 tablespoon sugar and cinnamon together and sprinkle over the apples. Cream butter, sugar, egg and salt until well blended. Add the flour and mix. Spread over the apples. Sprinkle nuts over the top of the pie and bake at 350 degrees for 45 minutes.

Chris Fee, Marion Public Library, Marion, IA

"Thy breathe is like the steame of apple-pyes."
The first written mention of a fruit pie. Robert Greene, *Arcadia,* 1590

Foolproof Pie Crust

4 cups flour
1¾ cups vegetable shortening
1 tablespoon sugar
2 teaspoons salt
1 tablespoon vinegar
1 egg
½ cup water

Mix first 4 ingredients with a fork. Mix next ingredients together. Combine the two with a fork. Chill. Can be kept 3 days in the refrigerator, or frozen. Yields 5 crusts

Judi Tjepkes, Gowrie Public Library, Gowrie, IA

Fudge Pie

1 cup sugar
¼ cup flour
¼ cup cocoa
2 eggs
1 stick of butter or margarine, melted
1 teaspoon vanilla
1 uncooked 8" pie shell

Beat eggs slightly, add butter and vanilla. Add dry ingredients and mix well. Pour into pie shell. Bake at 350 degrees for 35-40 minutes or until firm. Recipe may be tripled and put into two deep-dish pie shells; add 10-15 minutes to baking time.

Devon Murphy-Petersen, Waukee Public Library, Waukee, IA

Pumpkin Pie Custard (Sugar Free - Low Carb Version)

1 small can pumpkin
1 can evaporated skim milk
1 cup Splenda (granulated - not the packets)
1 teaspoon pumpkin pie spice
2 eggs
½ cup Bisquick or pancake mix

Spray pie plate or 9" square pan with cooking oil spray such as Pam. Preheat oven to 350 degrees. Combine all ingredients in bowl and mix by hand with whisk or use hand mixer. When mixture is smooth pour into baking pan. Bake for approximately 55 minutes. Cool, then eat and enjoy. (To make the recipe super low carb do not use the Bisquick/pancake mix. The mix gives the custard a firmer consistency so you can eat it like a crustless piece of pie.)

Valerie Smith, Lorain Public Library System, Lorain, OH

"A boy doesn't have to go to war to be a hero; he can say he doesn't like pie when he sees there isn't enough to go around."
E. B. Howe (1853-1937) American novelist

Rhubarb Custard Pie

4 cups (16-18 ounces) fresh or frozen rhubarb, cut in ½" pieces
2 large eggs
1½ cups sugar
2 tablespoons flour
2 tablespoons oil
1½ teaspoons vanilla

Prepare pie dough for a double crust pie. Line 11" pie pan with crust. Prick crust with fork. Break eggs into large bowl. Take pastry brush, dip in egg white, and paint bottom crust with egg white. Beat eggs with whisk until light. Beat in sugar, flour, oil, and vanilla. Stir in rhubarb. Pour filling into crust, cover with top crust, crimp, vent top. Sprinkle top crust with sugar. Bake at 410 degrees for 10 minutes. Reduce heat to 350 degrees for another 40-50 minutes.

Sheila Olson Merrell, Parkway North High School, St. Louis, MO

Sheila's Apple Pie

6-8 Granny Smith apples, peeled, cored, and sliced
1 cup sugar
2 tablespoons flour
1 teaspoon cinnamon
Dash of nutmeg
2 tablespoons butter

Prepare pie dough for a double crust pie. Combine sugar, flour, cinnamon, and nutmeg and mix into apples. Line large pie pan with bottom crust. Pour apple mixture into crust. Dot with butter. Cover with top crust, crimp, vent, and sprinkle with sugar. Bake at 410 degrees for 15 minutes, reduce heat to 350 degrees and continue to bake for 40-50 minutes.

Sheila Olson Merrell, Parkway North High School, St. Louis, MO

"Good apple pies are a considerable part of our domestic happiness."
Jane Austen (1775-1817) English novelist

Sheila's Never-Fail Pie Crust

1 cup vegetable shortening, such as Crisco
2½ cups flour
1 scant teaspoon salt
1 egg
¼ cup cold water
1 tablespoon white vinegar

Cut together the shortening, flour, and salt with a pastry blender until pea-sized in shape. In small bowl beat the egg, water, and vinegar. Add to flour mixture and mix to form a dough. Makes 2 double pie crusts.

Sheila Olson Merrell, Parkway North High School, St. Louis, MO

Surprise Pie

1 ready made pie crust
1 8-ounce container of fruit yogurt
1 8-ounce container of frozen whipped topping such as Cool Whip, thawed
Chopped or dried fruit to taste

Mix yogurt, whipped topping, and fruit together. Pour into pie crust. Refrigerate until set. A light and cool treat; vary the fruit and yogurt for a surprise!

Erin Zolotukhin-Ridgway, Saint Paul Public Library, St. Paul, MN

"If you wish to make an apple pie truly from scratch, you must first invent the universe."
Carl Sagan (1934-1996) *Cosmos*

Susie's Pie Crust

3 cups all purpose flour, divided
1 teaspoon salt
11/3 cup shortening, sweet butter, or a combination of the two
½ cup ice-cold water

In a large bowl mix salt and 2 ½ cups of flour. Cut in the shortening and/or butter until it resembles tiny peas. In a small bowl combine the remainder of the flour and water, pour into dry flour mixture, and mix with a fork until almost all is moist. Gather together into a ball so it can be then divided into 2 or 3 equal pieces and stored in the refrigerator until ready to roll out. This recipe can be refrigerated for a day or two, or frozen for a month. Yields 3 single pie crusts

Sue Padilla, Newton Public Library, Newton, IA

"The fine arts are five in number, namely: painting, sculpture, poetry, music, and architecture, the principal branch of the latter being pastry." Antonin Carême (Marie-Antoine Carême) (1783-1833) Founder and architect of French haute cuisine

641.8653 Brownies (Cookery)

Bookish Brownies

4 squares unsweetened chocolate (1 square=1 oz.)
¾ cup shortening
4 eggs
2 cups sugar
1 cup flour
1 teaspoon vanilla
Pinch salt

Melt chocolate and shortening in the microwave (probably about 5 minutes at 70% power, depending on the microwave). Or, you can melt them together slowly in a double boiler over hot water. Set aside. Beat together the eggs until thick and lemon-colored. Add the sugar, flour, chocolate mixture, vanilla, and salt. Mix well. Pour batter in a 13" x 9" inches pan that has been sprayed with a cooking spray (bottom of pan only.) Bake 25 minutes at 350 degrees (25 minutes is the secret to these brownies--they are a chewy, fudge-like brownie.) Frost when cool.

Frosting:

2 squares unsweetened baking chocolate
3 tablespoons water
12 large marshmallows (or 1 heaping cup of mini-marshmallows)
3 tablespoons butter
1 teaspoon vanilla
1¾ cup powdered sugar

Melt these slowly in a double boiler over hot water or in the microwave (approximately 5 minutes at 70% power). Stir together. (Mixture will be somewhat curdled.) Add vanilla and powdered sugar. Beat until well mixed.

The brownies are also good with a chocolate mint patty set on top to melt and spread.

Mary Herold, Cresco Public Library, Cresco, IA

"Research tells us fourteen out of any ten individuals likes chocolate."
Sandra Boynton (1953-) American children's author

Buttermilk Brownies

2 sticks butter
1 cup water
4 tablespoons cocoa
2 cups flour
2 cups sugar
½ teaspoon salt
2 eggs, beaten
1 teaspoon baking soda
1 teaspoon vanilla
½ cup buttermilk

In a two-quart saucepan bring the butter, water, and cocoa to a boil. Add the flour, sugar, salt, eggs, soda, vanilla, and buttermilk and mix until blended. Bake in a jelly-roll pan at 350 degrees for 20-30 minutes. Frost when cool.

Frosting

1 stick butter, melted
4 tablespoons cocoa
6 tablespoons buttermilk
1 pound powdered sugar
1 teaspoon vanilla

In a small saucepan melt the margarine, cocoa, and buttermilk. Remove from burner and add powdered sugar. Beat well and add vanilla. Frost while brownies are hot!

Connie Mataloni, Sibley Public Library, Sibley, IA

JJ's Utility Optmization Brownies

11 ounces butter
2 pounds, 3 ounces bittersweet chocolate
8 eggs
4 ½ ounces sugar
7 ounces all-purpose flour
1½ teaspoon real vanilla extract

Butter and flour a 2-quart baking dish. Melt butter and chocolate over hot water and let cool slightly. Whip eggs and sugar until very light and high -- they should at least double in bulk. Mix in vanilla very briefly. Fold in cooled chocolate and flour. Scrape into pan and smooth. Bake at 375 degrees until just set. Refrigerate overnight. These are good as above, but there's an even better way, albeit it's more trouble. Bake them 375 degrees until just set. Let them cool, then wrap them air-tight and let them sit, at room temperature. They improve with sitting, after about four days they are sublime.

A note on chocolate: because there's so high a proportion of chocolate in these, what chocolate you use matters. I favor Callebaut Dark, which is about 52% cocoa mass. They're quite good made with a 70% cocoa mass chocolate, but then they're not sweet enough for most people. One solution to this is to add sugar, another is to frost them with ganache:

Ganache

12 ounces chocolate, chopped into pieces the size of a quarter
1 cup heavy cream
1½ teaspoon vanilla extract

Put the chocolate in a heat proof bowl. Heat the cream until it just comes to a boil. Pour the cream over the chocolate and stir, slowly, until all the chocolate melts. Stir in the vanilla and let it set up at room temperature. Variables: It will take anywhere from 3-8 hours to set up, depending on the temperature of your kitchen and, once again, the chocolate. With a chocolate of higher than about 55% cocoa mass you'll need a little more cream, as you will if your chocolate is old.

(This recipe modified from one courtesy of Joann Carmody Vasquez)
These have won tolerable popularity with my classmates here at SI.

JJ Jacobson , MSI Program, School of Information, University of Michigan

"There are two kinds of people in this world. Those who love chocolate and communists."
Leslie Moak Murray in *Murray's Law* comic strip

Kahlua Brownies

2 sticks margarine
1 cup Kahlua
4 tablespoons cocoa
1 tablespoon vanilla
2 cups flour
2 cups sugar
2 eggs
½ cup sour milk
1 teaspoon baking soda

Frosting:

1 stick margarine
3 tablespoons milk
4 tablespoons cocoa
1 pound powdered sugar

In a saucepan or a microwave, bring 2 sticks of margarine, the water-Kahlua mix, 4 tablespoons cocoa, and vanilla to a boil. While still hot, add the flour and sugar and beat until blended. Add the eggs and beat. Add the sour milk and baking soda. Pour into a 13" x 9" baking pan, or a 16" x 12" shallow cookie sheet; batter will be thin. Bake at 400 degrees for 20 minutes. Meanwhile, prepare the frosting. In a saucepan or microwave, place the margarine, milk, and cocoa to a boil. Add in the powdered sugar and blend. Pour frosting on the brownies while still hot from the oven.

Kim Byers, patron, Hiawatha Public Library, Hiawatha, IA

"'Tis an ill cook that cannot lick his own fingers."
William Shakespeare, English poet and playwright (1564-1616) *Romeo and Juliet*

197

641.8653 Cake.

Almond Sherry Cake

1 package yellow cake mix (not pudding type)
4 large eggs
¾ cup cream sherry
¾ cup vegetable oil
1 package instant vanilla pudding mix
½ teaspoon nutmeg
1/3 cup brown sugar, packed
¼ cup flour
3 tablespoons firm butter
½ teaspoon cinnamon
¾ cup almonds, sliced

Grease and flour a 10" Bundt pan; set aside. Combine cake mix, eggs, sherry, oil, pudding mix, and nutmeg. Mix on low speed, 1 minute, scraping bowl constantly. Mix at medium speed approximately 3 minutes, scraping bowl occasionally. Pour half of the batter into the Bundt pan. Mix brown sugar, flour, butter, and cinnamon together until crumbly to make the streusel. Stir in almonds. Sprinkle the batter evenly with streusel filling. Pour in the remaining batter. Bake at 350 degrees for 45-50 minutes or until cake springs back when touched lightly. Cool on wire rack for 15 minutes. Remove from pan and cool completely on rack. Brush with sherry glaze; garnish with almonds.

Glaze:

2 cups powdered sugar, sifted
1/3 cup butter, melted
1 tablespoon cream sherry

Stir together and add 1 to 2 teaspoons of hot water until glaze is of desired consistency.

Ann Garas, patron, Rockford Public Library, Rockford, IL

"There is no sight more appealing than the sight of a woman making dinner for someone she loves."
Thomas Wolfe (1900-1938) American novelist

Apple-Cinnamon Crumb Cake

2 tart cooking apples, peeled and sliced
½ teaspoon lemon juice
1 tablespoon sugar
1 teaspoon cinnamon, divided
1¼ cups flour
2/3 cup sugar
1/8 teaspoon salt
¼ cup butter, chilled & cut in pieces
½ teaspoon baking powder
¼ teaspoon baking soda
1/3 cup nonfat plain yogurt
2 tablespoons water
1 large egg

Preheat oven to 350 degrees. Toss apple slices in a bowl with lemon juice, 1 tablespoon sugar and ½ teaspoon cinnamon. Spread slices evenly in the bottom of a 10" pie plate that has been coated with cooking spray. Combine flour, 2/3 cup sugar, and salt in a bowl; cut in butter with a pastry blender or two knives. Reserve ½ cup flour mixture for topping; set aside. Combine remaining flour mixture, baking powder, and baking soda; add yogurt, water, and egg. Beat at medium speed of a mixer until blended. Spread batter over apples. Combine reserved flour mixture and ½ teaspoon cinnamon. Sprinkle crumb mixture over batter. Bake at 350 degrees for 30 minutes. Cool on a wire rack. Cut in wedges to serve.

Cindi Carey Lacey Timberland Library, Lacey, WA

"The only real stumbling block is fear of failure. In cooking you've got to have a what-the-hell attitude."
Julia Child (1921-2004) Cookbook author and television cooking show host

Burnt Sugar Cake

1½ cups sugar
½ cup margarine or butter
3 eggs, separated and beaten
1 cup water
¼ cup burnt sugar*
2½ cups flour
2 teaspoon baking powder
1 teaspoon vanilla

Cream margarine and sugar. Add beaten egg yolks and burnt sugar. Sift together flour and baking powder and add to creamed mixture alternately with water beating after each addition. Add vanilla and fold in beaten egg whites. Pour into greased 13"x 9" or 2 round cake pans. Bake in 350 degree oven for 35-40 minutes.

*How to Make Burnt Sugar:
Use a heavy fry pan. Place over high heat. Add 1 cup sugar. Stir constantly until dark golden brown. Add 1 cup boiling water. Cook while stirring constantly for 3 minutes. Some of the burnt sugar may be saved and added to the frosting for flavor and color.

Maybeth Gilliam, Retired, Blairstown Public Library, Blairstown, IA

Chocolate Zucchini Cake

2 eggs
1¾ cups sugar
½ cup sour cream
2 cups flour
½ teaspoon cinnamon
½ teaspoon cloves
½ cup nuts, coarsely chopped
½ cup chocolate chips
1 cup vegetable oil
2 cups zucchini, grated
1 teaspoon vanilla
1 teaspoon baking soda
4 tablespoons cocoa
½ teaspoon salt

Cream oil, eggs, sugar, vanilla and sour cream. Add dry ingredients and zucchini. Pour into 13" x 9" pan and sprinkle nuts and chocolate chips on top. Bake at 325 degrees for 45-50 minutes.

Dee Davisson, Waukee Public Library, Waukee, IA

Cookies-and-Cream Cake

1 white cake mix
1 ¼ cup water
1/3 cup vegetable oil
3 egg whites
2 cups, about 20, Oreo cookies, crushed and divided
1 16-ounce can vanilla frosting

Preheat oven to 350 degrees. In a large bowl, combine cake mix, water, oil, and egg whites until smooth; gently stir in 1½ cups crushed cookies. Pour batter into greased-and-floured 13"x 9" cake pan. Bake 25-35 minutes or until toothpick inserted in center comes out clean. Cool completely. Mix together frosting and ½ cup Oreo cookies until well blended and spread over cake.

Jean Gullikson, Carnegie-Stout Public Library, Dubuque, IA

Death-By-Chocolate Cake

¾ cup sour cream
4 eggs
½ cup water
½ cup oil
1 chocolate cake mix
1 small box instant chocolate pudding
1 cup semisweet chocolate chips
Powdered sugar

Preheat oven to 350 degrees. Beat sour cream, eggs, water, and oil together in a large bowl until thoroughly mixed. Add cake mix and pudding mix. Stir in chocolate chips. Place batter in a greased and floured Bundt pan. Bake 45-55 minutes or until a fork inserted into cake comes out clean. While still hot, invert cake onto a serving platter. When cool, sift powdered sugar over top of cake.

Jean Gullikson, Carnegie-Stout Public Library, Dubuque, IA

"The appetites of the stomach and palate, far from diminishing as men grow older, go on increasing."
Cicero (106-43 B.C.E.) Roman statesman

Dirt Cake

1 box chocolate cake mix
1 large box instant chocolate pudding
1 large container of frozen whipped topping such as Cool Whip, thawed
1 package of Oreo or Hydrox cookies
1-2 packages of gummy worms
1 artificial flower, preferably a daisy

Prepare the cake and cut it into 1" squares. Prepare the pudding. Crush all of the cookies into large pieces ¼" reserving about 1 cup. Mix the large cookie pieces with the whipped topping. Crush the remaining cookies into a finer 'dirt.' Layer cake squares in a large, clean flower pot about 8"across (cover drainage hole with foil.) Layer chocolate pudding. Layer cookie/whipped topping mix. Toss in a few gummy worms. Repeat until these ingredients have been used. Cover with cookie 'dirt' and press the few gummy worms into the pot.

Charlotte Rabbitt, Peterborough Town Library, Peterborough, NH

Easy Apple Cake

½ cup margarine or shortening
1 cup sugar
½ cup brown sugar
2 eggs, beaten
2 teaspoons baking soda
1 cup sour milk or buttermilk
2 ¼ cups flour
½ teaspoon salt
1 teaspoon cinnamon
¼ teaspoon cloves
¼ teaspoon nutmeg
2 cups apples, chopped
¼ cup brown sugar
¼ cup granulated sugar
½ cup nuts

Cream together sugar and margarine. In a separate bowl mix the flour, salt, cinnamon, cloves, and nutmeg. Add the beaten eggs. Dissolve baking soda in sour milk or buttermilk. Add the milk mixture to the sugar/margarine mixture alternating with dry mixture until blended. Fold in apples. (Batter will be thick.) Pour mixture in a 13" x 9" pan. Prepare the topping by mixing the brown sugar, granulated sugar, and nuts. Sprinkle over the cake batter. Bake at 350 degrees for 30 minutes.

Linda Magley, patron, Mesa Family History Center Library, Mesa, AZ

Harriet Orr's Grandmother's Spice Cake

This cake was always the first thing to disappear at the Lion's Club ice cream social in my hometown of West Chester, Iowa.

2 ½ cups sugar, divided
2/3 cups solid vegetable shortening such as Crisco
4 eggs
1 cup buttermilk
2 cups flour
1 ½ teaspoon cinnamon, divided
½ teaspoon nutmeg
¼ teaspoon cloves
1 teaspoon baking soda
1 teaspoon hot water
½ cup nuts, coarsely chopped
½ cup sugar
½ teaspoon cinnamon
½ cup nuts, chopped

Beat 2 cups sugar, shortening and eggs until very light. Sift together flour, 1 teaspoon cinnamon, nutmeg and cloves in a large bowl and set aside. Add flour mixture alternately with buttermilk to the sugar, shortening and eggs. Dissolve baking soda in warm water and fold in to the batter. Add coarsely chopped nuts and stir to blend. Pour in a 13" x 9" pan. In a small bowl stir ½ cup sugar, ½ teaspoon cinnamon and ½ cup chopped nuts until mixed. Sprinkle evenly over the cake batter. Bake at 350 degrees for about 40 minutes.

Kathy Fisher, Keosauqua Public Library, Keosauqua, IA

"'What I like about gluttony,' a bishop I knew used to say, 'is that it doesn't hurt anyone else.'"
Monica Fulong (1930-2003) British author

Holiday Rum Cake

1 cup pecans, chopped and divided
1 ¾-ounce package vanilla instant pudding
1 box yellow butter cake mix such as Duncan Hines
½ cup white rum
½ cup water
½ cup cooking oil
4 eggs
1 cup sugar
½ stick butter
3 tablespoons water
¼ cup rum
½ cup pecans, chopped

Grease and flour Bundt pan (I use Baker's Joy for ease). Sprinkle ½ cup nuts into bottom of pan. Into large bowl, place cake and pudding mixes. Add ½ cup rum, water, oil, and eggs. Mix for 2 minutes on medium speed. Pour mixture into Bundt pan and bake at 325 degrees for 50-60 minutes. Meanwhile to prepare glaze, mix sugar, butter, 3 tablespoons water, ¼ cup rum, and ½ cup chopped pecans in a small saucepan and boil for 2 minutes until syrupy. Remove cake from oven when ready. Pour hot glaze over cake while it is still in the pan. Hot glaze causes cake to settle. Cool in pan for 30 minutes, then remove to serving plate.

Jennifer Hartshorn, District of Columbia Public Library-Martin Luther King, Jr. Memorial Library, Washington, DC

"On days when warmth is the most important need of the human heart, the kitchen is the place you can find it."
E.B. White (1899-1985) American author and poet

Hummingbird Cake

3 cups flour
2 cups sugar
1 teaspoon salt
1 teaspoon soda
1 teaspoon cinnamon
3 eggs, beaten
1½ cups vegetable oil
2½ teaspoons vanilla, divided
1 8½-ounce can crushed pineapple
2 cups pecans, chopped and divided
2 cups bananas, mashed
8 ounces cream cheese, softened
½ cup butter, softened
1 pound powdered sugar

Combine dry ingredients for cake in a large mixing bowl. Add eggs and oil, stirring until dry ingredients are moistened, but do not beat. Stir in 1½ teaspoons vanilla, pineapple, 1 cup nuts and bananas. Spoon batter into 3 well greased and floured 9" round cake pans. Bake at 350 degrees for 25 minutes or until cake tests done. Cool in pans 10 minutes, then remove and cool. Meanwhile combine cream cheese and butter in a small bowl and mix until smooth. Add powdered sugar and beat until light and fluffy. Stir in 1 teaspoon vanilla. When cake is cool, spread frosting between layers and on top and sides of cake. Sprinkle with remaining pecans.

Devon Murphy-Petersen, Waukee Public Library, Waukee, IA
Sue Padilla, Newton Public Library, Newton, IA

"When I am in trouble, eating is the only thing that consoles me. Indeed, when I am really in great trouble, as anyone who knows me intimately will tell you, I refuse everything except food and drink."
Oscar Wilde (1854-1900) Irish novelist and dramatist

Raw Apple Cake with Butter Sauce

2 cups sugar
½ cup margarine
2 eggs, beaten
2 cups flour
1 teaspoon baking soda
2-4 teaspoons cinnamon
1-2 teaspoons nutmeg
1 teaspoon salt
4 cups apples, finely chopped
1 cup pecans, chopped

Cream butter and sugar; add beaten eggs. Sift dry ingredients together and add to batter. Add apples and nuts. Bake in a greased 13" x 9" pan at 350 degrees for 15 minutes. Lower the oven to 300 degrees and continue baking for at least 45 minutes. Serve warm with butter sauce.

Butter Sauce

1 cup sugar
½ cup butter (no substitutions)
½ cup half and half
1 teaspoon vanilla

Cook together over low heat, stirring constantly until mixture coats spoon.

Denise Crawford, Glenwood Public Library, Glenwood, IA

"No one who cooks, cooks alone. Even at her most solitary, a cook in the kitchen is surrounded by generations of cooks past, the advice and menus of cooks present, the wisdom of cookbook writers."
Laurie Colwin (1944-1992) American author

Rhubarb Cake

¾ cup butter or margarine
1½ cups flour
4 tablespoons sugar, divided
2 egg yolks
6 cups rhubarb
2 cups sugar
9 tablespoons flour
½ cup cream
2 eggs

Mix butter or margarine, flour, 2 tablespoons sugar and egg yolks together; mix like a pie crust with pastry blender, or forks until crumbly. Press into 13" x 9" pan. Mix rhubarb, sugar, and flour. Place over crust mixture. Blend cream, 2 eggs and 2 tablespoons of sugar. Pour over the rhubarb and bake 350 degrees for about 1 hour.

Linda Magley, patron, Mesa Family History Center Library, Mesa, AZ

The traditional role of rhubarb was medicinal. Because of this the cost was high. In 1542, rhubarb sold for ten times the price of cinnamon in France and in 1657 rhubarb sold for over twice the price of opium in England. foodreference.com

Rum Cake

1 cup pecans, chopped
1 yellow cake mix
1 package instant vanilla pudding
4 eggs
½ cup cold water
½ cup oil
½ cup dark rum

Glaze:

¼ pound butter or margarine
¼ cup water
1 cup sugar
½ cup dark rum

Preheat oven to 325 degrees. Grease and flour tube pan. Sprinkle nuts over bottom of pan. Mix together remaining ingredients and pour over nuts. Bake 1 hour. Set on rack to cool. Prepare glaze; melt butter in saucepan; stir in water and sugar; heat to boiling. Boil 5 minutes stirring constantly. Take off heat, stir in rum. Invert cake on to a serving plate; prick top. Drizzle and brush glaze over top and sides.

Susan Kling, Marion Public Library, Marion, IA

Shelly's Krazy Kake

3 cups flour
2 cups sugar
½ teaspoon salt
2 teaspoons baking soda
1/3 cup cocoa
1 teaspoon vanilla
3 teaspoons vinegar
¾ cup salad oil
2 cups water

Sift together the flour, sugar, salt, baking soda and cocoa 3 times into large mixing bowl. Poke 3 holes in mix and pour in first hole: vanilla, second hole; vinegar, and third hole: salad oil Pour water over all and blend well. Bake in an ungreased 13" x 9" pan in a 350 degree oven for 30-35 minutes. Cool and frost with following:

Frosting #1

2 ½ tablespoons flour
½ cup milk
½ cup butter
½ cup sugar

Stir flour into milk and cook over low heat to a thick paste; cool. Cream butter and sugar and beat in the cooled milk mixture. Beat until fluffy, spread on cake.

Frosting #2

2 tablespoons cocoa
2 tablespoons white corn syrup
½ cup sugar
¼ cup milk
½ cup butter
1 teaspoon vanilla

Combine all ingredients in a saucepan. Bring slowly to a rolling boil, stirring constantly. Boil for 1 minute. Cool to lukewarm; add vanilla. Beat until thick. Pour over first frosting.

Linda Magley, patron, Mesa Family History Center Library, Mesa, AZ

Sour Cream Pound Cake

1 cup butter
3 cups sugar
6 eggs
1 cup sour cream with ¼ teaspoon baking soda dissolved in it
1 teaspoon vanilla extract
2 teaspoons almond extract
3 cups flour

Cream butter and sugar, add extracts. Add eggs one at a time, beating well after each addition. Add flour alternately with sour cream, beginning and ending with the flour. Pour into a greased and floured 10 " tube pan. Bake at 300 degrees for 90 minutes or until done.

Note: I have used fat free sour cream, substituted applesauce for part of the butter, and even used part egg-beaters. It all works.

Virginia Holsten, Vinton Public Library, Vinton, IA

Turtle Cake

1 box German chocolate cake mix
1 stick margarine, softened
1 14-ounce bag of caramels (Kraft works best)
1 cup chocolate chips
1 cup nuts
1 12-ounce can evaporated milk

Grease bottom of 13" x 9" baking pan. Mix dry cake mix with ½ can evaporated milk plus stick margarine (mix will be thick.) Pat ½ of this mixture into the baking pan. Bake 15 minutes at 350 degrees. While cake is baking, melt caramels and remaining evaporated milk. Remove from oven and spread warm caramel over cake. Sprinkle chocolate chips and nuts over the caramel topping. Add remaining cake batter over top with spoon. Bake 15-20 minutes at 350 degrees. Test with toothpick. Enjoy!

Margaret J. Ross, McNees Wallace & Nurick LLC, Harrisburg, PA

"Ponder well on this point: the pleasant hours of our life are all connected by a more or less tangible link, with some memory of the table."
Charles Pierre Monselet (1825-1888) French author

Wild About Coconut Cake

1 box white cake mix, prepared as directed
1 can Cream de Casa Cream of Coconut
1 12-ounce container frozen whipped topping such as Cool Whip, thawed
1 can sweetened condensed milk
1 small bag sweetened coconut

Follow directions on cake mix and bake in 13" x 9" pan. When removed from oven, poke a generous amount of holes with the end of a wooden spoon through the cake. Mix ½ can cream of coconut and ½ can sweetened condensed milk. Pour over cake. Cover with waxed paper and refrigerate to chill. Mix remaining cream of coconut with whipped topping and frost cake with this. Generously sprinkle loose coconut over the top. Refrigerate before serving.

Judy Havlik, Algona Community Schools, Algona, IA

641.8653 Icings, Cake.

Cake Decorating Frosting

2 pounds powdered sugar
¼ cup flour
1 teaspoon meringue powder
1¼ cups vegetable shorting
1 tablespoon white syrup
1 teaspoon white vanilla
1 teaspoon almond flavoring
Pinch of salt
½ cup cold water

Mix all ingredients for 3-5 minutes. Stir. Mix an additional 3-5 minutes. Makes enough to frost 2 cakes or frost and decorate a 2-layer cake.

Eileen Robinson, Marion Public Library, Marion, IA

"We owe much to the fruitful meditations of our sages, but a sane view of life is, after all, elaborated mainly in the kitchen."
Joseph Conrad (1857-1924) English novelist

Amanda's Scotcharoos

6 cups puffed rice cereal, such as Rice Krispies
6 ounces chocolate chips
6 ounces butterscotch chips
1 cup corn syrup
1 cup sugar
1 cup peanut butter
1 teaspoon vanilla

Bring sugar, peanut butter and corn syrup to a boil in a large pot and then immediately remove from heat. Mix in Rice Krispies. Pour into a 13" x 9" pan and spread evenly. Melt chocolate and butterscotch chips together in a medium bowl in the microwave; make sure they do not burn (melt in 30-second intervals.) Pour melted chips over the Rice Krispies mixture, and then smooth to cover. Let stand overnight or until set with a paper towel over the dish. Then cut into squares.

Amanda Gilreath, Waukee Public Library, Waukee, IA

Chocolate Crumb Bars

1 cup butter
2 cups flour
½ cup sugar
¼ teaspoon salt
1 teaspoon vanilla
1 bag (2 cups) chocolate chips
1 ¼ cups (14 ounces) sweetened condensed milk
1 cup nuts, chopped

Cream butter. Beat in flour, sugar, and salt until crumbly. Press 2 cups of the crumb mixture onto the bottom of a greased 13" x 9" pan. Reserve remaining mixture. Bake 10-12 minutes at 350 degrees until the edges are golden brown. Warm ½ cup chocolate chips and sweetened condensed milk in a saucepan over a low heat, stirring until smooth. Stir in vanilla. Spread over the hot crust. Stir nuts and remaining chips into the reserved crumb mixture. Sprinkle over the filling. Bake 25-30 minutes or until center is set. Cool pan on wire rack; cut when cool.

Lorraine Burdic, Jefferson County Library, Port Hadlock, WA

Coffee Bars

1 cup raisins
2/3 cup strong coffee
½ teaspoon cinnamon
2/3 cup shortening
1 cup sugar
2 eggs
1 ½ cups flour, sifted
½ teaspoon baking powder
½ teaspoon soda
¼ teaspoon salt
1½ cups powdered sugar
Strong coffee

Combine raisins, coffee, and cinnamon and set aside. Cream shortening and sugar well. Add eggs, one at a time, beating well after each addition. Sift together dry ingredients; stir into egg mixture alternately with the coffee and raisin mixture. Spread batter into a greased 10" x 15" x 1" jelly roll pan; bake 20-25 minutes at 350 degrees. While still warm, spread with coffee glaze made by adding enough strong coffee to 1½ cups powdered sugar to make a thin frosting. Cut when cool.

Jean Hampson, Marion Public Library, Marion, IA

Corn Flake Bars

1 cup white corn syrup
1 cup white sugar
1 cup creamy peanut butter
6 cups corn flakes
¾ cup semi-sweet chocolate chips
¾ cup butterscotch flavored chips

In a heavy saucepan, combine corn syrup, sugar, and peanut butter. Heat until the mixture just reaches a boil but do not boil. Remove from heat. Add corn flakes; stir to coat. Press into a well-greased 13" x 9" pan. Melt the chips in a double boiler or the microwave. Spread over the bars. *My all time favorite recipe to bring to work!*

Ann Hanson, Cook Memorial Public Library District, Libertyville, IL

"Do you know what breakfast cereal is made of? It's made of all those little curly wooden shavings you find in pencil sharpeners!"
Roald Dahl, British children's author (1916-1990*) Charlie and the Chocolate Factory,* 1964

Frangipane-Cherry Bars

Shortbread Crust

¾ cup butter (1 ½ sticks), softened (no substitutions)
¾ cup confectioners' sugar
1½ teaspoons vanilla extract
2¼ cups all-purpose flour

Frangipane Filling

1 tube, or can (7-8 ounces) almond paste, crumbled
½ cup granulated sugar
4 tablespoons butter, softened (no substitutions)
¼ teaspoon salt
2 large eggs
2 teaspoons vanilla extract
¼ cup all-purpose flour

Jam Layer

1 cup, (about a 12 ounce jar) sour-cherry jam
½ cup almonds, sliced

Preheat oven to 375 degrees. Grease 13" x 9" metal baking pan. Line pan with foil; grease foil. Prepare shortbread crust: In medium bowl, stir flour with confectioners' sugar. With pastry blender or two knives used scissor-fashion, cut in butter until mixture resembles fine crumbs. Press crumbs on bottom of pan to form crust. Bake crust 16-18 minutes or until light golden. Remove pan from oven; cool crust in pan on wire rack.
Meanwhile, prepare frangipane filling: In large bowl, with mixer at low speed, beat almond paste, sugar, butter, and salt until crumbly. Increase speed to medium, and beat until combined, scraping bowl frequently with rubber spatula, about 3 minutes (some tiny lumps of almond paste will remain). Beat in eggs and vanilla until smooth. Beat in flour just until combined.
Spread jam over crust in pan. Carefully pour almond-paste mixture over jam, spreading with small metal spatula if necessary. Sprinkle top with almonds.
Bake 25-30 minutes or until top is light golden. Cool in pan on wire rack.
When cool, transfer bars with foil to cutting board. Cut lengthwise into 8 strips, then cut each strip crosswise into 4 pieces. Store bars in a tightly covered container up to 2 weeks.

Susan Henricks, Carnegie-Stout Public Library, Dubuque, IA

213

Frangipane is a rich pastry cream flavored with ground almonds and used to fill or top pastries and cakes. The name has a very unusual origin. In the 16th century an Italian nobleman, Marquis Muzio Frangipani, created a perfume for scenting gloves. It was popular in Paris, and pastry cooks flavored pastry cream with almonds and called it 'frangipane,' presumably to take advantage of the scents popularity. foodreference.com

Lemon Bars

1 cup flour
½ cup butter or margarine softened
½ cup powdered sugar
2 eggs
1 cup sugar
½ teaspoon baking powder
¼ spoon salt
2 tablespoons fresh lemon juice

Heat oven to 350 degrees. Mix flour, butter, and powdered sugar, press evenly in bottom of ungreased 8" x 8" pan. (Use a 13" x 9" pan if doubling the recipe.) Bake 20 minutes. Beat remaining ingredients about 3 minutes or until light and fluffy. Pour over hot crust. Bake about 25 minutes longer or until no imprint remains when touched lightly in center. Cool, cut, and serve. 1 batch makes 16 cookies or double the recipe for 32

Linda Magley, patron, Mesa Family History Center Library, Mesa, AZ

Nestle Toll House Treat

1 package Nestle Toll House Cookie Dough (walnut chocolate chip, chocolate chip or cookie dough of your choice.)
Vegetable cooking spray, such as Pam
Peanut butter, creamy or crunchy, such as Reese's
1 ½ package Nestle Toll House morsels
Nuts, optional

Spray a 6" up to 9" non-stick baking pan lightly with vegetable cooking spray. Press cookie dough in the center of pan and press out to the edges. Double the baking time on label, but watch closely to keep from burning. Remove cookie and allow cooling. Melt chocolate morsels. Spread on a layer of peanut butter to the edges of the cookies, while it is still warm. Add the optional layer of nuts if you wish. Pour the melted chocolate all over the top and spread. Allow this to sit and cool. Refrigerate at least 1 hour. Cut in small squares; cover with plastic wrap.

Martha A. Boyd, Greensboro Public Library, Greensboro, NC

Peanut Butter Squares

1 cup corn syrup
1 cup brown sugar
1½ cups peanut butter
7 cups crispy rice cereal

Measure rice cereal into a very large bowl. Set aside. Combine corn syrup and sugar in a medium saucepan and cook over medium high heat, stirring occasionally until boiling. Lower heat and stir in peanut butter until smooth. (take off the heat if mixture appears to be sticking to the bottom of the pan.) Pour over cereal and mix with a sturdy spoon until all is coated. Pour and spread in a 13" x 9" baking pan. Coat palms of hands with butter or margarine and then press mixture to flatten and level in the pan so that the bars will hold together. Cut into squares while warm. Let cool in pan before serving.

Variations:

Spread melted semi-sweet chocolate chips over the top.
Add sunflower seeds or M & M candies to the mixture.
Use either smooth or chunky peanut butter.

Sue Padilla, Newton Public Library, Newton, IA

Peanut Squares II

4 cups Cheerios
2 cups Rice Krispies
2 cups peanuts
2 cups M & M candies
1 cup sugar
1 cup corn syrup
1½ cups peanut butter
1 teaspoon vanilla extract

Combine Cheerios, Rice Krispies, peanuts, and M & M candies in a very large bowl. Set aside. In a medium saucepan over medium heat, cook sugar and corn starch until it comes to a boil. Stir in peanut butter and vanilla. Pour the peanut butter mixture over the cereal mixture and stir with a heavy spoon until the cereal is well coated. Pour in a 13" x 9" pan. Coat palms of hands with butter or margarine and press the mixture in the pan so that the mix is level and holds together. Cut into squares while warm. Cool before serving.

Sue Padilla, Newton Public Library, Newton, IA

Rhubarb Dream Bars

2 cups flour
½ cup flour
1 cup margarine, melted
2 cups sugar
2/3 cup powdered sugar
¾ tablespoon salt
4 eggs
4 cups rhubarb, diced

Combine flour, margarine, and powdered sugar. Pat in a 13" x 9" baking pan sprayed with a cooking oil spray. Bake 350 degrees for 15 minutes or until edges begin to brown. Beat eggs. Add sugar and continue beating. Add flour and salt. Fold in rhubarb. Pour over baked layer and bake 45 minutes at 350 degrees. Cut into squares.

Judy Thompson, Manning Junior-Senior High School Library, Manning, IA

641.8654 Cookies.

Andes Crème de Menthe Chocolate Cookies

10 oz. bag Andes crème de menthe baking chips
1¼ cups butter, softened
2 cups sugar
2 eggs
2 teaspoons vanilla
2 cups plus 2 tablespoons all-purpose flour
¾ cup cocoa powder
1 teaspoon baking soda
½ teaspoon salt

Preheat oven to 350 degrees. In large bowl, cream butter and sugar. Beat in eggs and vanilla. Combine flour, cocoa, baking soda, and salt; gradually blend into creamed mixture. Stir in Andes baking chips. Drop by teaspoonfuls onto ungreased cookie sheets. Bake for 8-9 minutes. Do not over bake; cookies will be soft. They will puff during baking and flatten upon cooling. Cool on cookie sheets about 1 minute before removing to wire rack to cool completely. Yields 4 dozen.

Candice Michalik, Lynchburg Public Library Lynchburg, VA

"Part of the secret of success in life is to eat what you like and let the food fight it out inside." Mark Twain (Samuel Longhorne Clemens) (1835-1910) American author

Chocolate Chip Pudding Cookies

2 cups butter
1 ½ cups brown sugar, packed
½ cup sugar
2 small packages chocolate fudge instant pudding mix
2 teaspoons vanilla
2 teaspoons baking soda
4 ½ cups flour
1 12-ounce package chocolate chips
1 cup nuts, chopped

Cream the butter, brown and white sugars, pudding mix and vanilla until well blended. Add the baking soda and flour. Stir in the chocolate chips and nuts. Batter will be stiff. Drop by tablespoon on to cookie sheets. Bake at 350 degrees for 10-12 minutes.

Deb Leckband, Woodbury County Library, Moville, IA

Chocolate Oatmeal No-Bakes

1 stick butter or margarine 2 cups sugar
½ cup milk
½ cup cocoa powder
½ cup peanut butter, creamy or chunky
1 teaspoon vanilla
3 cups "old fashioned" oatmeal

Line two cookie sheets with aluminum foil. Use two soupspoons to scoop out the cookie mix. Have vanilla and peanut butter ready to add to hot mixture. Place sugar and cocoa in container with lid. Shake until the sugar and cocoa are well mixed. Melt butter in large pot. When butter is melted add the milk and the sugar/cocoa mix stirring until smooth. Cook over medium heat until mixture comes to a boil. Continue stirring for about two minutes maintaining a slow boil. Remove pan from heat. Immediately add vanilla; mix. Add the peanut butter and stir until the mixture is well blended. Stir in one cup of oatmeal at a time, mixing well between additions. Immediately start scooping heaping tablespoons of the mix on to the cookie sheets. Cool before serving. Someone you really like gets to lick the bowl.

"Central heating, French rubber goods and cookbooks are three amazing proofs of man's ingenuity in transforming necessity into art, and, of these, cookbooks are perhaps most lastingly delightful."
M.F.K. Fisher (1908-1992) *Serve it Forth*, 1937

Cream Cheese Cookies

1 cup butter or margarine
2 cups flour
1 teaspoon salt
3 tablespoons water
5 ounces cream cheese

Stir together the butter, flour, salt and water. Knead in the cream cheese. Roll out onto a floured surface to ¼" thickness. Cut into small circles by using a small cookie cutter or a small glass. Bake at 375 degrees for about 10 minutes. The top should be golden brown and the bottom semi-brown. Cool. Roll in powdered sugar. Yields 112 single cookies, or 56 filled

Cream Cheese Filling

3 ounces cream cheese, softened
1 tablespoon butter or margarine
1 teaspoon vanilla
2 cups powdered sugar

Stir until well blended. Use as filling between two cookies. Can be frozen before eating.

Faith, Jana, Kathi and Wanda, Red Oak Public Library, Red Oak, IA

Crunchy Chip Cookies

1 cup butter
½ cup sugar
1 ½ cups brown sugar, packed
2 eggs
1 ½ teaspoons vanilla
2 cups flour
1 teaspoon baking soda
½ teaspoon salt
2 cups quick-cooking oats
12 ounces chocolate chips
2 cups chow mien noodles

Beat butter and sugars until creamy and fluffy. Beat in eggs and vanilla. Gradually add sifted dry ingredients; mix well. Stir in oats, chocolate chips, and noodles. Drop by tablespoons onto greased cookie sheets 2" apart. Bake at 350 degrees for 15 minutes. Remove to wire rack to cool. Makes about 6 dozen

Cindi Carey, Lacey Timberland Library Lacey, Washington

Easy Peanut Butter Cookies.. for Unexpected Company

I use this recipe frequently. I am a busy person and when I need cookies in a hurry for church, or want to treat the gals at work, I whip these up. People read the recipe and think that I have left out an ingredient, but I haven't. This is it!

1 cup sugar
1 cup crunchy peanut butter
1 egg, beaten

Mix the sugar, peanut butter and egg together. Roll into balls. Place on a slightly greased cookie sheet about 2" apart. Press crosswise with a fork. Bake at 350 degrees until they are golden brown, about 12-15 minutes. Yields 2-2 ½ dozen.

Carolyn Walz, Estherville Public Library, Estherville, IA

Ginger Cookies

1 cup sugar
¾ cup shortening
1 egg
2 cups flour
2 teaspoons baking soda
¼ teaspoon salt
2 to 4 tablespoons molasses
¼ teaspoon cloves
1 teaspoon cinnamon
1 teaspoon ginger

Cream shortening and sugar and stir in the beaten egg. Add molasses. Sift remaining dry ingredients into this mixture. Mix well. Roll dough into walnut size balls, dipping side in sugar. Place sugar side up in pan. Bake 15-18 minutes at 350 degrees.

Judi Tjepkes, Gowrie Public Library, Gowrie, IA

"The kitchen is a country in which three are always discoveries to be made."
Grimod de la Reynière (1758-1838) French writer and famous gastronomist

Holiday Sugar Cookies

1½ cups powdered sugar, sifted
1 cup margarine
1 egg
1 teaspoon vanilla
½ teaspoon almond flavoring
2½ cups flour
1 teaspoon soda
1 teaspoon cream of tartar

Preheat oven to 375 degrees. Cream sugar and margarine. Mix in eggs and flavorings. Stir dry ingredients into sugar and margarine mixture. Refrigerate 2-3 hours. Roll dough using half a batch at a time. Cut. Bake 7-8 minutes.

Judi Tjepkes, Gowrie Public Library, Gowrie, IA

Lemon Drops

1 box lemon cake mix with pudding in the mix
2 eggs
½ cup vegetable oil

Mix ingredients together until blended. Shape heaping teaspoon of mix into ball with hands or scoop with small cookie scoop. Place balls on ungreased cookie sheet 2" apart. Flatten cookies with a glass dipped in sugar. Bake in 350 degree oven for 8-10 minutes or until edges are just barely browned.

My favorite emergency cookie recipe!

Cindy Dye, Greensboro Public Library, Greensboro, NC

"The duty of a good cusinier is to transmit to the next generation everything he has learned and experienced"
Fernand Point,1897-1955, French chef, Master of la grand cuisine and "Father of Novelle Cuisine"

Mint Chocolate Cookies

¾ cup butter
1½ cups brown sugar
2 tablespoons water
2 cups chocolate chips
2 eggs
2 ½ cups flour
1¼ teaspoons baking soda
½ teaspoon salt
Andes mints

Place butter, brown sugar, and water in a microwave safe bowl and microwave to melt ingredients. Add chocolate chips and stir until melted. Let cool 10 minutes. Using an electric mixer, add eggs, one at a time on high speed. Reduce to low and blend well for 2 minutes. Add flour, soda, and salt. Mix well and chill. When chilled, roll dough into balls; place on cookie sheet. Bake at 350 degrees for 6-8 minutes or until cookies have a cracked appearance. Remove from oven and immediately put an Andes mint on top. Let cool about 1 minute and swirl mint on top of the cookie to frost.

Linda Adams, Fayette Community Library, Fayette, IA

Oatmeal Crispies

1 cup shortening
1 cup brown sugar
1 cup white sugar
2 eggs, well beaten
1 teaspoon vanilla
1½ cup flour, sifted
1 teaspoon salt
1 teaspoon baking soda
3 cups quick oatmeal
½ cup nuts, chopped

Cream together shortening and sugars. Add eggs and vanilla; beat. Add flour, salt and soda. Add oats and nuts; stir to mix. Drop by teaspoonful onto lightly greased baking sheets. Bake at 350 degrees about 10 minutes.

Kathy Fisher, Keosauqua Public Library, Keosauqua, IA

Oatmeal Jumbos

1 cup peanut butter
½ cup butter
1½ cup brown sugar, packed
½ cup granulated sugar
1½ teaspoon baking powder
½ teaspoon baking soda
3 eggs
2 teaspoons vanilla
4 cups rolled oats
¾ cup peanuts or pecans, chopped
1½ cups M & M candies

In a mixing bowl beat peanut butter and butter with electric mixer 30 seconds. Add sugars, baking powder, and baking soda; beat until combined. Beat in eggs and vanilla. Stir in oats, then nuts and M & M candies. Drop dough by ¼ cup measure onto ungreased cookie sheets, about 4" apart. Bake in a 350 degree oven for 15 minutes or until the edges are light brown. Cool for 1 minute and transfer to a wire cooling rack. Cool. Makes 26 large cookies

Teresa Buckingham, Glenwood Public Library, Glenwood, IA

Old Fashioned Ginger Chews

4¾ cups flour
1 teaspoon cinnamon
2 teaspoons ginger
½ teaspoon cloves
1 teaspoon salt
3½ teaspoons baking soda
2 cups sugar
1 cup butter
2 eggs, beaten
1 cup light molasses
1 teaspoon vanilla

Mix together dry ingredients and set aside. Cream butter and sugar. Stir in eggs, molasses, and vanilla. Add dry ingredients and mix. Chill dough 1-2 hours. Roll into walnut-sized balls, and roll whole cookie in sugar. Place on greased baking sheet. Do not flatten. Bake at 350 degrees for 8-10 minutes. Makes 8 dozen

Susan Elgin, Waukee Public Library, Waukee, IA

Peanut Butter and M&M Cookies

¾ cup margarine or butter flavored shortening, such as Crisco
1 cup granulated sugar
1 cup brown sugar, firmly packed
½ cup peanut butter
2 eggs
2 teaspoons vanilla
2 ½ cups flour
1 teaspoon baking soda
½ teaspoon salt
1 16-ounce package M & M candies

Preheat oven to 350 degrees. Beat shortening, sugars and peanut butter in a large bowl with mixer on medium speed until light and fluffy. Blend in eggs and vanilla. Mix in flour baking soda and salt. Stir in M & M's. Drop by rounded tablespoonfuls onto ungreased cookie sheets. Bake 10-12 minutes or until lightly browned. Cool 2 minutes; remove from cookie sheets onto wire racks. Makes about 4 dozen

Candice Michalik, Lynchburg Public Library Lynchburg, VA

Pecan Tarts

1 3-ounce package cream cheese
½ cup butter
1 cup flour, sifted
1 egg
1 tablespoon butter, softened
¾ cup brown sugar
1 teaspoon vanilla
Dash salt
2/3 cup pecans, coarsely broken

Cheese Pastry: Let cream cheese and ½ cup butter soften at room temperature; blend. Stir in flour. Chill slightly, about 1 hour. Shape into 2 dozen 1" balls, place in tiny ungreased 1¾" muffin cups. Press dough on bottom and sides of cups.

Pecan Filling: Beat together egg, sugar, butter, vanilla, and salt just until smooth. Divide half the pecans among pastry-lined cups; add egg mixture and top with remaining pecans. Bake at 325 degrees for 25 minutes or until filling is set. Cool; remove from pans.

Linda Adams, Fayette Community Library, Fayette, IA

Potato Chip Cookies

½ pound butter or margarine
½ cup sugar
½ cup potato chips, crushed (hint, just leave them in the bag and crush them)
1 egg yolk
1½ cups flour
½ cup nuts
½ teaspoon vanilla

Mix in order given, drop by teaspoonfuls on cookie sheets and flatten with a floured fork. Bake at 350 degrees for 12-15 minutes. When cool, sprinkle with powdered sugar.

Linda Magley, patron, Family History Center Library,Mesa, AZ

Ranger Cookies

2 sticks margarine
1 cup sugar
1 cup brown sugar
2 eggs
1 teaspoon vanilla
2 cups flour
1 teaspoon baking soda
½ teaspoon baking powder
2 cups oatmeal
2 cups puffed rice cereal such as Rice Krispies
2 cups raisins or dates
2 cups pecans, chopped

Cream together the margarine, and sugars. Add eggs and vanilla, beat well. Add flour, soda, baking powder, and oatmeal; mix well. Stir in puffed rice cereal, raisins or dates, and pecans. Drop by tablespoon on cookie sheets. Bake at 350 degrees for 10 minutes.

Denise S. Crawford, Glenwood Public Library, Glenwood, IA

"The fact is that it takes more than ingredients and technique to cook a good meal. A good cook puts something of himself into the preparation – he cooks with enjoyment, anticipation, spontaneity, and he is willing to experiment." Pearl Bailey (1918-1990*) Pearl's Kitchen, 1973*

Sugar Cookies

1 cup powdered sugar
1 cup margarine
¾ cup white sugar
1 egg
1 teaspoon vanilla
¼ teaspoon lemon favoring
2¼ cups flour
1 teaspoon baking soda
1 teaspoon cream of tarter

Mix in order given. Roll in balls; flatten with sugared glass. Chilling not required. Bake at 350 degrees for 15 minutes.

Linda Adams, Fayette Community Library, Fayette, IA

Whole Wheat Sugar Cookies

1 cup sugar
1 teaspoon baking powder
½ teaspoon salt
½ teaspoon baking soda
½ teaspoon nutmeg
½ cup margarine or butter, softened
2 tablespoons milk
1 tablespoon lemon or orange peel, grated, optional
1 egg
2 cups whole wheat flour
2 tablespoons sugar
½ teaspoon cinnamon

Mix sugar, baking powder, salt, soda, nutmeg, margarine, milk, lemon or orange peel and egg until blended well. Stir in whole wheat flour. Roll into 1" balls and place on an ungreased cookie sheet about 2" apart. Flatten slightly. Mix the sugar and cinnamon and sprinkle over cookies before baking. Bake 8-10 minutes until light golden brown. Cookies will be soft in the center.

Sue Padilla, Newton Public Library, Newton, IA

"One of the very nicest things about life is the way we must regularly stop whatever we are doing and devote our attention to eating."
Luciano Pavarotti, Singer *My Own Story*, 1981

641.8659 Coffee cakes.

Apple Cinnamon Coffee Cake

2½ cups all-purpose flour
1 cup plus 2 tablespoons brown sugar, firmly packed
¾ cup sugar
4 teaspoons ground cinnamon, divided
¾ teaspoon salt
½ teaspoon ground ginger
¾ cup vegetable oil
1 teaspoon baking soda
1 teaspoon baking power
1 pound tart apples, peeled, cored, and chopped
1 cup buttermilk
1 large egg

Preheat oven to 325 degrees. Butter and flour 9" square pan. Mix flour, brown sugar, sugar, 2½ teaspoons cinnamon, salt, and ginger in a large bowl. Add oil and stir until mixture resembles coarse meal. Transfer ¾ cup of mixture to small bowl. Stir remaining 1½ teaspoons cinnamon into mixture in small bowl and reserve for topping. Mix baking soda and baking power into flour mixture. Add apples. Whisk buttermilk and egg in another small bowl to blend. Add to apple mixture and stir just until combined. Pour batter into prepared pan. Sprinkle reserved topping evenly over. Bake cake until tester inserted into center comes out clean, about 1 hour and 20 minutes. Can be served warm or at room temperature. Serves 8-10

Christine Lind Hage, Clinton-Macomb Public Library, Clinton Township, MI

"Food like a loving touch or a glimpse of divine power, has that ability to comfort."
Norman Kolpas, British cookbook writer

Danish Puff

My mother always made this on Christmas morning. It's not as complicated as it may seem and it sure is good!

½ cup butter, softened
2 cups all-purpose flour, divided
2 tablespoons water
½ cup butter
1 cup water
1 teaspoon almond extract
1 cup all-purpose flour
3 eggs
1½ cups powdered sugar
2 tablespoons butter, softened
1½ teaspoons vanilla
1-2 tablespoons warm water
Nuts, chopped

Preheat oven to 350 degrees. Cut ½ cup butter into 1 cup flour until particles are the size of small peas. Sprinkle 2 tablespoons water over the flour mixture; mix with fork. Gather pastry into a ball; divide in half. Pat each half into a 12" x 3" rectangle on an ungreased cookie sheet. (Rectangles should be about 3" apart.) Heat ½ cup butter and 1 cup water to a rolling boil; remove from heat. Quickly stir in almond extract and 1 cup of flour. Stir vigorously over low heat until mixture forms a ball, about 1 minute. Remove from heat. Add eggs; beat until smooth and glossy. Spread half over each of the rectangles. Bake until topping is crisp and brown, about one hour at 350 degrees; cool. (Topping will shrink and fall, forming the custardy top.) Meanwhile, mix powdered sugar, 2 tablespoons butter, and vanilla until smooth. Stir in 1-2 tablespoons of water, 1 teaspoon at a time, until glaze is smooth and of desired consistency. When puff is cool, spread with glaze and sprinkle with chopped nuts.

Kathy Fisher, Keosauqua Public Library, Keosauqua, IA

Easy Coffee Cake

1 box yellow cake mix
3 eggs
1 can of peach or apple pie filling
1/3 cup brown sugar
1 tablespoon flour
1 tablespoon margarine
1 teaspoon cinnamon

In a large bowl blend cake mix, eggs, and pie filling until blended. Pour into a 13" x 9" pan. Mix brown sugar, flour, margarine and cinnamon until crumbly. Sprinkle over batter. Bake for 25-30 minutes at 350 degrees.

Judi Tjepkes, Gowrie Public Library, Gowrie, IA

My Favorite Coffee Cake

1 box yellow cake mix
2 tablespoons flour
1 4-ounce package vanilla instant pudding mix
¾ cup oil
¾ cup water
4 eggs
1½ teaspoons butter extract, divided
2½ teaspoons vanilla extract, divided
½ cup sugar
2 teaspoons cinnamon
½ cup walnuts, chopped
¼ cup confectioners' sugar
2 tablespoons milk

Combine cake mix, flour, pudding mix, oil, water, eggs, 1 teaspoon butter extract and 2 teaspoons vanilla in mixer bowl; mix at high speed for 8 minutes. Mix sugar, cinnamon and walnuts in small bowl. Layer batter and walnut mixture 1/3 at a time in 12" tube pan sprayed with cooking spray. Bake at 350 degrees for 50 minutes. Remove to serving plate to cool. Blend confectioners' sugar, milk, ½ teaspoon butter extract and ½ teaspoon vanilla in bowl. Drizzle over cooled coffee cake.

Shellsburg Public Library, Shellsburg, IA

Sour Cream Coffee Cake

1½ cups flour
1 teaspoon baking powder
½ teaspoon salt
½ teaspoon baking soda
½ cup butter or margarine, divided
1 cup sugar
1 tablespoon grated lemon or orange rind
2 eggs
1 cup sour cream
2 cups Corn Flakes, Total, or Special K (your choice), crushed to make 1 cup crumbs
½ cup brown sugar
½ cup nuts
1 tablespoon flour
1 tablespoon cinnamon
3 tablespoons butter, melted

Combine 1½ cups flour, baking powder, salt, and baking soda. Set aside. Cream ¼ cup butter or margarine. Add sugar, rind, and eggs. Add dry ingredients to creamed mixture alternately with sour cream until well blended. Combine cereal, brown sugar, nuts, 1 tablespoon flour, cinnamon, and 3 tablespoons melted butter; mix well. Spread in a 13" x 9" baking pan. Sprinkle all but 1/3 cup of crumbs on top of batter. Cut through the batter several times. Add the remaining 1/3 cup of crumbs to top the batter. Bake at 350 degrees approximately 30 minutes.

Judy A. Chesley, Woodbury County Library, Moville, IA

"Serve the dinner backward, do anything, but for goodness sake, do something weird."
Elsa Maxwell (1883-1963) American columnist and professional hostess

641.874 Cocktails.

Apple Martini

1 shot vodka
1 shot apple Pucker
1 shot apple juice
½ shot melon liqueur

Shake ingredients with 2-3 ice cubes until very cold. Strain into martini glass and add a maraschino cherry.

Jesse Lewis, Palm Beach County Library System, West Palm Beach, FL

"Let us candidly admit that there are shameful blemishes on the American past, of which the worst by far is rum. Nevertheless, we have improved man's lot and enriched his civilization with rye, bourbon and the Martini cocktail. In all history has any other nation done so much?"
Bernard De Voto (1897-1955) American writer and critic

641.875 Beverages.

Favorite Punch

1 gallon raspberry sherbet
2 2-liter bottles 7-Up

Stir together in a punch bowl. Use whatever flavor of sherbet you want to get the desired color.

Denise S. Crawford, Glenwood Public Library, Glenwood, IA

Lemon-Lime Coolers

2¾ cups sugar
4½ cups cold water
1¼ cups fresh lime juice (from about 10 medium limes)
1 cup fresh lemon juice (from about 6 medium lemons)
1 lime, sliced

In a 2-quart saucepan, heat sugar and 4½ cups cold water to boiling over high heat, stirring occasionally. Cover saucepan and boil 3 minutes; remove from heat. Stir in lime and lemon juice into sugar syrup. Pour mixture into a large pitcher; cover and refrigerate until cold, about 3 hours. Add ice, stir in lime slices, and serve.

Susan Henricks, Carnegie-Stout Public Library, Dubuque, IA

Swedish Egg Coffee

7 cups water
1 egg
2 tablespoons water
1/3 cup regular grind coffee

Bring the 7 cups of water to boiling in a heavy, enameled coffeepot. Meanwhile, in a small bowl, beat the egg and 2 tablespoons of water. Stir the coffee into the egg and water mixture. When the water is boiling, add the coffee-egg mixture. Boil gently for 7 minutes. Remove from heat; add ½ cup of cold water. Grounds will settle to the bottom. Makes 10 servings

Susan Henricks, Carnegie-Stout Public Library, Dubuque, IA

"As soon as there is coffee in your stomach, there is a general commotion. Ideas begin to move . . . similes arise, the paper is covered. Coffee is your ally and writing ceases to be a struggle."
Honoré de Balzac (1799-1859) French novelist and short story author

Sweet Chai

1/3 cup water
2/3 cup whole milk
1 rounded teaspoon of Assam tea for each cup measure (plus a bit extra)
Fresh ginger chopped, or a dash powdered ginger, or crystallized ginger, chopped
One crushed cardamom pod, or a dash of powdered cardamom
One little piece clove
Enough sugar to make it sweet (one teaspoon per cup, I use demerara sugar)

Throw it all into a saucepan cold and bring slowly to a boil. When boiling turn up
the heat and swirl it around until it reaches the desired strength and the spices
provide a kick – about 5 minutes. Strain it into small glasses or cups.

GraceAnne Andreassi DeCandido, Blue Roses Consulting, NY, NY

"Ecstasy is a glass of tea and a piece of sugar in the mouth."
Alexander Pushkin (1799-1837) Russian author

641.875 Smoothies (Beverages)

Classic Smoothie

1 cup orange juice
1 cup fresh frozen strawberries, hulled and quartered
2 bananas

Pour the orange juice into a blender. Add the strawberries and bananas. Blend
until smooth.

Genevieve Henricks, Carnegie-Stout Public Library, Dubuque, IA

Berry Beauty

1 cup low-fat vanilla yogurt
½ cup grape juice
1 ½ cups fresh blueberries
1 cup fresh blackberries

Combine the yogurt and grape juice in a blender. Add the berries. Blend until smooth and strain through a sieve.

Genevieve Henricks, Carnegie-Stout Public Library, Dubuque, IA

Genevieve's "Orange Julius"

1 cup milk
½ cup sugar
1 6-ounce can frozen orange juice concentrate
10-20 ice cubes
1 tablespoon vanilla

Combine milk, sugar, orange juice concentrate, and ice cubes in a blender until smooth. Add vanilla and blend for 10 more seconds. Serve immediately.

Genevieve Henricks, Carnegie-Stout Public Library, Dubuque, IA

"We heard one evening, under the eye of the imperturbable Paul, a foreign lady ask for a milk chocolate drink to accompany a fillet of sole Cubat, the chefs speciality. Sacrilege! Just as well that Marcel Proust and Boni de Castellane were not here to see that."
Simon Arbellot de Vacqueur (1897-1965) French journalist

745.592 Toy making.

Bubbles

1 cup Joy or Dawn dish washing liquid
2 cups warm water
3 tablespoons glycerin
½ teaspoon sugar

Mix ingredients together and store in an airtight container. Use a plastic strawberry basket, colander, plastic six pack holder, funnel, plastic straw cut on a slant, or tape several straws together to form the bubbles.

"Play-Doh"

1 cup flour
1 tablespoon oil
1 cup water
½ teaspoon salt
2 teaspoons cream of tarter
Food coloring

Mix dry ingredients in a pan. Add wet ingredients and mix together. Cook over a low to medium heat Stir constantly until mixture forms a ball no more than five minutes. Make sure it doesn't dry it out too much. Add the food coloring while cooking; either paste or liquid color.

"Why, sometimes I've believed as many as six impossible things before breakfast."
Lewis Carroll (1832-1898) English author

From the archives of the Carnegie-Stout Public Library,
Dubuque, Iowa

808.0427 Essays.

Making Gravy

I was 15 when my parents and six brothers and sisters moved to 43 acres east of Des Moines. We moved from a three bedroom, modern house on a large and beautiful lot in Des Moines to a 2 bedroom house, barely modern with more running water from the 53 leaks in the roof than from the cistern, and the isolation of a half mile lane from a gravel road out in the country.

The water through the cistern was for bathing and flushing but not for drinking. We hauled drinking water for the 9 of us in five-gallon cans from town.

Mom always filled the water cans at her parents' house and stayed a bit to commiserate with them over the crowding, isolation and conditions at the 43 acres. My Dad loved that place as much as my Mom hated it.

One Sunday, I fixed dinner. I had three fresh chickens cut up and deep fat fried, mashed potatoes, corn-on-the-cob, and sliced tomatoes. There was tea nectar, cold milk, bread, and butter. I had everything ready except for the gravy. I did not know how to make gravy. Mom always did that but she had gone into town for water and was not back when everything else was ready.

Dad, John and Tom were bailing hay. Dad drove the old tractor and my brothers fed the wires into the baler. It was filthy work with the sweat acting like glue for the dirt and chaff. My brothers became barely recognizable after the first pass around the field. They had been at it quite a while and I knew they all wanted dinner.

I walked out and flagged Dad down. He shifted down and leaned over to hear me. I said that the chicken, mashed potatoes, corn and tomatoes were ready but I didn't know how to make the gravy and Mom wasn't back from town yet. He did some clutching and choking and cut that engine way back--till it just popped every now and again to prove it was still running. He took time right then to teach me how to make gravy.

He said; "I don't care whether you know how to make gravy or not. We are going to finish this pass and then come in for dinner. You will have gravy on the table."

I went back to the house. I made gravy. I knew gravy had something to do with flour and grease. I had two deep frying pans full of grease and chicken bits and I had flour. Mom came back. Dad and my brothers and sisters came to the dinner table.

Everyone ate. Everyone ate gravy. No one complained.   It was, however, about three years before you could eat my gravy without a knife and a fork.

My Dad taught me more than how to make gravy. He taught me that I could figure things out and did not have to stand around waiting for someone else. My Mom shared that belief and said it this way "You never know what you can do until you have to."

Patricia Coffie, Waverly Public Library, Waverly, IA

Or It Might Be Sweet: A Recipe For Getting By

My family's most memorable season, cuisine-wise, was the summer of 1968 when Mom subscribed to *Time-Life Foods of the World*, a series of full-color hardbound cookbooks that arrived in sturdy rectangular cardboard boxes every month or so. The Tet Offensive began in Vietnam, the Democratic National Convention exploded with riots in Chicago, and Apollo 8 took to the heavens for its graceful moon orbit that year. We got fat.

Jim, my stepfather, had fled the corporate world after his best friend collapsed and died in a rowboat while fishing with his son. "Tell your mother I love her," George moaned to little Dave, as the boy paddled for home. Life was brief and precious, even if you weren't stomping through a damp jungle with a gun over your shoulder. That's how Jim had begun to see it.

Mom was an improviser. About recipes she said, "Just remember, you have to eat it when you're done." I knew a metaphor when I heard one.

She had improvised, among other things, Jim: this much older man, well fixed for cash. I don't mean their relationship was casual or made up in some way, or not any more made up than others, (though it's true she was his secretary, true they eloped to Las Vegas). I mean my mother recognized her need for a man and our need for a provider, and she found a near perfect one in him. *Foods of the World* – the books themselves and those exotic meals that my mother created, more or less, from them – would have been impossible without Jim. The marriage lasted longer than he did.

That summer in 1968 I began my adaptation to life away from the city, in a shaded gatehouse on lonesome Kennedy Hill Road outside the quiet burg of Byron, Ill., with just-acquired stepfather Jim, my suddenly kitchen-bound mother and, soon enough, a yellow bus that wheezed up to our mailbox on Rural Route Two. At school, sun-speckled farm boys and girls would call me by a last name almost as new to me as it was to them.

That summer I explored the woods behind our house, acres of hilly forest with a shallow creek, shy deer, snakes, and a mansion along the Rock River that belonged to Mrs. Knight, our landlady and widow of the big-time Chicago lawyer. I peered in Mrs. Knight's windows. A long table in a dim, otherwise empty room was set with perfect china, silver and stemware.

That summer I met Scotty, the raw-boned hired man who herded Mrs. Knight's cows in the field north of our house. He squirted hot milk from an udder directly into my mouth. He told me if he caught my dog chasing his cows, he would kill it with one shot.

I can't remember what we ate from *Foods of the World* (I was a teenager and devoured everything, in large helpings) – only the fragrant steam and bright colors, the almost startling flavors and strange textures. Jim's way of saying, "What shall we enjoy tonight?" when he sat down. My mother's proud explanations, often read from the book. The cooking of Italy, provincial France, Japan, the British Isles. And one day, in the living room, Mom reaching under Jim's shirt from behind as he stared out the window. "We've all got one," she laughed. We stood there for a moment, shirts up, showing off our small round bellies to each other.

How to get from that point in time to the present, or how I did, I'm not sure. Mom's fondness for cooking and Jim's boredom led them to buy a Swedish restaurant in Rockford. We moved closer to the city. All of us worked happily but hard. The years disappeared.

One night, when the ink was barely dry on the Stockholm Inn's deed of sale, Mom said to Jim, "Can we change our mind? Is it too late?"

He studied her. She studied him back, the two of them taking stock of how the 12-hour days had aged them.

"No," he said. "Yes."

More years vanished. Jim lapsed into serious retirement, then died. Mom lapsed into something worse and followed him, later than she would have liked. And here I am in the spire of a wood-shingle Victorian at the base of Mt. Tamalpais, in a small town just across the Golden Gate Bridge from San Francisco, tapping away at an essay for – of all things – a cookbook.

Dusk. People meander the balmy street below. I want to shout at them, "The *Foods of the World* books are out of print, but can still be found on the dusty shelves of antiquarian stores!" They wouldn't understand. So I'll write instead of shouting it, and see if I can. Understand, that is, how it all happened.

How I grew up, got married, had kids, got divorced. Left northern Illinois for St. Louis for Atlanta for the mountains of southwest Colorado for California (first placid seaside Bolinas, then crazy Berkeley) and then back to suburban

Chicago. Belgium, France, Thailand, Laos, Cambodia. Now, the Promised Land again.

Of course, there isn't any "how." Like that kid set loose from the Byron gatehouse, I simply explored landscapes, those of the interior as much as the exterior. I fattened myself on life – all the bright colors and startling flavors and strange textures – while history got made in the distances around me.

I'm almost 50 years old. The other day I started thinking again about Dave. He lived with his father George and mother Mitzi beside the lake that opened into the Rock River, the same river Mrs. Knight's hollow mansion overlooked. After Dave's father died, I spent long afternoons fishing with him on the sloped bank near his house. We didn't take the boat out.

What happened to him? I like to think of Dave going on, remembering his father and that day they reached the shore too late but recalling it lightly – the way you might, near the end, revisit the saddest and the most glory-filled times of what gets improvised into the thing called "a life." We've all got one. It might be bitter or it might be sweet, but you have to eat it when you're done.

Randy Osborne, patron, Mill Valley Public Library, Mill Valley, CA

Randy Osborne lives in the San Francisco area, where he writes stories and takes long walks. In 2003 he published a chapbook zine, "Big Pinch World." He can be reached at randyosborne@hotmail.com.

Index

Beans *(continued)*

Pattie's beans, 57
peachy keen beans, 57
potluck beans, 14
tortellini bean salad, 167

Beau Monde Bread, 119

Bee Keeper's Sundae Sauce, 115

Beef *(See also ground beef)*

barbecued ribs, 10
best ever slow cooker stew, 11
crockpot beef Burgundy, 11
crockpot roast beef, 12
delicious pot roast, 13
Mongolian beef, 23
picadillo, 58
slow-roasted beef rib roast, 59

Beef Burgers, 169

Beer Bread, 119, 120

Bentonsport Bread, 120

Berry Beauty, 233

Best Ever Slow Cooker Stew, 11

Better Than Pumpkin Pie Dessert, 179

Beverages

apple martini, 230
berry beauty, 233
classic smoothie, 232
Di's homemade "Bailey's," 5
favorite punch, 230
Genevieve's Orange Julius, 233
lemon-lime coolers, 231
Swedish egg coffee, 231
sweet chai, 232

Big Apple Salad, 157

Breakfasts *(continued)*

easy egg casserole, 8
hootenanny pancakes, 140
New Orleans beignets, 126
scalloped eggs, 79
Scotch eggs with fresh herbs, 80

Broccoli

broccoli and rice casserole, 47
broccoli cheese soup, 105
broccoli holiday casserole, 48
broccoli salad, 157
broccoli with black olives, 48
cauliflower and broccoli casserole, 49

Broccoli and Rice Casserole, 47

Broccoli and Cheese Soup, 105

Broccoli Holiday Casserole, 48

Broccoli Salad, 157

Broccoli with Black Olives, 48

Brownies

bookish brownies, 194
buttermilk brownies, 195
JJ's utility optmization brownies, 196
Kahlua brownies, 197

Bubbles, 234

Burnt Sugar Cake, 200

Butterflied Shrimp in Wine, 90

Buttermilk Brownies, 195

Cajun Shrimp, 91

Cake

almond sherry cake, 198
apple-cinnamon coffee cake, 226
apple-cinnamon crumb cake, 199

Cake *(continued)*

Cake Decorating Frosting, 210

Calabacita, 62

Candy

Canine Carrot Cookies, 3

Canning

Captain's Stew with Rice, 91

Caramels, 172

Caramel Apple Salad, 158

Carrot Soufflé, 143

Carrots

carrot soufflé, 143

Casseroles

broccoli and rice casserole, 47
broccoli holiday casserole, 48
corn casserole, 147
cauliflower and broccoli casserole, 49
easy egg casserole, 8
farmer's casserole, 147
Greek potato and meat bake, 148
hamburger rice dish, 148
kitchen sink casserole, 149
mac and corn, 149
quick macaroni and cheese, 150
scalloped pineapple casserole, 150
special sweet potato casserole, 55
taco casserole, 151
tamale pie, 60

Cat Nip Cookies, 4

Cats- Food

catnip cookies, 4
crunchies for kitties, 4

Cauliflower and Broccoli Casserole, 49

Cavatini, 151

Chai

sweet chai, 232

Cheddar Cheese Bread, 121

Cheese

Asiago bread, 118
broccoli cheese soup, 105
cheddar cheese bread, 121
cheese ball, 97
cheese soufflé, 143

Cheese *(continued)*

cheese soup, 106
cheese spread, 97
fresh tomato and brie pasta, 153
gebna makleyah (fried cheese), 44
spinach and artichoke casserole/dip, 102
Swiss cheese spread, 103

Cheese Ball, 97

Cheese Soufflé, 143

Cheese Soup, 106

Cheese Spread, 97

Cheesecake

individual cherry cheesecakes, 175
Irish creme cheesecake, 176
Margarita cheesecake, 177

Cherries

cherries jubilee, 180
cherry blossoms, 180
cherry pie salad, 158
frangipane cherry bars, 213

Cherries Jubilee, 180

Cherry Blossoms, 180

Cherry Pie Salad, 158

Chicken

apricot chicken, 68
asparagus, 81
baked chicken breasts with stuffing and cheese, 68
breasts with pesto, 69
dumplings, 69
chunky chicken salad, 159
curry, 70
enchilada, 70
oven crusty chicken, 71

Cookies

Cookies and Cream Cake, 201

Corn

Corn Casserole, 147

Corn Flake Bars, 212

Corn Fritters, 17

Corn with Jalapeños and Cream, 17

Cottage Cheese

green stuff, 164
Italian cheese and ham pie, 29
Mom's special cottage cheese, 77
spinach and artichoke casserole/dip, 102
spinach casserole, 50
unbelievable salad, 168

Crab

crab in cream sauce au gratin, 92
crab rangoon, 98
crabbies, 99
DrWeb's spicy crab-potato pancakes, 139
shrimp and crab loaf, 102
4-3-2-1 dip, 96

Crab in Cream Sauce au Gratin, 92

Crab Rangoon, 98

Crabbies, 99

Cranberries

Christmas brunch French toast, 7
cranberry kisses, 173
cranberry waldorf salad, 160
pumpkin cranberry bread, 131
whole cranberry bread, 135

Cranberry Kisses, 173

Cranberry Waldorf Salad, 160

Cream Cheese

cheese ball, 97
cherry blossoms, 180
crab rangoon, 98
cream cheese cookies, 218
individual cherry cheesecakes, 175
Irish cream cheesecake, 176
Margarita cheesecake, 177
olive nut spread. 101
pink champagne salad, 166
scalloped corn and oysters, 18
shrimp and crab loaves, 102

Desserts *(continued)*

Pancakes

batty cakes, 138
DrWeb's Spicy crab-potato pancakes, 139
hootenanny pancakes, 140
mini Dutch apple pancakes, 140
Swedish pancakes, 35

Pansit Canton, 40

Pasta

cavatini, 151
chicken stew with tortellini, 107
creamy spaghetti and ham fiorentina, 152
Curt's spinach spaghetti, 152
fresh tomato and brie pasta, 153
Grandma Columbo's ravioli, 28
literary lasagna, 30
mac and corn casserole, 149
macaroni salad, 164
manicotti, 31
pasta with chicken, raisins and pistachios, 153
penne with yellow peppers and sweet onion, 154
quick macaroni and cheese, 150
Sarah's rigatoni con balsamica, 154
tortellini and vegetable soup, 16
tortellini bean salad, 167
turkey tetrazzini, 75

Pasta with Chicken, Raisins, and Pistachios, 153

Paté

chicken liver paté, 98
liver sausage paté, 100

Pattie's Beans, 57

Peaches

pêches à tonne (peaches with tuna), 86

Peachy Keen Beans, 57

Peanut Brittle, 175

Peanut Butter

easy peanut butter cookies for unexpected company, 219

Peanut Butter *(continued)*

Peanut Butter and Onion Sandwich, 170

Peanut Butter and M & M Cookies, 223

Peanut Butter Squares, 215

Peanut Squares II, 215

Peanuts

Pear Bread, 129

Pears

Pecan Muffins, 137

Pecan Tarts, 223

Pecan(s)

Pêches à Tonne (peaches with tuna), 86

Penne with Yellow Peppers and Sweet Onion, 154

Pepparkakor (Swedish Gingerbread Cookies), 34

Philippine

Picadillo, 58

State Library Gumbo Open Records Recipe, 23

Stew

chicken stew with tortellini, 107
hearty lentil stew, 21

Stir-Fry

chicken asparagus, 81
garlic pork with vegetables, 82
Mongolian beef, 83
Yang Chow fried rice, 84

Strawberries Romanoff, 186

Strawberry Apple Cobbler, 185

Streusel Raspberry Muffins, 138

Stromboli, 172

Stuffed Vienna Bread, 134

Sugar Cookies, 225

Super Easy Corn Chowder, 111

Sushi, 38

Susie's Pie Crust, 193

Surprise Pie, 192

Swedish

fingerklatchens (Swedish), 33
Jansson's frestelse (temptation), 33
mjuk pepparkaka (Swedish soft gingerbread), 35
pepparkakor (Swedish gingerbread cookies), 34
sill salad (herring salad), 34
Swedish egg coffee, 231
Swedish pancakes, 35

Swedish Egg Coffee, 231

Swedish Pancakes, 35

Swedish Soft Gingerbread (Mjuk Pepparkaka), 35

Sweet Chai, 232

Vegetarian

Zucchini

Acknowledgements

Special thanks to Chef James T. Ehler, who describes himself as a Webmaster, cook, chef, writer, and computer nerd. I'd like to add library lover and supporter. His web site foodreference.com and generosity in sharing his material put the frosting on this cookbook.

Denette Kellogg, Carnegie-Stout Public Library donated her time and expertise to help edit, format, and most importantly, do the techie stuff to make the cover what it is. Without her, well, Dewey Cooks may have been coverless.

My family, Rich, Genevieve, and Natalie let me "do my thing" over the past year in putting this book together. After three months, I lost track of the hours. They were patient and didn't remind me just how many they were.

Most of all, I need to thank Genevieve (aka Pie), editor extraordinaire! She caught stuff to correct that I didn't know existed. The process was not painless. I was accused of writing totally in running fragments and non-parallels, using no verbs, adjectives, or adverbs. Punctuation, well, if used was definitely wrong. Just when I thought I'd heard all the critique I could handle she told me, "You have a real thing with gerunds. I mean, gerunds are okay, but you need to know when and how to use them." "Huh?" I responded confused, "A what?" "A gerund!!" she declared. "Oh, you mean those grrrrr UNDS?" Thanks, Pie, more than I can correctly write for your help. You are the best. I could not have completed this alone.

Any remaining typos or errors, I take full responsibility. I know of one BIG one . . . let me know if you find it.

"When I get a little money, I buy books.
And if there is any left over,
I buy food.

Desiderius Erasmus (1466 – 1536)